Conscience of a Progressive

The Author

Clement Wulf-Soulage is a business author, newspaper columnist and former university lecturer. He lived in Germany for 17 years, and taught courses in business economics, business communications and marketing at various universities in the country including the University of Göttingen, University of Applied Sciences and Arts (HAWK Göttingen/Hildesheim) and the Private University of Applied Sciences (PFH Göttingen), a higher-learning institution for entrepreneurs and business starters.

The Saint Lucian author has also conducted hundreds of business communication, academic writing and presentation seminars for a variety of corporate clients, public academic institutions and language academies in Germany including the Institute for International Training and Communications (IBK), the Göttingen Graduate School of Social Sciences and the Community College for Further Education (VHS).

During his 11-year stint at the VHS, he tutored students for the advanced international language and business certificates offered by the University of Cambridge in England.

Wulf-Soulage is the author of two business books: Market Economy: English for International Economics; and Management English Intelligence: English for International Management.

He speaks fluent German, and in his spare time, enjoys reading history and autobiographies. Further, he is an avid researcher on subjects ranging from economic growth and social development – to globalization and foreign policy.

Conscience of a Progressive

Clement Wulf-Soulage

Clement Wulf-Soulage
Conscience of a Progressive

ISBN: 9-781-5334-5936-7

General Editor: Richard Brown

Review Editor: Clement Wulf-Soulage

Cover Design: Martin Munzel

Cover Image: Lucia Wulf/Leslie Wulf

Interior Design: Johann-Christian Hanke

All rights reserved.

1st Edition 2016, Gleichen

© 2016 by Espresso Tutorials GmbH

URL: *www.espresso-tutorials.com*

Feedback
We greatly appreciate any kind of feedback you have concerning this book. Please mail us at *info@espresso-tutorials.com*.

Table of Contents

CONSCIENCE OF A PROGRESSIVE

"Sufficiently well-equipped to always rise above the din and make his points from global, regional or national perspectives, this author doesn't genuflect to the political whims and fancies of the day's gubernatorial make-up. His arguments and offerings for thought are usually based on fact, not fiction. Widely read and well taught, his words of wisdom normally appeal for sober consideration of the issues he comments on."

– Earl Bousquet, Veteran Caribbean Editor and Journalist
  Saint Lucia Medal of Honour (Gold)

For my son
Clement Jr. (CJ)

PROLOGUE

The Progressive in Me

The term "PROGRESSIVE" has its roots in the word "progress" and the idea of making things better. It implies support for equality, change and reform. A timeless progressive vision is: "Government of the people, by the people, and for the people."

Hillary Clinton likes to say: "I'm a progressive who likes to get things done." For me, this statement exemplifies what drives social progress and economic development – execution and implementation.

Progressive people are interested in structured change and sustainable development. You're a progressive thinker if you can use searchlight intelligence to think up new ways of doing things and if you're open to change. People who are "progressives" favour reform, civil liberties, human resource development and political enlightenment.

John Halpin of the Centre for American Progress writes that "Progressivism is a non-ideological, pragmatic system of thought grounded in solving problems and maintaining strong values within society. It's a dynamic concept giving the LEADERSHIP of an up-and-coming generation the tools to make a nation's future brighter for all."

Mainstream literature explains that "Progressivism has historically been associated with science, rationality and an approach to government and society reliant on knowledge and empirical methods. Progressives tended to be people with a broad education and understanding of the world."

Pathways to Progress

As Saint Lucia approaches its 40th anniversary of political independence in 2019, let's prepare for that milestone by committing ourselves to a process of educational transformation and mental renewal. Hopefully, our island by then would have experienced a new coming of age. Let's make the next decade the one that ushered in the mentality change needed for us to develop and to progress as a nation. Let's inspire our children to do more, dream more, be more and become more.

All of us must demonstrate an interest in the future direction of our country by participating in its governance and development. It is the responsibility of every patriotic citizen to contribute to the vitality and well being of Saint Lucia, for the love of country. Above all, national leaders in all spheres of society need to look beyond the horizon and prepare long-term projections in pursuit of sustainable development goals in the areas of education, healthcare, family care, ecology and agriculture.

The progressive and inspirational ideas in this ebullient book pave the way forward for a fundamental rethink and upgrade in the democratic, governance and organisational mindsets of a young and beautiful nation – whose rigour, talent and feasibility remain unharnessed. Undaunted in spirit by past colonial and political misgivings, we the people believe the time is ripe for a new and progressive nation exultant in economic hope. If so inclined, you can call it a revolution or even a new national consciousness, but the fact remains that the results must embrace and address major changes in economy, industry, socio-political institutions and the culture of information and debate.

For the sake of our country, civil society and the business community need to urge the leaders of all political parties to tone down the current blame-driven politics and instead demonstrate to the electorate that they have real ambition for the society and economy – and the policies to tackle the toxic twosome of high unemployment and low investment. The people want to see programmes and constructive ideas that will support the creation of the skilled jobs needed, equip their children with the education and skills they need for the future and anchor value-creating enterprises in Saint Lucia. In short, the people want to hear what the big picture is for the truly critical issues such as the economy, the justice system and the police force.

There is a general feeling that our political, religious and educational leaders have failed our citizens. The society is now clamouring for social and economic remodelling and political renewal. For such sweeping reforms, however, we'll need a crop of both tactical and visionary young leaders armed with medium and long term management plans to end poverty and illiteracy, increase national income, build the economic infrastructure, attract foreign investment, educate the masses, upgrade our health system and strengthen our local and national institutions.

Quite urgently, we need to modernise the police force, cut bureaucracy and invest more in information technology to improve efficiency and effectiveness in the public service, and to foster greater educational productivity in schools and colleges.

Economic growth requires a sound economic base of engineering skills, and this cannot be achieved without an increase in the number of engineers and scientists. We need to develop an economy that actually designs, builds, and sells stuff.

Saint Lucia needs to become a more dynamic and productive nation – one averse to wasting resources (labour, opportunity, time, materials, land). There is no doubt that government can and must play a vital role in promoting an efficient economy, but the brunt of the effort must be on the shoulders of responsible citizens, functioning institutions and an unfettered private sector.

As I will argue, politics is about the education and mass mobilisation of people for the common good, which will result in greater awareness of developmental issues, protection of national and community interests and the collective embrace of a value system.

It is no secret that Saint Lucia is divided along political fault lines, and that divisiveness is causing much social disharmony and civil disorder. You don't need a poll to know that the vast majority of Saint Lucians are weary of the dead zone that politics has become; in which narrow interests vie for advantage and ideological minorities seek to impose their own versions of absolute truth.

This publication of disarmingly blunt and trenchant commentaries is my way of appealing to the political and business directorate to change their present mindset in the interest of progressive governance. I express some of my most profound thoughts on the system of democracy – arguing that the fundamental fact about this system is that it must at all times rest on the will and support of the people.

At a time of rising anxiety among the youth and with the onset of signs and symptoms of a broken society, there is no doubt in my mind that a bona-fide national conversation needs to be started to identify the circumstances and causes of the social breakdown – and evidence-based policies instituted to change the trajectory of events before they reach a critical stage.

The future of this country depends on how well we take care of our youth today. I am tired of seeing a country of only 236 square miles in area let the talents of young people go to waste. Moreover, I am weary of seeing young people waste their youth on the young.

Let us once again give our young people a reason to believe in themselves and in the future of their country. It is sad that so many of them consider politics to be a waste of time, an unnecessary burden, about corruption and just making noise. I hope through positive political transformation that their definition of politics will change to one of public service, scope for the country's bright future, what they can do for their country and the most desirable burden to carry for the good of the State.

This collection makes enlightening and sobering reading and a lot of time, energy and resources have been invested in its preparation. I do hope that you will be informed and inspired by what you read.

Clement Wulf-Soulage
May, 2016

CHAPTER 1 – ECONOMIC AND BUSINESS AFFAIRS

1. How Keynes Changed the World

January 2016 marked the 80th anniversary of the Keynesian Revolution, spearheaded by the British economist John Maynard Keynes – who is widely regarded as the founder of macroeconomics. The groundbreaking and momentous year in history was 1936 when he published his magnum opus, "The General Theory of Employment, Interest and Money" – a book whose theorem and postulates still populate economic textbooks, dominate fiscal discussions and shape macroeconomic policy.

A year before publishing his seminal work, this clairvoyant of the dismal science had written a letter to Irish playwright and controversialist Bernard Shaw, expressing the following sentiments: "I believe myself to be writing a book on economic theory which will largely revolutionize – not, I suppose, at once but in the course of the next ten years – the way the world thinks about its economic problems."

Lo and behold, it turns out that he was indeed right about the transformative impact of his theories – and his forecasting wasn't by any measure an act of sheer hubris.

For as long as macroeconomics has been around, there have been few more hotly debated topics than what role the STATE should play in the economy, notwithstanding the fact that prominent economists the world over have provided plenty of examples of market failure (climate change, healthcare and housing, for instance) that seemed to have justified direct government intervention through fiscal policy, as well as through regulations and conditionalities.

Citing the need to moderate booms and busts, the main plank of Keynes' economic theory is that government intervention through active fiscal policy can stabilize an economy – and that spending by households, businesses and the government is the most important economic driving force – effectively countering the idea that free markets would automatically provide full employment and price stability, as the monetarists and neo-liberals believe.

Considered to be the intellectual founding father of the IMF and the World Bank, Keynes was insistent that "the market is a kind of wild animal" that needs to be tamed, and governments can and should prevent recessions and depressions through demand management – effectively arguing that demand creates its own supply – in direct opposition to Jean Baptiste Say's Law which posits that supply creates its own demand. Further, Keynes maintained that inadequate overall demand could lead to prolonged periods of high unemployment and that state intervention is necessary to moderate the vicissitudes of the business cycle.

Keynesianism, whose prominent proponents include Nobel Prize-winning economists Paul Samuelson, Joseph Stiglitz and Paul Krugman, came to life in the 1930s in response to the debilitating depression which ravaged the American economy and subjected many to a life of misery and destitution. By historical account, President Franklin D. Roosevelt's New Deal (a relief, recovery and reform plan to rescue the United States from the Great Depression) was flavoured by Keynesian ideas, although the true extent of its impact is still being debated today. The Great Recession of 2007–2009, triggered by the financial dysfunctions and infelicities of American capitalism, saw the return of Keynesian policies by way of large stimulus packages (increased government spending and subsidies, and reduced taxes) which brought some of the world's traumatized economies back to life.

The Columbia University Professor Joseph Stiglitz, who has consistently called for fiscal expansion during hard economic times especially when monetary policy is constrained, argues in a trenchant piece for the British Guardian entitled, "After The Financial Crisis We Were All Keynesians": "A bloated and dysfunctional financial system had misallocated capital and, rather than managing risk, had actually created it. Financial deregulation – together with easy money – had contributed to excessive risk-taking. Monetary policy would be relatively ineffective in reviving the economy, even if still-easier money might prevent the financial system's total collapse. Thus, greater reliance on fiscal policy – increased government spending – would be necessary. Five years later, while some are congratulating themselves on avoiding another depression, no one in Europe or the United States can claim that prosperity has returned...Yes, we were all Keynesians – but all too briefly. Fiscal stimulus was replaced by austerity, with predictable – and predicted – adverse effects on economic performance."

John Cassidy, an economist and author of the book, "How Markets Fail: The Logic of Economic Calamities", shared a similar view when he wrote in The New Yorker: "In the real world that rarely intrudes upon conservative economists and voters, both parties (and all Presidents) are Keynesians. Whenever the economy falters and private-sector spending declines, they use the tax-and-spending system to inject more demand into the economy. In 1981, Ronald Reagan did precisely this, slashing taxes and increasing defence spending. Between 2001 and 2003, George W. Bush followed the same script, introducing three sets of tax cuts and starting two wars. In February, 2009, Barack Obama introduced his stimulus. The real policy debate isn't about Keynesianism versus the free market, it is about magnitudes and techniques: How much stimulus is necessary? And how should it be divided between government spending and tax cuts?"

Of course, Keynesian economics is not without its fierce critics and some of its ideas haven't found resonance everywhere. The view that governments can "manage" demand has been categorically rejected by a school of thought called Monetarism – led by the late Nobel laureate Milton Friedman and the Neo-Liberals headed by the late Friedrich Hayek (another Nobel laureate and student colleague of our own Sir Arthur Lewis) – which contends that government should "keep its hands off the economy, cut back on regulations, and instead allow the free market – supply and demand – to determine prices and wages."

Perturbed by the fact that governments were often unable or unwilling to provide short-term relief to their people in times of recession, Keynes was exasperated by the view that, "provided the government doesn't interfere, in the long run the economy is an equilibrium which will eventual return to a point of balance" – to which he once replied: "Long run is a misleading guide to current affairs. In the long run we are all dead."

Not surprisingly, some of Keynes' policies have been labelled "left wing" and there are even suggestions that his main work be rewritten, as some mainstream economists and policymakers have cited theories that have been discredited, and ideas that have allegedly strangulated the free market. But, I ask in earnest, have we ever truly lived in a free market economy?

Writing in Forbes Business Magazine, Peter Ferrara bemoans what he sees as the failure of Keynesian economic policies to spur growth: "By the 1970s, Keynesian policies had produced double digit unemployment, double digit inflation, and double digit interest rates, all at the same time, along with four successive worsening recessions from 1969 to 1982. Keynesian monetary policy involves running up the money supply to increase demand, with artificially lowered interest rates promoting more spending. That is where the inflation came from. Ronald Reagan explicitly scrapped Keynesian economics for the more modern supply-side economics, which holds that economic growth results from incentives meant to boost production."

Be that as it may, some of the economic ideas of Keynes have survived the test of time and have become immortalized in the lecture halls of universities as well as in the finance ministries of governments around the world. Paul Samuelson is quoted to have said, "Funeral by funeral, theory advances" – and so have the works of Keynes. Although he never won the Nobel Prize in Economics (the prize was first awarded in 1969, long after his death), his theories are an established fixture in economics education and his ideas have shaped the course of history. By any metric that mattered, John Maynard Keynes was the greatest economist of the 20th century. If indeed he had an Achilles heel, it was his "State" theory. That is, the assumption that the "State" always cares about its people.

2. Can a Nation Grow Without Developing?

It has often been acknowledged by disputatious economists the world over that if ever there was a controversial economic indicator from the statistics world, GDP is it. Not only is the concept of Gross Domestic Product (GDP) considered narrow and outdated in mainstream economics, some economists also view it as woefully unreliable, citing its failure to factor in social welfare and the development of human capital. A German economist famously called the idea of GDP "laboured and overwrought", as it measures income but not equality, growth but not development, and it ignores values like social cohesion and the environment.

Yet, governments, businesses and probably most people swear by it. As an indication of the level of distrust and scepticism expressed with regard to this statistical icon, the tiny remote Himalayan kingdom of Bhutan invented its own Gross National Happiness (GNH) index in 1972. The idea was to use happiness and other non-economic aspects of wellbeing as a measure of good governance and social prosperity, given the obvious limitations of GDP.

Consider the following analogy: Discerning parents would understand the difference between the growth and development of their child. In the first crucial years, the child becomes bigger and actually grows physically. It may even be a source of happiness to them if the child is growing very fast. But after about 18 to 20 years, they don't want the child to grow any more; they want the child to develop – to become wiser; to learn foreign languages; to learn how to have important love relationships; to be a good parent; and so forth. Similarly, if an undeveloped country or corporation was flooded with money it would be richer but no more developed. On the other hand, if a well developed country or corporation was suddenly deprived of wealth, it would not be less developed.

Unfortunately, in the economic sphere, we haven't made this distinction between "growth" and "development". Economic growth in many instances, whether market-led or government-facilitated, is still widely confused with economic development, even by economists themselves. The term "economic growth" is more widely used internationally since quite a few economists believe it to be a necessary condition for development. But is this ostensible intellectual gospel always true especially in the context of developing countries? Does growth come before development or do they occur simultaneously?

Of course, there has been endless debate and discussion on the use and application of the two terms. Some economists have even gone as far as to suggest that there is no relation between the two. Yet, I believe growth and development do not have to conflict; they can reinforce each other.

In other words, growth and development are neither mutually exclusive nor are they perfectly correlated. Research has shown that high economic growth may not necessarily result in increased economic development of the overall population, and targeting human development indicators will not automatically translate into higher level of economic growth. Further, some economists believe that a lack of resources can limit growth but not development. The more developed individuals, organisations or societies become, the less they depend on resources and the more they can do with whatever resources they have.

So what is development then? First and foremost, development is both a human condition and a progressive mindset that facilitates people upliftment, cultural advancement, and the harmonious and social integration of society. The concept of economic development as used by mainstream economists explains the "increase in the standard of living in a nation's population with sustained growth from a simple, low-income economy to a modern, high-income economy. It is typically measured in terms of work and income, but also includes improvements in human development, education, health, choice, and environmental sustainability."

The six factors that constitute economic development are education, incentives, quality of life, infrastructure, health and social cohesion. Some economists speak of the four Ts of development namely: talent, technology, tolerance and thinking.

Essentially, economic development alleviates and elevates people from low standards of living into proper and effective members of civil society. Since the notion of development implies more a matter of learning than earning, the famous German economist Hans-Werner Sinn believes it may be more relevant to measure progress and quality of life in developing nations. Promoted and sustained through social and technological progress, economic development implies a change in the way goods and services are produced, but not an increase in their actual production.

Of crucial importance is the fact that development nowadays is defined in the context of sustainability which means meeting the needs of the present without compromising future needs. The main idea behind sustainability is to shift the path of progress from growth, which is not sustainable, toward development, which can be. The sustainable economy must at some point stop growing, but it need not stop developing.

Adair Turner, former head of the Confederation of British Industry (CBI), said in the 2008 book "Do Good Lives Have to Cost the Earth" that we need to "dethrone growth" and place more importance on social justice, ecological sustainability and prosperity.

In contrast, economic growth entails only an increase in quantitative output; it may or may not involve development. Consequently, as economist Amartya Sen points out, "Economic growth is one aspect of the process of economic development."

As I mentioned before, GDP is an indicator for economic growth, and thereby is not single-handedly expedient for economic development. My economics professor used to argue that economic growth is a more relevant metric for progress in developed countries. However, the two famous Indian-American economists, Jagdish Bhagwati and Arvind Panagariya seem to think that growth is especially important for developing countries. They maintained that economic growth – measured by GDP – constitutes the foundation for any meaningful development and the reduction of poverty in developing nations. Only on the basis of fast growth, they say, redistributive reforms for poverty alleviation and human capital as well as capacity building become viable.

Now I admit that I am an unswerving believer in economic development. However, I also believe that growth is crucial for economic and social stability. Although there are no explicit indicators for economic development, the Human Development Index (HDI) is a popular and reasonable measure which covers GDP, education, life expectancy and purchasing power parity. The HDI also takes into account the literacy rate & life expectancy which affect productivity, and could lead to economic growth. It also leads to the creation of more opportunities in the sectors of education, healthcare, employment and the conservation of the environment.

So what are the prerequisites for economic development? Most economists concur that strategic (long-term) planning, technology, political conditions and the attitude of the people are necessary; all being major determinants for nation-building. In all fairness, lifting the poor out of poverty and making them self-sufficient is not a task that the government can do on its own. The private sector, think tanks and civil society are equally responsible partners in helping promote and sustain the economic health of a nation.

Finally, does growth create development? There are different opinions on that question. First the "yes" side believes that growth causes development because some of the increase in income gets spent on human development such as education and health. Conversely, the "no" side assert that poor countries have experienced economic growth with little or no economic development, indicating that they have functioned mainly as resource-providers to wealthy industrialized countries. They provide Angola as an example, where it is one of the fastest growing countries through its huge oil fields, but there is nearly no development.

It has become conventional wisdom that the idea of taking economic growth for granted and focusing just on social development is a mistake. Conversely, taking economic development for granted while focusing just on GDP growth through industrialization is equally risky.

3. The Middle Class: Who They Are and Why They Matter

You may have realized that during every election cycle in the United States, presidential hopefuls on both sides of the political divide vow to defend the middleclass (a fluid group of people who are not poor but not truly rich), and often promote economic agendas promising tax relief and other incentives for that demographic. Invariably, praising the middle class has been a staple of American politics since the mid-forties, and the concerns shared by its members have echoed those of the country at large.

Barack Obama pushed for "middle-class economics" during his presidential campaign in 2008, believing that growing income polarization in America threatens economic stability and thwarts social progress. In fact, when he took office in 2009, revival of middle class jobs was one of his mantras. In a "State of the Union" speech in 2015, President Obama explained, "Middle-class economics means helping working families feel more secure in a world of constant change. That means helping folks afford childcare, college, health care, a home, retirement – and my budget will address each of these issues, lowering the taxes of working families and putting thousands of dollars back into their pockets each year."

In many developed countries like the UK and Germany, political parties are often elected to office on a "middle class" campaign pitch. In burnishing their economic credentials, they strategically focus on the strength of the middle class as a stabilizing influence on society as well as a source of economic growth. Historically, the middle class has been at the forefront of great social causes. In France, for instance, the middle classes helped drive the French Revolution that overthrew the monarchy and established a republic.

The corollary is that a strong middle class comprising of teachers, doctors, entrepreneurs, supervisors, managers and other professionals, forms the backbone of an economy and provides a stable consumer base (a source of demand for goods and services) that drives productive investment. Against the backdrop of rising inequality, it is middle class workers who grow the economy and promote the development of human capital and a well educated population, not the rich. Further, the strength of an economy can be measured directly by the strength of its middle class, which usually translates to better governance, bigger tax intakes, deeper credit markets, and greater spending in social sectors, such as public health and education. Moreover, a strong middle class supports inclusive political and economic institutions, which underpin economic growth.

Yet, though often mentioned in political speeches and policy proposals, the term is famously difficult to define and can mean different things to different people. In fact, the common measures of what constitutes middle class vary significantly among cultures.

Germany, a country with a religious fervour for the working class, has taught us that if you want a thriving middle class, you need to build an industrial base. In America, education plays a role in who is deemed to be "middle class". "Having long-term financial security by staying out of debt, balancing spending with income, and saving for the future" was chosen by the American enterprise Institute as the best indicator of whether a person falls into the middle class as opposed to simply owning a home and a car.

Brazilian economist Eduardo Giannetti da Fonseca, describes members of the middle class as: "People who are not resigned to a life of poverty, who are prepared to make sacrifices to create a better life for themselves, but who have not started with life's material problems solved, because they have material assets to make their lives easy."

At any rate, alarm bells have been sounding for quite a while now over the economic plight of the middle class, especially their reduced capacity to consume. Globally, the fact that this target group is falling behind and may have now become a vulnerable class is probably a reflection of the failure of governmental policy and economic liberalism. There is evidence that the trouble started decades ago, long before the financial crisis of 2008. The financial crisis may have simply exacerbated the problem.

The Washington Post poignantly states that "The middle class took America to the moon. Then something went horribly wrong." The British Guardian indulged our attention recently when it wrote, "Who are the new middle classes around the world? You'd be surprised how poor some are."

Despite a World Bank report released in 2012 that revealed the middle class in Latin America and the Caribbean grew to an estimated 152 million in 2009, compared to 103 million in 2003, an increase of 50 percent, Barbadian economist Clyde Mascoll thinks that for the first time in the history of Barbados the middle class is in crisis. "Since 2007 middle-class Barbados has been under severe pressure living on a fixed income. This does not mean that poor people are not hurting because, by extension, they are hurting; because people who have more are hurting, the poor are even hurting more. Since Independence this is the first time that we are experiencing a middle-class or a middle-income crisis. It has to be addressed".

The Jamaican Gleaner laments in a recent piece entitled: Looking Back, Looking Forward – The Dwindling Middle Class, "What many people have long accepted is that Jamaica's middle class is in a state of flux, with most persons realistically falling in the less distinguished category of working poor or underemployed."

The World Bank report which I cited earlier identifies three strategies which governments could employ "to gain the support of the middle class for a fairer and more legitimate social contract:"

- Explicitly incorporate the goal of equal opportunities into public policy to break the perception that the system is rigged in favour of the most privileged.
- Embark on a second generation of reforms to the social protection system – including both social assistance and social insurance – to overcome fragmentation and thus enhance fairness and efficiency.
- Break the vicious cycle of low taxation and low quality of public services by investing some of the region's commodity windfall to improve the quality of public services, service and administration

"Some of the key factors favouring the upward mobility in Latin America were higher levels of education among workers; higher employment in the formal sector; more people living in urban areas; more women in the labour force; and smaller families."

Understanding which policies create, expand and protect the middle class has become more important than ever. The new progressive thinking is that it takes more than economic growth to reach the middle class; targeted social policy is imperative.

Recent analysis of socio-economic hierarchy shows that entrepreneurship and invention are rooted in the middle class, and that the purchasing power of that target group is something that economic policy should seek to harness and exploit. It's any wonder why the rise in middle-class worker productivity has generated much of the wealth in the BRIC nations, according to the International Labour Organization (ILO).

Saint Lucia is not immune from the effects of the declining middle class. If economic history is any guide, an actual rise in middle class jobs is crucial in spurring the kind of sustainable growth needed in our economy. But again, how can this happen when there is hardly any talk about the middle class. I am not even aware of the commissioning of any study to find out what is happening to that demographic and how it may have been transformed in recent years. Is the middle class in Saint Lucia the "silent majority"? Have they become more vocal politically or are they gasping for air? Do we even have an official definition for "middle class"?

Whatever the answers to those questions are, let's hope that politicians don't see the middle class as something to create with the gains of economic growth, as opposed to an actual source of economic growth.

4. SMEs – The Answer to Unemployment

Much has been written about the pivotal role that small and medium sized enterprises (SMEs) play in the economic development of Saint Lucia. Not only are they crucial for nation building, but also for national innovativeness and competitiveness. Socio-economic paradigm shifts cannot happen without them; and poverty cannot be reduced without them. They are what produce a country's middle class. Therefore, there is little doubt that SMEs, when treated as an economic sector, can become the engine of social and economic growth.

Still, our record at generating start-ups or at quickly turning smallish firms into medium size firms is average. In all fairness, over the years several useful programmes and policies have been put in place to guide and assist SMEs in realizing their full business potential and in generating employment.

Evidence of this sector's importance is found in the "Industrial Policy of Saint Lucia" where it states: "The micro and small enterprise sector is the backbone of the St. Lucian industrial economy." According to Saint Lucia's Ministry of Commerce and Industry, over 80% of businesses on the island are SMEs operating in areas such as construction, agriculture, transportation, manufacturing, hospitality and cosmetology.

However there is still an incredible amount of work to be done in terms of institutional incentives, access, information and value generation. The Small Enterprise Development Unit (SEDU) has identified some of the challenges SMEs face including lack of market research & information, human resource constraints, poor cash flow management and limited access to finance. Recently, the Saint Lucia Trade Export Promotion Agency (TEPA) in collaboration with the Caribbean Export Development Agency (CEDA) held training programmes for small and medium sized businesses with a view to building capacity in exporters and enterprises, thereby helping them grow and become more competitive.

A TEPA press release on the programme read, "The initiative will seek to raise the level of productivity and profitability within SMEs, through the Experiential Learning Methodology (i. e. case study based and driven by practical examples and assignments."

I believe such efforts are commendable especially since it has become crystal clear that accessing international markets is no longer simply an option for Saint Lucian SMEs, but an economic necessity. Saint Lucian companies can no longer afford to focus solely on domestic and regional markets. If they wish to grow, they must take steps towards increasing scale and scope, and trading internationally.

The critical question I suppose is: How can we promote an enterprise culture or forge an entrepreneurial spirit in Saint Lucia which can help catapult greater wealth and job creation?

It's quite instructive how governments around the world have responded to the challenges of SMEs against the backdrop of globalization, competition and technology. In order to assist SMEs, policymakers' attention has focused on supporting working capital, easing access to finance and implementing a better regulation agenda that addresses issues such as licensing, registration and taxation. They have also been hard at work in providing SMEs with the tools and skills needed to become better suppliers and distributors.

SMEs particularly in the agricultural sector in Saint Lucia continue to struggle to access growth capital. Both policy-makers and financial institutions need to do more to help these enterprises access finance. The Saint Lucia Chamber of Commerce, Industry and Agriculture has a huge role to play here. Notwithstanding the good work it has done over the years, I believe that now more than ever, with the assistance of the ministry of international trade, it can provide even more crucial support to SMEs seeking to expand through the provision of the following services: international networking opportunities, trade documentation services, international trade training, and the facilitation of trade missions. Particularly useful would be the development of knowledge and information resources to guide SMEs through the red tape challenge associated with international activity, and to help them access all appropriate sources of funding.

In terms of the role the education system can play in fostering entrepreneurial growth, perhaps the time has come for us to introduce "manufacturing science" and "entrepreneurship" into our various curricula at all levels of our school system. As is most evident in countries like India, Germany and increasingly China, courses in manufacturing science are critical in developing early entrepreneurial and creativity skills to help young people start their own business rather than waiting for someone else to provide them with a job. Statistical evidence in emerging economies has demonstrated that manufacturing has the largest multiplier of all sectors of the economy and is of vital importance in maintaining a nation's innovative capacity. Manufacturing employs workers at all skill and education levels and may be critical to other high value-added sectors of the economy including our vital tourism industry.

In a Voice newspaper article in 2015, I wrote: "The answer to our unemployment woes may well lie within the sphere of private sector business nurturing and development. Although foreign direct investment (FDI) is essential, more critical is the support and incentives provided to entrepreneurs, and small and medium size enterprises (SMEs), either through targeted business development policies or fiscal stimuli. SMEs are the lifeblood of a country's economy; they are essential to generating good jobs. Long recognized as crucial to economic development, entrepreneurs and SMEs are increasingly seen as crucial for sustainable recovery and for a strong middle class, a source of economic growth. A strong middle class provides a stable consumer base that drives productive investment. Hence, tax policy is one of the most obvious policy levers that policymakers control to alter the incentives of firms and entrepreneurs. When business tax structures are well-designed, government facilitates investment in the emerging firms that create jobs."

Saint Lucia has the potential to build its SMEs on the strength and initiative of its creative arts industry. Unfortunately, the lack of technical, structural and financial investment in the creative and literary arts industry (perhaps due in the first place to scarce financial resources) bodes ill for our local economy since it could have given this country a unique advantage in a world evermore reliant on the knowledge economy. For all we know, this could be the elusive answer to our unemployment problem. The point is if we are to truly make an economic success of the creative industries in Saint Lucia, we must aim to strengthen the sector, promote intellectual property rights and invest in the next generation of content creators to keep the flow of IP coming. The economic benefits could be huge.

Research on the subject of the importance and success of SMEs in many developed and emerging economies has left us with three general lessons. First, you do not need to try to build your own version of Silicon Valley to prosper; it is often better to focus on your traditional strengths in "old-fashioned" industries. Second, niches that appear tiny can produce huge global markets. The third lesson is that developing nations can secure and preserve high-quality jobs in a vast array of local industries so long as they are willing to focus and innovate.

5. When the Most Productive Sector is the Weakest Link

Economic development does not come easy especially when a country has no mineral resources and lacks a solid manufacturing base for export production. Over the course of time, the experiences and successes of resource-poor countries have pointed to the need for sectoral support policies that help create a network of commercial interdependence, skilfully weaving together the manufacturing, agriculture and service sectors. Although the various outcomes of many of these economic policies manifest the constant challenge of keeping unemployment low, they nonetheless predicate a change of perspective in the manner in which development should be approached. In the final analysis, adopting a lateral and creative mindset may be just as critical as the imperatives of technology and organization in the quest for prosperity and economic growth.

On the face of it, the tourism industry has done well in recent times and has helped keep our struggling economy somewhat afloat, as agriculture and manufacturing have declined. The World Travel and Tourism Council (WTCC) estimates that in Saint Lucia, tourism's contribution to GDP was 65 per cent in 2014, supporting 10,000 jobs – and is forecast to rise further in 2015. Impressive you might think, but how much of that wealth trickles down from tourism to the other economic sectors? Can tourism be a real driver for recovery when the other productive sectors are not performing?

The 2014/2015 Social and Economic Review states that "the island recorded 1.034 million visitors in 2014, the highest in the history of tourist arrivals for the destination as record numbers were realized for both stay-over and yacht arrivals." Despite this impressive result, the other economic sectors continue to be far removed from the country's success in tourism. Today, the linkage with primary agricultural production and manufacturing remains weak. Given the significant patterns of consumption and resource utilization in tourism, there is enormous potential for agriculture, agribusiness, small-scale manufacturing and the creative industries to supply the inputs needed to produce tourism and leisure services through forward, backward and horizontal linkages – resulting in greater resource efficiency and encouraging large-scale production. Further, the knowledge spillovers from linkages through the application of innovation and new technologies will benefit small businesses and farmer co-operatives by helping reduce their production costs and increasing revenue.

Since independence, our island has struggled with problems associated with development, and these have been particularly exacerbated by the absence of an inter-sectoral growth strategy. Plenty of economic literature has been produced citing how the establishment of sustainable and beneficial linkages among the productive sectors could enable the utilisation of the ability of the tourism industry to diversify our local economy, and thereby stimulate employment through local sourcing (insourcing) and leveraging more economic activity.

The tourism industry must be viewed as both a source of income and a basis and catalyst for greater inter-sectoral development. By now, one would have thought that the island's main source of foreign exchange earnings would be effectively linked to other parts of the economy, having replaced the agricultural sector as the economic mainstay. But unfortunately tourism is still a disjointed industry – and the nation's economic structures are poorly designed to achieve the desired inter-sectoral synergies. The linear and short-termist mindset of economic policymakers as well as the sectoral approach to development have not worked and need to be reviewed and rethought. It is now time to adopt a non-linear approach to growth where sustainable, integrated tourism becomes a new paradigm for holistic and inclusive development in Saint Lucia.

I am thinking, by now the growth of the tourism industry should have led to the growth of agribusiness as well as the growth of the creative and cultural industries. I am at a loss for words as to why successive administrations didn't see the bigger picture and recognize the need to vigorously implement policies and programmes to pursue true economic sustainability, especially since tourism's potential linkage effects renders the industry a viable economic development strategy. Why haven't we worked harder to overcome the obstacles blocking inter-sectoral linkages, since many economists believe this approach to be our sole means of long-term survival? We should have used the tourism industry – bolstered by educational and industrial linkages – as a development tool, especially as we have no real viable alternatives for economic development.

Stuart McCook, in a trenchant review of the book, Last Resorts: The Cost of Tourism in the Caribbean authored by Polly Pattulo, posits the view that what Caribbean tourism presently engenders among other industries is not "linkages" but indeed "leakages". He poignantly states: "Two important measures of the economic effects of the tourist industry are 'leakage' and 'linkage'. Leakage is the proportion of import expenditures to export earnings. Many Caribbean nations import goods and services to sustain the tourist industry: the average leakage for the region is 70 percent. In some cases, such as the Bahamas, leakage is as high as 90 percent. Countries that can provide more of the goods and services locally have a much lower leakage rate: Jamaica's leakage in 1994 was 37 percent. Linkage refers to the ways in which the tourist industry utilizes locally produced goods and services rather than importing them."

It's worth noting that annually more than US$2 billion is spent by CARICOM countries on food imports, although their combined population is only six million people. If ever we needed evidence of the neglect and underdevelopment of the agricultural sector in the region, this is it. Not only have Caribbean governments failed to facilitate and exploit inter-sectoral linkage synergies, they have also done precious little to promote food security in the region.

Right here in Saint Lucia, I really can't recall (over the years) any sustained and persistent attempts by way of programmes and policies to increase the use of local produce in tourism enterprises. After so many years of lamenting the structural deficiencies in the system, there are still no salient signs of change – tourism and the other economic sectors seem set to exist side by side without touching. The intermediary support structures that would have enabled buyers and suppliers to come together are conspicuously lacking.

In further deploring the weak interface between tourism and agriculture as well as the absence of tourism-induced improvements to industrial and export systems, Stuart McCook maintains: "More could be done to stimulate linkages in the tourist economy, particularly with the agricultural sector. In resorts and on cruise ships, tourists are more likely to eat tropical fruit imported from other parts of the world than that produced locally. Local agriculture, long geared to the export market, has had difficulty shifting to meet the tastes of the tourist industry. In fundamental terms, the Caribbean produces what it does not eat, and eats what it does not produce. Nonetheless, recent efforts in Jamaica and Grenada suggest that it is possible to strengthen the linkages between the agricultural economy and the tourist industry."

Without viable policies that address the driving forces behind linkage industries, sustainable development in the Caribbean islands will remain a pipedream. I strongly believe in order to fully understand the economic impact of linkage industries, policy makers and businesses will need to acquire accurate and reliable data on tourism and examine the overall causal and correlational relationships with other sectors. Assessing the economic impact of tourism will help to inform the conduct of stimulus policies in response to economic recessions and international crises.

Like I said before, the "old ways" of economic development no longer work. If we are to achieve our stated economic objectives, i. e. create new jobs, raise income levels, diversify the economy, sustain local businesses and help them grow, and create new business, the new approach to development will have to be one where old problems are thought of in new ways, and ideas that had not been questioned before, rethought. Unfortunately, with all the great promise that tourism holds for our resource-starved nation, I'm afraid it is still the weakest link in our economic system.

6. All Development is Local

The preponderant view of the general population is that the weaknesses of the Saint Lucian state are particularly apparent at the local level and that promises of governance reform in the public sector have been mere palliatives. By any measure, the greatest failure of our governance system resides in the dysfunctional state of local government – an institution considered by many as the most fundamental form of grass-roots democracy and the lodestar of community welfare. As far back as 1945, the West India Royal Commission wrote that "The improvement of the social conditions in these territories depends in a large measure on co-operation between the central administration and the people through properly constituted and well-conducted local authorities." Even the renowned Jamaican scholar, the late Professor Rex Nettleford noted in 1998 that "Local government is an investment in human capability for self-governance over the long haul in building a nation and a society."

Not surprisingly, one of the things I've recognized about the political structure of progressive and successful economies around the world is their well-oiled local government machinery – a structure viewed as critically important to their productive economic development thrust. Besides, the conventional wisdom is that the institutions of local government are significant for the realization of people-centred development in developing nations. So what exactly is wrong with local government in Saint Lucia and why does it portend failure for the national economy?

Firstly and ironically, the question of how towns and villages are structured and governed to deliver services to their residents isn't something our constitution specifically addresses. This of course is not the case in many European and Asian countries, where local government has been entrenched and strengthened as a full sphere of government in more recent constitutions.

For too long, our efforts as a nation have been focussed on the performance and productive capacity of the national economy rather than the stability and strengthening of local economies. Despite the enormous role that local government has been proven to play in national development and democratic empowerment, town and village councils around the island continue to lack vigour and are poorly capacitated to undertake expansive administrative responsibilities and resource mobilization, whether it be in dealing with the perennial problems at the Soufriere Hospital or in addressing the dire need for reliable portable water supply in Dennery North. As it stands, our communities are governed directly by the Saint Lucia Parliament without a system of local government to develop, administer, and maintain infrastructure and public facilities such as parochial roads, bridges, drains and gullies, etc. Most, if not all major decision-making authority rests in the hands of a concentrated group of leaders and decision makers in the parliament or legislature.

I'm sure you're also asking, shouldn't a vibrant democracy be giving more power back to the people at the local level where the economic and social impact are likely to be most pronounced? Today within the modern nation-state, government should operate at many different levels, ranging from villages to districts, towns and cities. By now, through ordinary legislation, every single district on the island should have had elected mayors with executive and administrative functions, assisted by a town clerk and overseen by a district council comprising of business owners, bankers and representatives of the clergy. This governance model, bolstered by a system of accountability, has been a winning formula to create vibrant and thriving communities, and has been proven to deliver economic results by getting government down to the grassroots and giving rural dwellers a sense of belonging. Critically, with the right checks and balances and due process policies, politicians can be prevented from carving out for themselves little pools of patronage and misusing funds for their own purposes.

Ever the avid promoter of good governance and community-led local development (CLLD) , the World Bank, through its local economic development (LED) initiatives, offers local governments, the private sector, non-governmental organizations and the local community the opportunity to work together to improve local economies. According to the global institution, "the aim of LED is to enhance competitiveness and thus encourage sustainable growth that is inclusive... LED is about communities continually improving their investment climate and business through an enabling environment to enhance their competitiveness, retain jobs and improve incomes. It is a process by which public, business and non-governmental sector partners work collectively to create better conditions for economic growth and employment generation." Further, the bank believes that "most development – and most pro-poor public services that people rely on day to day – takes place at the local level, whether it is schools for children, health care for mothers and children, seeds and fertilizer for farmers, or access to clean water and sanitation."

Alas, we have paid too much attention to the institutions and operations of central government and not enough to whether (and how) these efforts trickle down to local communities where the process of empowerment and transformation actually begins. Perhaps we should borrow a page from the Dominican Republic where the capital Santo Domingo and other municipalities have been given ample power to decide how to spend public money in their areas so they can meet the local people's needs. In developing countries like Ghana and Nigeria, local government is the first door that people knock on when they need assistance from the government.

In more ways than one, the failure of decentralisation in Saint Lucia has impacted the way in which essential services are both delivered and accessed. I believe the time has come for us to look seriously at how powers, functions, responsibilities and resources can be effectively transferred from the capital city to local communities to ensure the effectiveness and efficiency of governmental services and processes, particularly in the face of increasing aggregate duties and pressures of central government. The rural-to-urban migration of people for educational, social and economic reasons has engendered a myriad of problems from urban congestion to social misery, further hampering the efforts of the authorities at supplying water, housing and health care.

It's now clear that our long-term success in addressing the aforementioned community issues hinges on our efforts to establish local government agencies that supply public needs. Life in our towns and villages can be made a lot more bearable and attractive by investing more in agriculture and horticulture, housing, recreational activities and public services.

In the quest to service the developmental needs of our people, we'll need rational discourse at the town hall level so that communities can become sufficiently empowered to take responsibility for their own destiny.

I have little doubt that we can build and develop our nation's human capital, social amenities and civil society if local governments from Gros-Islet to Vieux-Fort are equipped and allowed to perform their fundamental roles with respect to public health, education, poverty eradication, issuance of licences, etc. Without effective local government, the authorities will remain isolated from the people they seek to represent and administer. Evidently, it still holds true that the closer a representative government is to the people, the better it works. In the final analysis, we can all appreciate that all development, like all politics, is local.

7. Development is a Mindset

In recognition of performance efficiency as one of the great unquestioned socio-economic virtues of our age, Thomas L. Friedman explains in his book, The World Is Flat: "Every morning in Africa, a gazelle wakes up. It knows it must run faster than the fastest lion or it will be killed. Every morning a lion wakes up. It knows it must outrun the slowest gazelle or it will starve to death. It doesn't matter whether you are a lion or a gazelle. When the sun comes up, you better start running."

The gazelles I suspect Friedman had in mind are small island states like Saint Lucia with their inherent structural vulnerabilities, limited capital resources and rapidly declining rates of productivity. The lions on the other hand, are the developed and emerging economies with their insatiable appetites for huge capital inflows, natural resources and productivity growth.

The lions, restless and merciless in their quest to conquer and survive, lie unpretentiously on the great plains of globalization, and are waiting to make the kill. How will small states fight back and do they have a chance at survival? Can we continue to bury our proverbial heads in the sand and ignore our deficiencies in economic competitiveness and productivity? No one owes us anything; hence we need to keep moving to secure the changes and benefits that we want and need.

The broader question is whether our mindset and work practices are compatible with economic productivity and efficiency. Because productivity is considered a key source of economic growth and competitiveness, the efficiency of firms and organizations depend not only on a well-trained workforce, but also on professionalism, critical thinking and strong work ethics. How do you shift the mindset of a people or institutions to align with critical national developmental needs?

Shifting mindsets to align with a country's macroeconomic objectives can be challenging, but not impossible. The best approach is to start with the leaders, managers and supervisors at all levels of the organization, in order to ensure congruent understanding of national purpose, and align leadership mindset with capability. The inescapable truth is that we can never get anywhere close to the ranks of emerging economies if our work ethic is lacking.

A poor work ethic hinders economic progress the same way it cripples productivity, and hence competitiveness becomes a difficult game to play. In fact, the latest research shows that poor work ethic in the wider Caribbean is the region's worst enemy and has become an economic pandemic. Compounding the problem are bad working conditions, poor leadership and supervision, as well as inadequate and weak institutions.

I have always maintained that in order for nations to progress and achieve their full potential, the four Ts of development (talent, technology, tolerance and thinking) must be leveraged sufficiently, and must remain the bottom line of any development thrust. To foster productivity, governments and organizations need to provide people with the enablers required to get there – a plan, skillsets, toolsets, and efficiency in the transitional process.

Why isn't there a national educational thrust to educate Saint Lucians on the importance of punctuality, consistency and reliability? Indeed, these are the true underpinnings of productivity and not necessarily the much trumpeted ideas of input to output ratio or production efficiency. In today's age of deadlines and tight schedules, time management is essential for business execution and organizational effectiveness. From all indications, punctuality doesn't seem to be a traditional virtue of Saint Lucians and there seems to be no great sense of urgency surrounding due dates and appointments.

This counter-productive mindset is everywhere to be noticed, from the lack of punctuality of government ministers to start official events to the tardiness of doctors and lawyers in the private sector. The structure of our daily lives, which is based on accepting things as they come, could also be the cause of such an approach to the concept of time and reliability. According to island thinking, if things do not go according to plan, there is no point in getting upset. Time, for many people, is something to share rather than something to steal.

Another issue of importance is the need to start pruning the regulatory forest in order to eliminate superfluous bureaucracy. Take for example the huge amount of paperwork and time required to conduct a transaction at a commercial bank here on the island. How can you even plan your day productively when you are frustratingly held up at commercial banks and asked to produce all sorts of utterly pointless documents for a simple financial transaction?

Then there is the issue of customer service both in the public and private sectors, where people believe that they're doing the customer a favour. Simple things like acknowledging a customer or asking whether or not one has already received service are in many ways foreign concepts. Even the practice of subjecting Saint Lucian nationals to pointless paperwork and questions at our two airports is rather preposterous.

Moreover, if Saint Lucia is serious about improving productivity and competing with the rest of the world, it should start by cleaning up its holiday calendar. The number of public holidays celebrated during the course of the year is having a knock-on effect on business productivity and in turn, on the economy. Can't some public holidays be made half-days? There is a case to be more flexible and to move holidays to a Friday or Monday so they do not break up the week in that way, causing small and medium-sized enterprises to lose production days.

Changes in technology are a major source of permanent increases in productivity. However, the digital revolution has yet to fulfil its promise of higher productivity in the island.

The public service is the primary front office agent in small nation-states like ours. Any blueprint for enhancing public sector efficiency must embrace the imperative of Business Process Re-engineering (BPR), which encompasses a new orientation in delivering public services based on the simplification of procedures geared towards providing better quality service, increasing speed, reducing cost and transforming the workforce culture. Both long-overdue and indispensable, BPR can help optimize public service efficiency by eliminating duplication of functions and obliterating forms of work that do not add value to the service rendered to the public.

Furthermore, we can improve national productivity by building better infrastructure (four-lane highways to ease the flow of traffic), reducing the size of the informal economy, and efficiently adopting new technologies.

An idea whose time has come is the proper naming of streets island-wide and the swift introduction of postal codes and addresses to increase logistical efficiency in the island. If we get it right, the benefits can be enormous.

Lest we forget, development is a mindset; a frame of mind needed in the pursuit of personal advancement and social transformation. It shapes our weltanschauung and fosters democratic dynamism in our important national institutions. In seeking a regional competitive edge, we need to become lateral and strategic thinkers guided by international standards and procedures; and develop more focus, vision and priorities in our commercial dealings.

For a while now, I have followed the productivity debate in Saint Lucia and remain unconvinced that we have addressed the fundamental requirements for national efficiency. "Productivity isn't everything, but in the long-run it is almost everything," said Paul Krugman in his book "The Age of Diminished Expectations". The more productive an economy is, the more effectively it uses capital and labour.

Productivity growth is the key to unlocking sustainable growth in our small island. Rising productivity is the key to making possible permanent increases in the standard of living. Most experts concur that some basic steps such as better training and supervision, improved communications, sufficient staff and greater autonomy and freedom can go a long way in improving worker morale. These may be small steps for workers, but a giant leap for national productivity.

8. Are Retirees Distorting the Labour Market?

Finding economic solutions to the developmental challenges of so-called Third World countries was the life-long and celestial vocation of Sir Arthur Lewis, an illustrious son of this soil whose birthday and outstanding achievements are celebrated annually here in his home country. Having contributed immensely to the field of labour economics, Sir Arthur was also known for his intellectual tenacity and was aptly nicknamed "Consultant Physician of the Ailing Economics". Although his various labour-market analyses didn't exactly deal with retirement economics, I nonetheless shudder to think what the good doctor would have said about the phenomenon (an ailment to some) known in the parlance of economics as the "lump of labour".

Now for those of us who are not altogether acquainted with this bizarre term, it is the improbable contention that if a group enters the labour market and stays in it beyond their normal retirement date, others will be unable to gain employment. Whether or not this idea is considered a fallacy by many economists today, the fact remains it has been widely discussed in academic circles, albeit without final resolution.

At any rate, the theory of the "lump of labour" has been revisited and expanded to reflect the paradigm shift of the 65+ generation taking on new full-time jobs even when their "real" careers are over. In other words, the workers retire at 65, start to collect their retirement benefits, and then another company hires them – irrespective of the fact that unemployment levels are high and universities are churning out armies of qualified manpower. But whereas dynamic economies like the United States and Germany with their advanced labour markets have the capacity to absorb such potential risks and costs, this development in small fragile countries is bound to create a drag on the labour market – in effect having unintended consequences on the economy in terms of employment, investment and consumption.

So has our labour market been impacted by this trend? Base on anecdotal evidence, I believe it has, if only partially. At a time of high unemployment in Saint Lucia, we have started to witness a phenomenon whereby the older generation refuses to shuffle quietly into retirement – instead opting to pursue a second career by taking on another full-time job, even while receiving reasonably generous pension benefits. Now it would be understandable if a cash-strapped pensioner decided to accept a job in order to bring in needed income or to make up for lost wealth. However, when former highly-paid executives or public servants (often with few or no kids) take on late employment despite receiving generous pension benefits, we need to examine whether this may be distorting the labour market and affecting the chances of the younger generation in getting a foot in the door. From the face of it, I rather suspect that younger workers are already getting the "shorter" end of the stick during this economic slowdown than older ones.

However, let me hasten to add that already, plenty economists have outrightly rejected the notion that stretched-out boomer careers are displacing the younger generation. In fact, research on developed economies show that droves of older workers aren't to blame for high unemployment. No less an authority than Paul Krugman has deconstructed this argument – skewering the idea and believing it to be one peddled mostly by the economically naïve left. According to Krugman who, like Sir Arthur, is a Nobel-Prize winner: "The "lump-of-labour thinking – and the policy paralysis it encourages – feeds protectionism. If the public no longer believes that the economy can create new jobs, it will demand that we protect old jobs from new competitors…"

Yet, the evidence from various research studies doesn't always reflect the realities of especially small, vulnerable economies with underdeveloped social welfare systems, weak product and labour markets, sclerotic private sectors and poorly-functioning institutions.

On the other hand, there are economists who share the opinion of Rick Newman, a senior economics writer who has worked for U.S.

News & World Report and who covered the 2008 financial meltdown as well as the Great Recession, that "the economy can only support so many jobs, and as older workers stay on the payroll longer, it impedes the creation of new jobs, many of which would go to younger workers. Older people remaining on the job later in life are stealing jobs from young people."

Of course, I don't necessarily agree with that crass perspective, but we still do need to know for a fact what impact or profound consequences this trend is having on our resource-constrained society and economy. Needless to say, we cannot just assume that every piece of (one-size-fits-all) research commissioned and carried out in developed countries invariably apply to us, especially given the size and nature of our economy, and our level of development. The same way the presumed consequences of technological progress on employment is still a subject of much heated debate today, we shouldn't be quick to dismiss any argument as fallacious, in the absence of longitudinal research into our real circumstances. In our own local context, we need to find out whether well-off retirees are in fact restricting job opportunities for younger workers as they stay in the workforce longer.

In some European countries where it has been observed that pensioners don't always stay retired, governments have instituted measures to deal with the issue by imposing higher taxes on net incomes which exceed a certain threshold after retirement. In other instances, there are regulations which stipulate transition periods of up two years in which elders are obliged to train the junior workforce. Furthermore, working after the retirement age in some developed countries like Germany, even while receiving a comfortable retirement package will affect your social security benefits.

Against the backdrop of high unemployment and fiscal pressures, labour markets have undergone major and frequent changes – and there is no rule that demand one group should make way for another. Saint Lucia saw its own major changes in the labour market in 2015 when the retirement age for the receipt of a full National Insurance pension was increased over a 15 year period from 60 to 65 years. Still, in the current environment of unemployment and low investment, there is an enduring need for small islands like ours to find ways to assess and stabilize their job markets with the support of strong labour-market institutions and (supply-sided) active labour-market policies. We need to find out what's behind the continued high unemployment – whether it's really a structural problem, the fault of ill-advised economic policy or the outcome of the changing character of the global business cycle.

9. Are Commercial Banks Out of Balance?

Many people rightly attribute the financial crisis of 2008 to "greed", Wall Street (meaning the banks), and free-market capitalism. In the absence of effective regulations, the reckless financial practices of both conventional and shadow banks (hedge funds and credit insurance provider, for instance) brought untold misery to millions of people around the globe. Still it's clear that many banks haven't learnt much from the Great Recession and continue to use shady practices that cost customers substantial sums of money. It seems like consumers might be trying to hide from the banks, but the banks keep coming up with creative ways to pick their pockets.

Now if you asked Saint Lucians how they view the local banking industry, most people would probably let off steam by deploring the deceptive overcharging practices and account fees imposed on them. Moreover, they feel that companies involved in the financial industry take advantage of consumers for their own financial gain.

I'll be the first to admit that walking into a commercial bank on the island isn't often a delightful experience. Retail banking is not what it used to be. The relationship between banks and customers no longer feels personal. Above all, poor branch access, shoddy customer service and the automation of banking services are representative of how bank-customer behaviour has changed. Perhaps this is one of the reasons why consumers do not have the same kind of loyalty they used to have.

With so much banter in the media about how little people think of the banking industry, it can be easy for individual banks to sidestep responsibility for their less-than-stellar image.

Much of the problem has stemmed from an attitudinal shift away from the customer and towards money-making. It has become clear that having an aggressive sales culture which more often than usual rips off customers, has cost banks dearly especially in terms of their reputation and trustworthiness.

For an increasing number of people in our country, financial resources are hard to come by these days in the present economic climate and it's even harder when everyone has to put up with outrageous and unlawful fees and charges just to operate their bank accounts. Why should any customer have to pay a fee for opening or even operating an account at a bank? Isn't the notion of free customer accounts and accepting deposits for financial value creation the very basis for the operations of commercial banks? Why are local banks short-changing customers in that regard?

Allegations have been made about excessive bank overdraft fees as well. Financial institutions may be manipulating your transactions to charge you an overdraft fee. Some of the tactics being employed by the banks lead to penalty fees such as allowing customers to overdraw on their accounts then charging them, and delaying processing payments to allow accounts to go into the red and incur fees. Some institutions even go as far as putting account holders in overdraft protection programmes they didn't ask for. Isn't there a regulatory body that can tell us whether most of these fees are legally enforceable?

Why have some local commercial banks placed a maximum limit of 300 euros on foreign cash transactions? In a nation where tourism is the biggest service industry and where attracting foreign direct investment has been made an urgent priority, how does this help particularly when there is so much emphasis these days on the "ease of doing business"? What this means is that a visitor who wants to change 500 euros will now need to go to two different banks in other to conduct a simple transaction. Just think of the consequences this can have for restaurants, boutiques and other tourism-dependent businesses?

While many bank branches have disappeared causing much inconvenience to loyal customers, bureaucratic redtape has increased in terms of the processing of transactions, making eventual reforms both imperative and inevitable. Why do customers in this modern age of banking have to waste so much time just to conduct a simple transaction? This is truly an issue of productivity, needless to say that inefficient banks cost consumers and businesses significantly in terms of time and productivity. One would have thought that the advent of technology would have fundamentally changed the delivery systems banks use to interact with their customers and would have transformed the banking industry from "paper" banks to digitized and networked banking services. Technology was supposed to reduce the cost of banking for both banks and customers, but as it appears the value impact of technology at local banks is yet to be felt.

For banks – like with most other businesses – customer engagement is the true driving force behind financial outcomes. Given the rough patch that banks are going through, I would think that customer service would be seen as an attitude rather than a department. Banks need to change their image as unconscionable institutions whose only concerns are profit maximization and cost reduction. A culture shift back towards putting customers first is needed for trust to be regained; and you can't simply change that culture by making announcements from the top.

Given all the aforementioned issues confronting local banks, is it any wonder that credit unions have become hugely popular? These member-owned co-operatives now provide customers with a range of useful services at low cost including current accounts, payroll deductions, standing orders and even insurance. On its website, the Laborie Co-operative Credit Union declares, "We are not a bank, we are better. To others you are a risk, to us you are family."

I believe banks can play a bigger role in addressing the social challenges of our time. Retail banks used to be organisations embedded in communities and played a social role, but now there is a transaction and trading based culture instead of relationships. One can't help feeling that there is culture of "socially useless" banks that have become disconnected from the real economy.

10. Diaspora Capital – Wheresoever You May Roam!

The business environment is more globalized, interconnected and interdependent than ever before. Globalization has fostered greater rates of mobility and an increasing reliance on networks for commerce and economic interaction. The global economic crisis of 2008, as well as the European currency and sovereign debt crisis of 2009 demonstrated that it is no longer possible for any nation state to consider itself an 'island', nor is it possible to be immune from the vicissitudes and mutability of global economics.

The term "diaspora" is not a pretty one, but the dividend potential of the concept of "diaspora capital" is huge and promising. Diaspora networks can serve as a potent economic force for re-engaging disconnected citizens and driving national change. Thus, engagement with the Saint Lucian Diaspora offers a strategic advantage in multiple areas. Given the growing magnitude of international migration, there is now both an opportunity and a tremendous need to fully utilize the skills, experiences, insights and connections of the Saint Lucian Diaspora in fostering economic growth, reducing poverty and increasing trade.

Increasingly, the economic and foreign policy of several developed and developing nations reflect the rise of truly transnational populations, and many of these governments have made pandering to diasporas a foreign policy priority. In fact, Canada openly boasts of adopting a full-on **diaspora-driven foreign policy** shaped out of a combination of its interest and values, and its attentiveness to the sensitivities of the country's diverse and sundry ethnic and immigrant communities.

The global zeitgeist demands that Saint Lucia engages its diaspora population and astutely recognizes the role its foreign nationals can play in nation building and transnational business networking. Not only should the diaspora be seen as a source of finance through remittances and financial transfers, but critically also as true development partners who can help transfer technology and skills back to the homeland.

Having studied, lived and worked in developed and progressive societies over the years, our emigrant compatriots would have been able to observe, practise and see what it takes organizationally and ideologically to fashion a society and economy from parochialism into the mainstream. We will all agree that there is an urgent need for Saint Lucia to improve its balance of payments and fiscal position by attracting more foreign direct investment and by searching for new trading opportunities both regionally and internationally. I believe this is where the diaspora network can help position Saint Lucia strategically and facilitate exporters in accessing new markets.

I was indeed delighted to read that the Government of Saint Lucia has recognized the need to make greater use of its global citizens by developing a diaspora policy, with a view to promoting business opportunities abroad and creating a framework for nation branding. In the same vein, I must commend the Saint Lucia Tourist Board for realizing through its **"Se Sannou"** programme the valuable resource that is the diaspora community in helping to showcase the island's tourism product and promote vital cultural linkages. This is a clear signal of the Government's interest in increasing collaboration with the diaspora community to capitalize on their potential for development. Having lived overseas myself, I have no doubt that diaspora networks are in a good position to influence people's perception and image of a country. Connections do help perceptibility and flexibility. Essentially, the idea is that through global diasporal conferences and through diplomatic missions abroad, we can reach out to our people who have migrated and empower them to build our nation and sell our consumer and investment products **"wheresoever they may roam"**.

Since the attainment of national independence in 1979, thousands of our compatriots have migrated to the United Kingdom, Canada and the United States. Appreciably through the years, they would have acquired the appropriate mindset, skillset and toolset; established links and developed an understanding of the internal dynamics of these nations. Invariably, such tapping of human resources would have the potential to reverse the brain drain by facilitating knowledge sharing and technology. The opportunity presents itself where the idea of the brain drain is transformed into a kind of brain circulation or brain exchange sustained through information and communications technology. We can even think of this approach as the new "foreign exchange".

Crucially, I would suggest that a special government unit or department is established to deal exclusively with the business and corporate diaspora. Alternatively this can take the form of a sub-ministry committed to sourcing talent and equipping both nationals and ex-nationals abroad with the collaborative tools necessary to sell the island and attract investors. By now it should be clear that the road to economic development in the 21st century is paved with concrete notions of strategic collaboration, joint ventures and foreign partnerships.

At the launch of the Global Diaspora Strategies Toolkit which coincided with the Hillary Clinton Global Diaspora Forum in 2011, Kingsley Aikins of the Diaspora Forum provided the following invaluable advice to governments: "There is growing awareness now that there is such a concept as 'diaspora capital' to go alongside financial, human and social capital. Countries are coming to the realization that this is a resource to be researched, cultivated, solicited and stewarded. Many see this as a way of addressing tough domestic economic challenges and as a key piece of their economic recovery. They also see it as more than just economic remittances as there are also social remittances in the form of ideas, values, beliefs and practices."

Embracing the diaspora as a national asset is certainly not a new phenomenon, as countries such as Israel, India, Ireland and China have led the field for some time. Even the continent of Africa has launched creative business ventures engineered by its ever active "Diaspora Marketplace" initiative. We can take a leaf from the book of the African diasporas since they are at the forefront of economic reform and change, and are one of the most active communities of citizens outside of their countries. Owing to their great success stories of strategic partnerships, entrepreneurial ventures and foreign direct investment, a host of different institutions and African nations are calling them on more and more, particularly in the attempt of gathering forces to foster human development in Africa. Additionally, through the important efforts of the diasporas, the continent has acknowledged the critical role of remittances in economic development and hence, has taken steps to reduce the cost of remittance transfers.

Finally, research confirms that diasporas themselves invest back at home and spread money, too. Migrants into rich countries not only send cash to their families; they also help companies in their host country operate in their home country. In some cases, they may be instrumental in identifying investors for their countries. For instance, a lot of foreign direct investment in China still passes through the Chinese Diaspora, and modern communications make these networks an even more powerful tool of business and economic development.

11. Categorical Imperative or New Deal?

The sword of Damocles, I'm afraid, will continue to hang over our collective heads lest we renounce the Kantian posture that fiscal consolidation is the nation's categorical imperative at this time. Contrary to what the "fiscal hawks" or "deficit scolds" from all sections of society have argued, what we need for a rapid, powerful recovery is a burst of government spending to help JUMP-START the economy. Like a boxer squaring the ring, our nation needs to tackle head-on the demand management tools of spending, taxation, subsidy and stimulus.

Alas, Saint Lucia risks a deeper recession if a package of economic measures are not put together to stimulate the weaker parts of the economy. The objective of this stimulus package would be to reinvigorate the private sector through tax breaks and spending projects and prevent or reverse a recession by boosting employment and spending. We owe it to the unemployed.

Support for SMEs

The answer to our unemployment woes may well lie within the sphere of private sector business nurturing and development. Although foreign direct investment (FDI) is essential, more critical is the support and incentives provided to entrepreneurs, and small and medium size enterprises (SMEs), either through targeted business development policies or fiscal stimuli. SMEs are the lifeblood of a country's economy; they are essential to generating good jobs. Long recognized as crucial to economic development, entrepreneurs and SMEs are increasingly seen as crucial for sustainable recovery and for a strong middle class, the source of economic growth. A strong middle class provides a stable consumer base that drives productive investment. Hence, tax policy is one of the most obvious policy levers that policymakers control to alter the incentives of firms and entrepreneurs. When business tax structures are well-designed, government facilitates investment in the emerging firms that create jobs.

Focus on job creation

Saint Lucia's economic policy is marked by a tradition in which the supply side has played an important role, as opposed to the demand side which has been less in focus. This needs to change. The current political fixation on fiscal consolidation is wrong. The focus should be on JOB CREATION and getting the economy humming again. The future prospects of today's youth are being eroded with each passing month. Every month that this economic drag goes on inflicts continuing and cumulative damage on our society, damage measured not just in present pain but in a degraded future.

Deficits do matter, but not the way you think

The essence of the notion that deficits don't matter in times of economic turmoil can be distilled from the ferment of contributions made by illustrious economists. The corollary must be true that economies need to adjust for the business cycle. In the scary months that followed the perceived point of world recession in 2008, many governments agreed that the sudden collapse in private and investment spending had to be offset, and they turned to expansionary fiscal and monetary policy.

Lately, Christine Lagarde, the Managing Director of the International Monetary Fund has made progressive remarks about cyclically adjusted budget deficits citing "today, we understand better than before how a restrictive fiscal policy weighs on growth." Pointedly, in calling for greater financial stimulus to revive a moribund economy, Paul Krugman has made reference to "the lesson that the Obama administration unfortunately failed to learn until very late in the game – that the economic strategy that works best politically isn't the strategy that finds approval with focus groups; it's the strategy that delivers results."

With the benefit of hindsight, world renowned macroeconomists now believe that bigger deficits don't necessarily undermine confidence in an economy. In fact, recent research demonstrates that bond market confidence might even rise on the prospect of faster growth. Both consumer and business confidence would actually rise if policy turned to boosting the real economy. This can be mainly prosaic investments in roads, water systems, town beautification, community projects, etc. Remember, it's about the short and medium terms and doesn't have to be any visionary projects. It is actually alright to incur a deficit as a result of investment spending on health care, education and infrastructural development. After all, these are the seeds of growth. Unemployment programmes and social welfare are also critical for a short-term economic boost driven by increased consumption and spending. Put money in the hands of people in distress and there's a good chance they will spend it, which is exactly what we need to see happen.

Move to medium-scale manufacturing
In the long-term, the way forward is clear. Our priority must be to get ourselves back on the path of inclusive and sustainable growth. Saint Lucia's deep-seated structural problems are paralyzing consumption and investment, and change must come sooner rather than later. There has been too much investment in recent years in hotels and retail companies and too little in manufacturing industries, which has left the structure of the economy "distorted." By now we should have already moved from small-scale to medium-scale manufacturing.

Monetary policy assistance
Furthermore, in the aggregate design and scheme of things, we cannot downplay the need for more competitiveness and facilitation in our financial marketplace. In order to ease the credit crunch affecting small businesses and prospective entrepreneurs, the Eastern Caribbean Central Bank (ECCB) needs to provide more monetary policy assistance to the OECS territories. Interest rates in Saint Lucia are simply too high for

new business investments and private spending. Moreover, the regulatory forest must be pruned in order to eliminate superfluous bureaucracy and facilitate the conduct of private business in the country.

As a precursor to sensible economic policymaking, politicians, policy makers and the media are expected to be consistently well informed about the latest academic debates, or preferably even a step ahead of them. Economic policy divisions must have access to specialized knowledge and contacts at universities, banks and associations, as well as think tanks in the Caribbean and around the world. The veritable mountain of references available can help governments weather economic storms, and explains the anatomy of financial crises and budget deficits.

A new deal

I hold steadfastly to the view that Saint Lucia should move slower on fiscal consolidation to counteract the economic effects of structures and circumstances currently throttling growth in the country. Injecting more money into the heart of the economy and thereby improving the underlying economic conditions is an urgent priority. We need a certain Rooseveltian resolve based on a new deal. In other words, a willingness to be aggressive and experiment with economic policy – in short, to do whatever is necessary to get the country moving again.

12. PPP – Timely Solution to Pressing Fiscal Gaps

Barbadian government officials have often been heard quipping about meetings between private sector groups and the Government that have become so commonplace that they are barely noticed by ordinary Barbadians. Essentially, the common thinking underpinning this prevailing circumstance is that when a country's infrastructure is struggling, the private sector through partnerships with the Government can chip in, which should result in increased scope for public savings, reduced policy uncertainty, promotion of innovation and the creation of wealth. Further, public-private partnerships are more likely to deliver projects on time and on budget, as well as guarantee maintenance standards for the life of the asset.

First sought after during the macroeconomic dislocation of the 1970s and 1980s, public-private partnerships, also known as PPPs or P3s, are long-term contracts between a government and a private party to deliver an infrastructure service — involving the sharing of risks and rewards among the contracting parties. Such joint ventures and partnering arrangements add value to existing capital stock through synergies between public authorities and private sector companies – in particular, through the integration and cross transfer of public and private sector skills, knowledge and expertise.

To all intents and purposes, many nations are now seeking innovative ways to place their economies on a path of economic growth. Facing limited capacities to meet the growing demand for infrastructural development, governments are now tapping private sector participation with a view to combining the strength of state resources in the provision of public goods, with that of the private sector – in particular, its ability to move swiftly and deliver high-quality services on time. What seems true is that the most amazing innovations and successes have and continue to come from PPPs. One can well appreciate that when investors have their own money in the game, they have a major incentive to avoid budget overruns and missed deadlines because this cuts into profits.

Since the establishment of Invest Barbados in 2007, there have been concrete steps taken through the Social Compact to facilitate public/private dialogue in order to establish the institutional framework necessary to expedite the efficient and cost-effective delivery of projects. Despite the structural economic problems Barbados faces, it is widely believed that such public-private alliances may have significantly addressed some of the shortcomings in government policy designed to sow the seeds of growth.

The relative achievement of Barbados as an example of a country that has employed public-private alliances has brought into sharp focus the significant shift in development thinking and practice. Recognizing that the country's pressing problems were far too complex and resource-intensive to be addressed by the public sector alone, the Barbadian Government worked together with the private sector to ensure the country was able to secure better access for its tourism service providers and investors under the CARIFORUM-EU Economic Partnership Agreement (EPA).

Further afield, the success stories of countries that have reaped the economic benefits of public-private partnerships are myriad. Ghana's public-private dialogue, for instance, resulted in a public-private partnership and a highly successful initiative to integrate customs services.

This resulted in boosting Ghana's ratings as a good place to do business and increasing government tax revenues.

Similarly, the Government of Canada established *PPP Canada* in 2008 through the Canada Business Corporations Act. According to the country's Finance Ministry, "Under the auspices of the Act, Canada has embarked on many P3 projects, ranging from bio-fuel development, to water treatment facilities, mass transit systems, and bridge construction."

By published account, other countries where PPPs have become enshrined in legal frameworks and government policies are Ireland, Finland, Sweden, Australia, New Zealand, Spain, Malaysia and Singapore.

Not surprisingly, the financial crisis of 2008-11 has brought about renewed interest in PPPs in both developed and developing countries. As a result of that debilitating recession, governments had to contend with higher borrowing costs, lower levels of credit and reduced international capital flows. This made it all the more urgent to find innovative ways to combine public and private financing to meet the mounting demand for infrastructure. The World Bank admits, "Given the present fiscal constraints and the need to stabilize debt-to-GDP ratio, governments are increasingly turning to the private sector as an alternative source of funding to meet infrastructural needs in order to spur badly needed economic growth."

In our own neck of the woods, PPPs can become a game-changer both in terms of the transfer of operational and financial risks and in the pursuit of developmental goals. Given the capacity constraints and financial bottlenecks facing the Saint Lucian economy, PPPs can help meet fiscal and growth targets through higher productivity of labour and capital resources in the delivery of projects.

Recently, the International Finance Corporation (IFC), a member of the World Bank Group, was chosen as the lead advisor to assist the Saint Lucia Air and Sea Ports Authority (SLASPA) and the Government of Saint Lucia to structure a public-private partnership for the redevelopment and operation of the Hewanorra International Airport (HIA). The Government of Saint Lucia has said that the redevelopment of Hewanorra International Airport will support Saint Lucia's long term economic and social development. This course of action will stand us in good stead since I believe it to be a way of gradually exposing state owned resources and the Government of Saint Lucia to increasing levels of private sector participation (especially foreign) and exploring PPPs as a way of introducing private sector technology and innovation in providing better public services through improved operational efficiency. Hence, the private capital-public good model is a good economic approach that will redound to the benefit of taxpayers.

However, PPPs also involve significant risks and may not be right for all projects. In some instances PPPs may not be the lowest-cost way to procure infrastructure. At any rate, there is a tremendous need for thorough project administration and due diligence carried out by a professional and independent agency to help the State navigate the complex world of public-private partnership and to make sure deals are structured properly so the public gets the best return on its investment in infrastructure. Information will have to be furnished on how these contracts work, who benefits and who pays. There are cases in other countries including the United States where public leaders failed to ask the right questions to ensure they were getting a good deal. Public risk has to be priced fairly; otherwise, taxpayers will never know whether PPPs are any cheaper than building things the conventional way.

Public-private collaboration has been a key driver in countries' strategies for diversification, competitiveness and development, and for successful integration into the global economy. It is now time to move from dialogue to action.

13. Is C.I.P a Solution Waiting for a Problem?

I remember having an animated discussion in December of 2014 with a Maltese friend about his country's decision to attract foreign direct investment through a programme of economic citizenship. Citizenship, he quipped quixotically, should have nothing to do with economics.

In laying out his case against what he called "citizenship for sale", he maintained that a nation's character should be formed and guarded by its shared social values and cultural identity; and that both the gift and privilege of owning a national passport are sacrosancties.

The rhetoric grew more heated when I mentioned that my cash-strapped island home may be considering the possibility of marketing itself as a Caribbean paradise with the promise of sea water, sand, sun and interim passports – by introducing investment citizenship in tandem with initiatives already taken by sister islands like St. Kitts and Nevis, Antigua, Dominica and Grenada.

Obviously caught in the eye of an economic storm, Malta has embarked on a programme of economic citizenship whereby foreigners from outside the European Union can now buy Maltese citizenship for 650,000 euros. The controversial law also gives buyers the right of free movement within Europe, much to the chagrin of the other European member states.

According to Prime Minister Joseph Muscat, the programme's goal is to raise revenue for the country and attract "high-value" individuals who will invest there. Predictably, critics have accused the government of pawning the national birthright and surrendering to the destructive forces of "nomad capitalism".

With our collective backs already against a tenuous wall of economic vulnerability, should Saint Lucia and the rest of the Caribbean pursue this new economic and investment model? Should the Caribbean region become havens for investment citizenship?

For opportunistic global high-flyers who wish to open offshore financial accounts or expatriate in a given tax year, economic citizenship can make some sense. The principle is quite simple: wealthy foreigners can obtain a passport for a financial investment with or without residency requirement. Based on current broad policy guidelines, the economic contribution takes the form of a direct non-refundable payment made to the government. In exchange, investors and their families are granted full citizenship. They'll have the same rights as natural citizens, the right to establish business, and work and live how they want. In effect, just like they have diversified their investment portfolios, they can also diversify their passport portfolios.

Still reeling from the impact of the global financial and economic crisis, several countries are now developing strategies to help mitigate the effects of the global economic slowdown. While a few Caribbean governments have decided that the heft of the applicant's wallet is the answer to their economic woes, several economists view economic citizenship as the bastard children of economic policy.

Indeed, there is much consensus out there that foreign direct investment and economic citizenship make strange bedfellows. The question I suppose is whether or not it would be far better and more sustainable to focus on building capacity for the trading of goods and services rather than engaging in the practice of trading passports.

Alas, much controversy has been stirred in proffering the "cash for citizenship" concept as a way of raising revenue to either fix government budget deficits or attract investment capital into a country. According to research done by the British Broadcasting Corporation (BBC), by far the cheapest deal for citizenship is on the tiny Caribbean island of Dominica. For an investment of $ 100,000 plus various fees, as well as an in-person interview on the island, citizenship can be bought.

As much as the current debate on investment citizenship is essential and opportune, the fundamental question we need to ask is what precisely citizenship means today for a society and what values are associated with nationality. In order to own a Saint Lucian passport in the future, will it no longer be necessary for a person to be born here or become a naturalized citizen; and could the requirement be met by simply being able to afford and purchase a passport?

Sharing citizenship with people you have nothing in common with sounds like a sardonic business model. Maybe I am a bit conservative and at odds with the new economic zeitgeist, but I see nationality as a derivative of social and cultural circumstances, and therefore cannot be sacrificed on the altar of economic opportunism and commercial expediency. Citizenship is the character of an individual viewed as a member of society, with all the duties, obligations and functions that accompany those rights. Many other freedoms inhere in humanity and in citizenship, and neither economics nor commerce should interfere with them.

That notwithstanding, I do sense that Saint Lucians are a bit fickle about allowing high net-worth individuals express entry because they may be able to create a few (menial) jobs and seemingly generate some economic momentum in the place.

Basically, there are three big snags with the idea of economic citizenship. Firstly, issues of transparency and accountability are still cast in a cloud of suspicion. Secondly the question of whether these islands will and can attract the right people is disquieting. And finally, how do we reconcile the putative economic gains with the resulting social costs?

It is essential for a small nation to assess its political dynamics thoroughly before proceeding to offer economic citizenship. Not only does Saint Lucia lack the structural and capital resources to countenance a socio-economic backlash, it also lacks the legal efficiency and institutional support necessary for the functionality of economic citizenship.

According to which criteria will we determine who qualifies for an investment passport? Who decides how and when passports should be issued and under what circumstances are exceptions made? Who will conduct the necessary and crucial background checks? Will a future government be able to repeal the economic citizenship programme, or indeed revoke any citizenship granted by its predecessor?

In an age of money laundering and international terrorism, how will we ensure that we attract the right investors without jeopardising the safety and security of our beloved island? I'm sure that worldwide, there are enough millionaires whom Saint Lucia would love to pay court to, and who would wish to protect their assets from tax collectors, but at what price?

With the passage of time, I fear that the screening process will be short-changed and compromised, and criminals and terrorists will use the system to circumvent immigration rules, resulting in diplomatic conflict with the E.U. and the U.S., and the potential danger of sanctions being imposed on us. In St Kitts and Nevis, the programme has recently been singled out by the U.S. Treasury, which has cautioned that "Iranian nationals could be obtaining passports and then use them to travel to the U.S. or make investments, which could violate US sanctions."

Furthermore, how do we hope to address the questions of social injustice and inequality that have hitherto failed to indulge our nation's attention? Doesn't economic citizenship have the potential to threaten the already tenuous social harmony and exacerbate the economic inequality in this country? Our size, geography and limited resources cannot help us buffer the impact of any economic policy mistakes.

Moreover, I fear the fragmentation of social coherence, perpetuated by the new rich elite who may not likely be Caribbean nationals but probably Russians, Chinese and Arabs. I fear that we'll allow real estate Saint Lucia to be gobbled up (if this hasn't already happened) by some wealthy foreign elite who are socially disengaged and show loyalty only to their wealth and profits.

Experts are predicting that the sale of passports will increase dramatically in the coming year. This particular model seems to be so promising meanwhile that several large firms have now introduced "Investor Immigration Services" where they render passport mediation services to "high value" individuals in exchange for huge commissions. The International firm Henley and Partners, for example, advise clients on the best place to spend their money and estimates that every year, several thousand people spend a collective $2bn (£1.2bn; 1.5bn euros) to add a second, or even third, passport to their collection.

Despite the many promised financial and economic benefits, there is scant evidence that economic citizenship actually works. Without structural reforms and outward-oriented trade policies, economic citizenship will not provide the region with the momentum necessary to reverse the current downward economic spiral.

14. CSME – Still an Empty Shell after 25 Years

The CARICOM Single Market and Economy (CSME) was intended to benefit the people of the region by providing more and better opportunities to produce and sell their goods and services, and to attract investment in a larger economic space. Sir Ronald Sanders, a regional diplomat, hit the nail on the head when he wrote recently that: "Foreign investors would be more greatly attracted to a larger regional market than to the individual small markets of most CARICOM countries. It would be one effective way of creating a larger economic space for the employment of young people."

Let me hasten to add that without critical mass, political solidarity and unification of economic policies, international investors will view us simply as isolated islands (or what David Rudder calls tiny theatres of conflict and confusion) with no real investment and economic scope. Bottom line: Companies often locate in particular countries precisely because they are part of an efficient and functioning single market and economy.

In a world where size, scope and geographic proximity matter for the luring of foreign direct investment (FDI), trading blocs and economic single markets are an unavoidable necessity. Not only do single markets serve as facilitators for the free movement of goods, people, capital and technology, they are critically important for trade, investment and jobs. Membership of a single market is commonly assumed to be a key factor in encouraging foreign investors to choose to invest in a region. An increase in foreign direct investment benefits the economies of participating countries on account of larger markets – resulting in lower costs to manufacture products locally, market access and trade creation.

Yet, it is most shameful that the CSME, an integrated development strategy envisioned by heads of CARICOM countries more than 25 years ago, has only partially been implemented and exploited. To the chagrin of CARICOM nationals, the critical institutional constructs such as labour and capital mobility, aviation, integration of the services market and the harmonization of economic policies have been given scant attention, if not altogether lip service. Although many of the initial ideals are credible, successive governments in the region have not been able to muster the courage and will to complete the process of the CSME. Economic integration, foreign policy co-ordination, functional co-operation and security – the four pillars upon which the idea of CARICOM was first established in 1973 – are yet to be fully grounded and strengthened. Of further disquiet is the fact that every CARICOM country seems to have those preconceived notions of political autonomy and economic self-determination. Rather than co-operate and collaborate, each island would rather go it alone and render itself insignificant; a circumstance Herbert W. Marsh in his bestselling book, David and Goliath: Underdogs, Misfits, and the Art of Battling Giants, calls the Big-fish-little-pond (BFLPE) effect.

Unfortunately, the issue is always with regard to the level of commitment and processes to implementation, and this has been dismal. Unlike many developing and emerging nations in various parts of the world, the nations of CARICOM have failed to use the region to their economic and geopolitical advantage. Hence, CARICOM nationals have become increasingly exasperated by the limitations and constraints of the CARICOM Single Market. Presently, CARICOM is viewed as a talk shop that makes agreements that are not followed through with action or implementation. Further, it is believed the best brains of the region are wasted in meaningless meetings, conferences and workshops that consume scarce resources. Given the weakness and lack of leadership effectiveness in CARICOM, new options and models of integration are being sought such as Petro Caribe and ALBA, to the detriment of the solidarity and complementarity of CARICOM.

One repeated chord in the symphony of shock and dismay is the lack of collective commitment among CARICOM member countries at the levels of institutions and sectors to the sharing of a single economic space. Trinidad should have taken a lead role in the CSME, but has not. Jamaica seems far away from everything and has never taken a lead role in any integration movement. As a matter of fact, some observers in the region believe that individual countries may be deliberately placing restrictions on the free flow of intra-regional trade to the disadvantage of others. Ramesh Dookhoo, President of the Guyana Manufacturing and Services Association (GMSA) has made his displeasure known publicly:

"Trinidad and Tobago, for example, clearly believes that it is the only country that ought to enjoy the privilege of unhindered access to intra-regional markets under the single market arrangement. The stronger producing countries of the region are seeking to impose their economic strengths on the region's less developed economies without going the distance to promote products from those weaker economies. If we are to create this single economic space, the concept of harmonization of the economic environment is paramount. Unless we take these steps we are heading for a situation of massive trade distortions." Mr. Dookhoo does not believe that the Georgetown-based Caribbean Community Secretariat is doing "as much as it should" to synergise the needs and opportunities of the various countries in the region. "We are, for example, all absorbing the high costs of extra-regional food imports without seriously pursuing intra-regional opportunities to develop regional food security and, by extension, reduce the high cost of extra-regional food imports."

Taken as a whole, the lack of initiative and will of the CSME to promote growth, competitiveness and jobs have resulted in grave social dislocations and missed opportunities in economic development throughout the region. The CSME was supposed to be a single market space within which Caribbean-based businesses and professionals in the private sector operated with minimum barriers and costs. If the single market had worked as it was intended, there would be substantial gains in investment and market opportunities extending beyond the borders of any one member country. Since sustainable jobs are linked directly or indirectly with trade within a single market, Saint Lucia would have expanded its economy more quickly because a more functional single market would have encouraged more foreign direct investment into the island.

Growth is the most important factor in the eradication of unemployment. The base of all economic development is investment. The future challenges of economic development give rise to three foundational principles on which economic development investments should be based: exports, productivity and sustainability. Being mindful of the challenges of small island states, there hasn't been any significant co-ordination of foreign and investment policy in the region (both at the CARICOM and OECS levels), and sadly we are still stuck in the eighties' mindset of preferential treatment in trade matters. The Caribbean in fact gives the impression in the developed world that the region has conflicting foreign policies and priorities, enjoys a laid back, carefree lifestyle based in part on a parasitic relationship with the industrialized world from which it has no intention of diverting. Even China seems to have a strategy for the Caribbean. But do we have a strategy for China?

Maintaining the status quo means to advocate reinforcing poverty. In projecting the quality of life required in the Caribbean, we should ask ourselves about our collective Caribbean destiny in the next crucial ten years. The grandiose speeches about the single destiny of the Caribbean must be translated into more concrete steps to collaborate and deal collectively with the rapidly changing circumstances of global alliances and competing interests.

15. ECCB Leadership – Thinking Outside the Bank

While central banks have a monopoly on the issuance of fiat money, the people who actually lead such banks cannot be said to be sole custodians of economic and financial knowledge.

Since the dawn of free-market financial ingenuity, central banks around the world have demonstrated through their policy of term limits, rotational leadership and succession planning that when it comes to monetary policy and economic management, there is indeed no monopoly of wisdom. Just recently, the governing British Conservative Party proposed a one-term limit for the governor of the Bank of England in an effort to ensure and promote good corporate governance and democratic accountability.

Alan Greenspan, the financial maestro himself, who served as Fed Chairman from 1987 to 2006, and whose easy-money policies have been blamed for the sub-prime mortgage crisis, had limited use despite being praised by President Reagan during a White House ceremony as "an economist's economist".

It's also quite instructive to observe that until now, the European Central Bank has had three governors since its establishment in 1998. In the Caribbean region, the Central Bank of Barbados has seen no less than five governors since its inception in 1972 and the Central Bank of Trinidad and Tobago has had eight in its fifty-one year existence.

The Eastern Caribbean Central Bank (ECCB) on the other hand, has had Sir Dwight Venner at the helm since 1989, making him the longest serving central bank chief in the world. Most people wouldn't even remember Sir Cecil Jacobs who served as the venerable institution's first Governor from 1973 to 1989.

Sir Dwight has often belaboured the point that the ECCB and the OECS economies need to make significant policy adjustments and I do agree. However, I believe a leadership adjustment at the helm of the institution might be more critical at this juncture to help foster greater institutional vibrancy and improve the way the system responds to financial innovation and future crises.

Essentially, the ECCB was established as the monetary authority for eight countries namely: Anguilla, Antigua and Barbuda, Dominica, Grenada, Montserrat, St. Kitts and Nevis, Saint Lucia and St. Vincent and the Grenadines. Notwithstanding the financial and economic crisis in 2007-08 which severely affected OECS economies, Sir Dwight has done reasonably well in maintaining the stability of the Eastern Caribbean Currency Union (ECCU) financial system. As far back as I can remember, the EC Dollar has been pegged to the US dollar at a rate of $2.65, and $2.70 since 1976, unlike Guyana, Trinidad and Tobago and Jamaica where catastrophic currency devaluations have occurred.

Yet, central banks today are much more than monetary institutions managing exchange-rate mechanisms and risks. In reality, they have become economic change-agents and pacesetters that are expected to use financial innovation and growth strategies to bolster private and public sector dynamism and advance the socio-economic interests of their respective member states. Given the economic stagnation and loss of competitiveness of the economies of the OECS, it's not at all farfetched to conclude that the ECCB has been inadequate in stimulating economic growth and bringing job security to the OECS region.

Regrettably, some economic policy mistakes have been made as well in terms of regional trade financing. As it stands, OECS WTO Members do not have national programmes for export credit, insurance or guarantees. The export insurance facility provided by the Eastern Caribbean Central Bank (ECCB) for manufacturing exports, covering political and commercial risks was terminated in 2009.

The view has been expressed that Sir Dwight's long tenure spanning 26 years may be affecting positive change, transparency and democratic governance within the ECCB; and this may be so despite his significant contribution to the regional bank to date. Furthermore, there is the urgent need for the bank to expand its communication with the public as well as its relationship with its stakeholders.

By and large, institutional leaders who remain in office for so long often have a tendency to become self-centred and narrow-minded, the consequence of which could be the creation of a risk-adverse culture that squelches creativity and inadvertently contributes to group-think.

Going forward, I strongly believe the institution needs a fresh face with a new and reformed mandate to take on the challenges of debt management and monetary reforms, and spearhead a growth agenda aimed at sustained and balanced economic growth in the region. Assuming Sir Dwight is replaced or retires soon, the new Governor of the ECCB must be someone with proven experience in dealing with international economic matters, particularly in tough times.

Moreover, after nearly three decades under the stewardship of Sir Dwight, the regional monetary authority needs fresh ways of thinking about organizational effectiveness, systemic risks and financial markets. Self-evidently, the new leadership will have its work cut out for it and will need to face up to the challenges facing the region particularly as more public calls are made by regional economists and politicians who clamour for a revaluation of the artificially high exchange rate regime; which has allegedly contributed to high unemployment, weak economies dependent on foreign grants and loans, many small businesses being forced to close down, and very high public debt.

Ivan O'Neal, Leader of the St. Vincent and the Grenadines (SVG) Green Party strongly believes that the pegging of the EC Dollar to the US Dollar has partly worked to our disadvantage: "We have to take the bull by the horns, restructure our economies and devalue the EC Dollar to EC$ 3 to US$ 1. The overpriced EC Dollar has been a major obstacle to St. Vincent and the Grenadines' development, and it has stifled economic growth and sustainable development. Devaluation of the EC Dollar is a must", he states.

At any rate, the call for new leadership at the ECCB is nothing new. Sir James Mitchell, former Prime Minister of St. Vincent and the Grenadines first called for Sir Dwight's resignation in 2013. In a national interview, he remonstrated: "Where was the Central Bank with the destruction of the middle class by CLICO and British American in St. Vincent and throughout the Caribbean? Where is the Central Bank in all that? I suppose he will say now he has nothing to do with building societies. Dwight Venner has been there too long. He is the longest serving central bank governor in the world. We need fresh thinking and fresh vigilance in these financial institutions."

When asked about his perspective on Sir Dwight's lengthy tenure, he pointed out: "I was one of the persons who put him there, but...same way we have to look for succession in politics, we have to look for succession in our institutions. And it is very, very sad what has happened there with Building & Loan."

Further, it is alleged that the Central Bank has been bedevilled by internal issues concerning governance, transparency, conflict of interest and staff turnover, even as commercial bank charges across the OECS are prohibitively high and growth is limping along in a few of the states of the ECCU.

A while back, an SVG Newspaper reported that an unsigned letter from a concerned employee of the bank was addressed to the Prime Minister of St. Vincent & The Grenadines, Dr. Ralph Gonsalves in his capacity as Chairman of the Eastern Caribbean Monetary Council and was written under the headline banner, "Terrorism at the Eastern Caribbean Central Bank."

Based on the newspaper source, the contents of the letter read: "Board members cannot be allowed to continue to collect board fees only to make the easy decisions and leave the hard ones. The time has come for new leadership, new ideas, new enthusiasm, new initiatives, new methods and new people in key positions. We have seen this kind of change take place on a regular basis at all the other central banks in the Region. We however, continue to do the same thing, the same way, with the same people and expect a different result. That will not happen. Hard decisions have to be made by real leaders to propel our Bank and our Region forward... The Bank is in very serious trouble. Productivity is at an all time low, employees are leaving at an unprecedented rate, its ability to attract new quality employees is at an unprecedented low, some departments of the Bank have now become totally ineffective; most persons in management are job hunting."

The region clearly needs a new growth thrust and the ECCB can help deliver it through renewed vigour and the more creative use of monetary policy. Principally, the challenge concerns the driving forces, visions and processes that fuel large-scale economic transformation and institutional effectiveness. Although I believe in the fullness of time, Sir Dwight will go down as one of the great economic leaders in the Caribbean, it is now time to hand over the reigns of the ECCU economies to someone else.

NB: Sir Dwight Venner resigned as Governor of the ECCB on November 30, 2015. The Monetary Council has since appointed Mr. Timothy Antoine as the new Governor.

16. The Economics of Corruption

In 1999, I had the privilege of attending an insightful seminar and workshop dubbed "The Economics of Corruption" conducted by the globe-trotting Professor Johann Graf Lambsdorff – internationally renowned for his work on measuring corruption and the behavioural economics of reform. What made this seminar particularly interesting and memorable is the fact that Graf Lambsdorff himself had designed the Corruption Perceptions Index on behalf of Transparency International, the global corruption watchdog – and had supervised its production until 2008.

Present at the workshop were advanced level students and public officials (including permanent secretaries) from around the world who came seeking to understand the anatomy of corruption (demand and supply theories) and how it affects public welfare, productivity, capital flows and economic growth. I recall participating in a trenchant discussion on "Corruption and Reciprocity" where each participant was asked to identify and report on an egregious case of corruption in their respective countries.

Of course, I had no difficulty at the time finding a corruption narrative, as just a few years previously, Saint Lucia had been rocked by a scandal over the use of United Nations funds which had implicated the country's then UN Ambassador along with several senior government officials.

At any rate, one of the points Graf Lambsdorff drove home was the fact that developed countries were just as guilty as developing countries on corruption – generally defined as the misuse of public power for private benefit. As in most developed countries, the issue is not specifically bribery or embezzlement, but a lessening of political transparency in campaign finance, regulatory oversight and lobbying. For too long, we have harboured the myth that corruption only happens in poor, developing nations saddled with cumbersome regulations, excessive bureaucracy and market restrictions – exacerbated by poor governance structures and weak institutions.

But it would appear that industrialized nations have developed more sophisticated ways to conceal their own corruption, which makes it harder to track. In the years leading to the introduction of the Euro, creative accounting machinated wisely by the Greek political establishment was used to mask the true extent of the deficit and circumvent the EU Maastricht deficit rules. In May 2015, several FIFA officials were arrested in raids at a hotel in Zurich over allegations of racketeering, wire fraud and money-laundering conspiracies spanning 24 years. Also just recently, the German Football Association President resigned over a controversial €6.7m payment to FIFA that was allegedly used to bribe officials to vote for Germany's World Cup bid. What these developments demonstrate is that corruption transcends geographical and cultural boundaries and has assumed a single global standard.

Even so, corruption research in economics has a long history – centering around what actually determines graft, the cataclysm it has wrought on society and how it can be reduced in the most effective and efficient way. The challenge this global epidemic poses to contemporary society is tremendous as it can easily undermine good governance and lead to unsustainable wastage of scarce resources. Further, research has revealed the negative impact of corruption on levels of investment, which is "the most important causal link to the impact of corruption on the growth of GDP." Alas, in some countries, corruption has become a way of life – hampering development to the point where special government departments and ministries have had to be set up to deal solely with the problem.

The Indian government, for instance, has set up special councils to deal with the scourge of corruption because they believe that it, like cancer, can metastasize beyond the confines of officialdom to infect the behaviour of the general population. Moreover, it threatens to distort public policy – systematically percolating into vital sectors and industries in the economy, and hurting those who can afford it least. In other words, not only does corruption exacerbate the inequality trifecta (income, wealth and opportunity) and affect the provision of basic public services, it also affects the poor disproportionately (in essence a tax on the poor). When economic conditions are bad in a country where political corruption is widespread, it's only a question of time before violence erupts. On that calculus, the Arab Spring amounted to a mass uprising against kleptocratic practices.

Citing the "invisible foot" (which shows that the unreliability of corrupt counterparts induces honesty and good governance) as a novel strategy to fight corruption, Graf Lambsdorff believes that poor institutional conditions can provide fertile ground for corruption to flourish; however they are often not the basis but themselves a consequence of corruption. In addition, he has identified the following as fundamental causes of corrupt behaviour: lack of press freedom, availability of raw materials, a culture of reciprocity, lack of rights for women and lack of judicial independence.

Many questions have also been raised in terms of the correlation between corruption and international aid. When international donors provide aid packages without proper monitoring and assessment mechanisms, this can open the door to opportunism leading to graft and corruption. According to the Department for International Development in the UK: "Weak governance emerges from the evidence review as one of the fundamental leading causes of corruption. The political and economic opportunities that different political systems present, as well as the strength and effectiveness of state, social and economic institutions, shape the conditions in which corruption can thrive. Centralisation of power, lack of political competition and weak accountability mechanisms afford too much discretion."

Transparency International, the global corruption watchdog, has developed several tools including the Corruption Perceptions Index (how corrupt the public sector is perceived to be), Bribe Payers Index, Global Corruption Barometer and Financial Secrecy Index – used to measure and monitor corruption around the world. The institution has reported that corruption still remains a global threat whereby "bribes and backroom deals don't just steal resources from the most vulnerable – they undermine justice and economic development, and destroy public trust in government and leaders."

In its 2013 report, the Berlin-based institution explains: "The Corruption Perceptions Index 2013 serves as a reminder that the abuse of power, secret dealings and bribery continue to ravage societies around the world. No country has a perfect score, and two-thirds of countries score below 50. This indicates a serious, worldwide corruption problem."

In 2013, St. Lucia ranked 22 among 177 countries in the world retaining the same ranking and score of 2012. However, in the 2014 index, which Denmark, New Zealand and Finland topped as the least corrupt nations, Saint Lucia together with Brunei and Equatorial Guinea were not included owing to insufficient survey information. For that year, Sudan, North Korea and Somalia ended at the bottom of the list.

Although there isn't sufficient evidence to show whether corruption is truly a men's game, it is generally accepted that higher levels of women participation is public life are associated with lower levels of corruption. Still, by any measure, corruption is genderless and cuts across political parties, cultures and countries. Going on the conclusions of Graf Lambsdorff, "corruption is highly context-specific as it depends on the institutional setup, stage of development, but also norms and culture." For the developing world especially, targeting the problem can help governments unlock critical funds for sustainable development.

17. The IMF's New Groove

Since its founding in Bretton Woods in 1945, the International Monetary Fund (IMF) has acquired a somewhat shady reputation for its obstinate and doctrinal approach to economic and financial crisis management. The alleged inept performance of the Fund has elicited derision from prominent economists the world over, so much so that its acronym has been re-labelled "Its Mostly Fiscal".

To most people, the very mention of the name "IMF" conjures up an image of economic subjugation, social hardship and relentless financial austerity. Its dreaded structural adjustment programmes (SAP) first introduced in the 1980s have been blamed for the economic carnage that menaced many developing nations especially in Africa, where doses of economic medicine were prescribed advocating the premature removal of controls on capital flows, and then imposing harsh and inappropriate measures on the countries that were forced by capital outflows to borrow from it. These economic policy conditionalities were highly controversial, leading many to question the efficacy of the "tough love" policies of the Fund.

The former French President Francois Mitterand admitted that the debt repayments demanded by the IMF since the 1980s have been a major mechanism for the transfer of wealth from the South to the North. It is estimated that during that period debt repayments drained about US$ 160 billion each year from "developing" countries. This was about 2.5 times the total development aid that these countries received.

Long criticized for its lack of accountability and transparency, the Fund has also faced serious questions about its relevance and theological devotion to outdated and discredited economic policies.

The prominent American economist Jeffrey Sachs believes that the IMF has a poor record in nursing fiscally-challenged countries back to financial health and may have helped detonate the Indonesian crisis in 1997. Likewise, the Nobel Prize-winning economist Joseph E. Stiglitz notes in his book, Making Globalization Work that "advanced industrial countries, through international organizations like the International Monetary Fund (IMF), the World Trade Organization (WTO), and the World Bank, were not only not doing all that they could to help these [developing] countries but were sometimes making their life more difficult. IMF programs had clearly worsened the East Asian crisis, and the shock therapy "they had pushed in the former Soviet Union and its satellites played an important role in the failure of the transition."

However, all these misgivings were based on the Fund's performance before the global economic crisis of 2007. Since then a major shift has occurred in the global economic landscape, with the emergence of the IMF as a leading player in the response to what has become known as the "Great Recession. Consequently, many commentators have hailed the rejuvenated IMF as a "phoenix rising" against the backdrop of the collapse of the financial system which led to an economic contraction that spread outside the original group of crisis countries including Iceland and Greece. For all intents and purposes, the Great Recession of 2007/2008 will always be remembered as the debilitating crisis which led to the unprecedented downgrade of Greece to emerging market status by S&P Dow Jones Indices, Morgan Stanley Capital Index (MSCI) and Russell Indexes.

It is fair to say that during the global financial crisis of 2007/2008, the role played by the Fund was outstanding. Fortunately, the Frenchman Dominique Strauss-Kahn was in the right place at the right time when he assumed the stewardship of the IMF in November 2007 and gave it a new lease on life just as its influence on the world stage was waning. Arguably, he provided a human face to the organization and embarked on a number of transformational reforms.

One of those reforms concerned the credit basis of the fund which was structurally extended to reflect the increasing importance of emerging market economies. Crucially, the reforms produced a combined shift of 9 percent of quota shares to dynamic emerging market and developing countries. In fact, when Mr. Strauss-Kahn took over the reins, the outstanding credit at the fund was US$ 10 billion as opposed to US$ 91 billion fours years earlier. Upon leaving office, the figure was at US$ 84 billion. Owing to prudent economic management, the total capital of the fund had quadrupled to US$ 250 billion. Particularly significant was Mr. Strauss-Kahn's controversial call for fiscal stimulus in early 2008. One shudders to think where we might be if it had not been heard.

Despite the good results achieved on the watch of Mr. Strauss-Kahn, a lot more needs to be done especially as it relates to the selection of the best possible candidate for the job of managing director from a world-wide pool. Since its inception, the IMF has been under the helm of a (Western) European whereas the World Bank has been headed by an American. We are all hoping that further reforms undertaken by the new managing director will address this outmoded approach to govern-ance of a leading international financial institution.

Regarded as an augury of good things to come, his successor Chris-tine Lagarde, another French national, has continued his legacy, register-ing two significant achievements in her first 15 months as managing director, first when she sounded the alarm in 2012 that European banks needed to be recapitalized to meet the challenge of the region's debt crisis and second when she succeeded in mobilizing nearly US$ 500 billion of new resources to ensure that the global lender could respond to future emergencies.

Nevertheless, there is still the widespread misconception that the IMF "army" simply matches into a country and imposes its will on the gov-ernment and the people. The fact is the IMF doesn't just impose its remedy on a nation unless it is invited to help restore economic and fiscal health. Countries generally turn to the Fund for financing when they have run into balance of payments problems and require counsel for economic stabilization and the pursuit of a growth agenda. These difficulties may have come about due to external shocks, for instance a rise in the price of energy or economic policy choices that have led to economic imbalances and vulnerabilities in the economy.

Despite the economic challenges Saint Lucia faces, we can consider ourselves blessed that we haven't gone cap in hand to the IMF. Unfortu-nately, the same cannot be said about some of our sister islands includ-ing Grenada and Antigua. That notwithstanding, the Fund has made a case to the Saint Lucia Government advising a reduction in the wage bill and the amount spent on transfers and subsidies in the region. A statement released by the IMF in 2014 recommended "ambitious, credible medium term fiscal consolidation to put public debt on a sustainable path and create the fiscal space for counter cyclical policies."

The new IMF under the sterling and forward-thinking leadership of both Christine Lagarde and her predecessor Dominique Strauss-Kahn has been given a bit more orientation, although it still has a long way to go in adopting an even-handed approach in the way it deals with developing economies and emerging markets. Since the Great Recession of 2007/2008, there has been every indication that the Fund has begun to restructure and shift its own tasks to reflect a fundamentally-changed environment.

18. The Anatomy and Insanity of Debt

The Grammy Award-winning American singer James Taylor has had his fair share of life misfortunes. As a survivor of drug addiction, divorce and bankruptcy, he epitomises how fortunes can change quickly when finances and debt aren't managed prudently and sustainably. His life predicaments inexorably demonstrate how easily a debt spiral can become an existential threat capable of subjecting an individual or nation to a life of servitude, destitution and illusory freedom. Having dragged himself from the jaws of defeat eventually, the singer has made the following exhortation: "People should watch out for three things. Avoid a major addiction, don't get so deeply into debt that it controls your life, and don't start a family before you're ready to settle down."

Sound and judicious advice indeed, except that the world has already become incorrigibly addicted to debt, and the relentless control it has over the lives of families, institutions and nations is rather discombobulating.

By all accounts, hundreds of countries have either defaulted on their debt or restructured it, from France in 1558 to Argentina in 2002. Some countries have been subjected to impoverishment and oppression on account of their desire for emancipation and freedom. Haiti, the first black independent republic in the Western Hemisphere was threatened in 1825 into paying reparations to France amounting to 150 million gold francs (estimated at the time to be ten times the country's annual revenues) in exchange for national sovereignty and freedom. The debt as we now know crippled the Caribbean nation, which did not finish paying it off to French and American banks until 1947. This set the stage for the economic misery and underdevelopment that have plagued Haiti up to this present day; a lesson that history is not as distant as it may seem.

Since the financial crisis began in 2007, debt-to-GDP has risen in 41 of 47 big economies, according to McKinsey, a consultancy firm. Of course, small island developing states in the Caribbean have not been spared the debt onslaught (whether self-inflicted or otherwise) with Saint Lucia recording public sector outstanding liabilities of $2,811.1 million at the end of 2014; an increase of 4.0 percent ($107.0 million) over the previous year. As a percentage of GDP, the official debt stood at 73.7 percent in 2014 compared to 67.6 percent in 2007. This begs the question: How will small vulnerable states like ours face the growing challenges of high debt and low growth? How can emerging and middle income states reconcile local democracy with international debt obligations?

Today, the entire global financial system resembles a colossal spiral of debt. For every extra dollar of output, the world churns out more than a dollar of debt. Soon there will be as much debt as money. Recent figures indicate that the total indebtedness of the world, including all parts of the public and private sectors is a mind-boggling $223.3 trillion, amounting to 313% of global gross domestic product. Now how do you take on a giant of that size a lot bigger than what David was up against?

For several decades now, this debilitating debt crisis has had a pernicious effect on most of the world's impoverished nations, retarding economic development and draining scarce resources from health, education and other important services. In the financial corridors of the world, the problems of debt-afflicted nations may be expressed in terms of capital flows, debt-service ratios and credit earnings, but the reality of the matter is that debt obligations are about the lives of billions of "real" people around the world. But if debt is an ingenious substitute for the chain and the whip of the slave-driver, as Ambrose Bierce puts it, why is the world so addicted to borrowing?

Mostly, economists attribute the current debt-mania to factors ranging from fiscal constraints and limited investment options to easy money made possible by frequent short-term interest rate reductions and quantitative easing by central banks in the last decade. Further, when one considers the huge reserves countries such as China have built, one will appreciate the need to invest that money abroad; securities which the Americans are only too happy to purchase in the form of treasury bills, notes and bonds. On a micro level, because bond and loan interest are tax-deductible, firms around the world, the argument goes, have a greater incentive to issue debt instead of equity.

Yet the contentious and burning question still remains: How much debt is too much debt? In a research paper, Harvard Professors Kenneth Rogoff and Carmen Reinhart have even established a number, a "threshold," or "magical limit": They wrote that growth suffers when government debt exceeds more than 90 percent of a country's gross domestic product. Can that measure be applied to Saint Lucia as it is to emerging and developed nations, given our country's size, nature and level of development?

Paul Krugman, the Nobel-winning economist has argued that the relationship between debt and growth varies significantly between countries, and the average "rule" as suggested by Reinhart and Rogoff, has little meaning or policy relevance. He believes that bigger fiscal deficits don't necessarily undermine confidence in an economy. In fact, based on his research findings, bond market confidence might even rise on the prospect of faster growth. At the height of the debate on growth, debt and austerity, he maintained: "What the Reinhart-Rogoff affair shows is the extent to which austerity has been sold on false pretenses. For three years, the turn to austerity has been presented not as a choice but as a necessity. Economic research, austerity advocates insisted, showed that terrible things happen once debt exceeds 90 percent of G.D.P. But "economic research" showed no such thing; a couple of economists made that assertion, while many others disagreed. Policy makers abandoned the unemployed and turned to austerity because they wanted to, not because they had to."

Distressingly, while we have seen how the world (mis)manages austerity, there isn't much structural clarity on the matter of sovereign defaults. We know for a fact that countries have been defaulting on their debt since time immemorial and recent history has certainly seen its share. Notwithstanding the valiant efforts of the Paris Club of Creditors to coordinate and find solutions to the payment difficulties experienced by both debtor and creditor nations, sovereign defaults are bad news for everyone. As history will attest, failure to repay can lay the groundwork for the seizure of the debtor's foreign assets or even military invasions.

Nonetheless, governments tend to default for a variety of different reasons, ranging from a simple reversal of global capital flows to constraints of revenue structure. Argentina defaulted on its $132 billion debt in 2002 at the depth of the worst economic crisis in the country's history. The Icelandic financial crisis involved the default of all three of the country's major privately owned commercial banks in late 2008. The Greek debt crisis was triggered by misrepresentation, corruption and malfeasance in the management of the country's liabilities. Puerto Rico is now facing its first bond default in its history after missing a $58 million bond payment in 2015.

Of course by any measure, the global financial crisis of 2007–08 created huge economic headaches for everyone, unleashing a credit crunch and plunging the world into debt, foreclosures and crippling unemployment.

Contrary to popular thinking, the Greek economic malaise has not been the worst experienced in Europe. Ironically, the German economic historian Albrecht Ritschl, Professor of Economic History at the London School of Economics, has argued consistently that Germany has been the worst debtor nation of the past century, having benefited from debt relief and international support initiated and facilitated by the Young, Dawes and Marshall Plans. According to Ritschl, "Germany's resurgence has only been possible through waiving extensive debt payments and stopping reparations to its World War II victims."

So where do rating agencies come in all of this? How is a country's creditworthiness rated? Do the rating agencies really give credit where credit is due? Interestingly a sovereign rating assessment is based in equal measure on a government's willingness to pay as its ability to do so. Japan for instance, with debt of 237 percent of GDP, and a huge current deficit in 2013 was rated more highly than Turkey with a debt-to-GDP ratio of 37.7 percent in the same year. Economists attribute this peculiar circumstance to a nation's history of paying back its debts and even the nature of its creditors. In the case of Japan, most of its government debt is owned by its citizens.

In any event, the best way of coping with too much debt is to spur growth through infrastructure development, education and health care. Sensible fiscal, monetary and investment policies obviously play a major role in sowing the seeds of growth. Experience has taught us that a fiscal policy that is too restrictive will weigh on growth. In the end however, the best advice for financial prudence is captured in the maxim by

Thomas Jefferson that you should "never spend your money before you have it."

19. Between Debt and the Deep Blue Caribbean Sea

Thoughts of a Caribbean dream holiday instantly conjure up clichéd images of swaying palm trees, sparkling turquoise blue seas and white sandy beaches. However, realistic thoughts of the region's economic landscape produce images of tidal waves of unemployment, anaemic investment environments and mountains of debt.

The debt crisis in the Caribbean – from the Bahamas in the north to Guyana in the south – is what has now been dubbed "the silent crisis", particularly as the region has become relatively inconspicuous in attracting transformative and sustainable investments (Caribbean share of world FDI has been declining since the late 1990s) amid the constraints of a stagnant financial-services industry, underdeveloped physical and social infrastructure and high debt-servicing obligations.

Hit by downturns in tourism following the 9-11 terrorist attacks and the then global financial crisis, the Caribbean region has slowly but surely become one of the most indebted in the world, with liabilities often far beyond what is safe for such small, vulnerable and undiversified economies.

But that's hardly the whole of it. The Caribbean is one of the most disaster-prone regions in the world – costing annually the equivalent of 2 per cent of GDP. The rating agency Moody's explains that: "The industries in which Caribbean economies specialize are highly cyclical in nature, exposed to external shocks, and dependent on the performance of the external economic environment. Therefore, Caribbean countries remain vulnerable to external shocks and balance of payments difficulties, and their economic performance will continue to exhibit cyclical features."

A negative balance of payments essentially means that an economy lives beyond its means and consumes more than it actually produces. In the absence of natural resources and organic economic growth, debt-ridden economies in the region need to borrow abroad, often at prohibitive interest rates in order to finance consumption – making them prone to fiscal and economic crises – and in the event of such crises, compelling them to undergo painful economic, structural and fiscal readjustments.

Yet despite the position of Moody's and other international institutions – and irrespective of the fact that investors have long exploited the high returns on Caribbean bonds and speculated that they can repurchase those regional securities in the face of sovereign bond payment difficulties – others believe that the Caribbean region has no one but itself to blame for the anaemic growth and unsustainable levels of debt. In a report on the region entitled "The Silent Debt Crisis", the U.S. rating agency Moody's provides some further perspective: "Unlike elsewhere, the build-up of debt in the Caribbean region was not sudden or caused by the global financial crisis. It happened gradually and almost unnoticeably over many years."

Further, Moody's estimates that "the debt-to-GDP ratio is over 60 per cent for 12 of the 20 Caribbean countries for which it has data. Six have debt-to-GDP ratios of over 80 per cent, and four have over 100 per cent."

Going on World Bank statistics, the average level of debt of Caribbean nations in relation to the size of their economies stands around 70 per cent, whereby Jamaica, Antigua and Barbuda and Grenada have already passed the 93 per cent mark. In June 2015, Saint Lucia's public debt stock stood at $2.8 billion, representing an increase from December 2014. In 2010, its debt-to-GDP ratio was 60.4 percent; however in 2014 it reached 73.5 per cent. The same unsustainable trend can be observed in Saint Vincent and the Grenadines where in 2010, the debt-to-GDP ratio was at 65.4 per cent, but increased to 78.1 per cent in 2014.

The World Economic Forum (WEF) recently examined the issue of financial stability and the lurking risks of rising levels of national debt worldwide, as it believes that the level of gross indebtedness in relation to GDP shows whether a country can pay back its debts without seeking fresh loans. As of January 2016, Jamaica and Barbados, according to the WEF, were among the 17 worst country debtors in the world, along with Greece, Italy and Portugal.

Of further disquiet is the fact that since 2006, Jamaica and Belize alone have carried out two debt-restructuring programmes totalling US$9.5 billion. Likewise, Antigua and Barbuda, St Kitts and Nevis as well as Grenada have had to default and restructure their debts in the last two decades. Moody's has said that "if history is to serve as a guide, more defaults are likely by the highly indebted countries in the region".

Barbados, one of the more prosperous and developed islands in the Eastern Caribbean, has had to struggle with a gross debt-to-GDP ratio of over 130 percent (including securities held by the National Insurance Scheme) – a perilously high figure for a small island, despite it having gone through an austerity programme that saw the sacking of one per cent of its public servants and the imposition of fiscal and structural adjustments.

Not to be outdone is Jamaica, whose national debt hovers around 139 per cent of GDP, and which has become a byword for fiscal and economic mismanagement over the past forty years (such is the extent of debt's hold on the Caribbean psyche). Against the backdrop of increasing crime, corruption and unemployment, the country has struggled to both meet its international financial obligations and secure additional finance on the international capital markets. Curiously, at the end of last year, the Jamaican Share Index rose by 77 per cent, prompting financial analysts to suspect that "specific entities" may have bought large amounts of securities to artificially boost the index.

At any rate, as I have said before, there is little doubt that the debilitating debt crisis has had a pernicious effect on the overall growth potential of the region – retarding its economic development and further inhibiting its ability to respond to adverse external shocks, as well as draining scarce resources from health, education and other important services. Above all, the reality of the matter is that the debt obligations of regional economies are about the lives of millions of "real" people, who increasingly feel that they have been left stranded on the high blue seas by their own governments and exploited by importunate international creditors.

20. More BRICS in the G-7 Wall

They've got size, demographics and economic momentum. Together they comprise more than 3 billion people or 41.4 percent of the world's population, more than a quarter of the world's land area over three continents, and account for more than 25 percent of global GDP. Despite the fact that much of the political power today is concentrated in their hands, they were noticeably absent at the G-7 summit held from

June 7–8, 2015 in the picturesque Schloss Elmau at the foot of Germany's highest mountain, the Zugspitze.

Yes, dear reader, you guessed right, I am referring to the BRICS group of emerging economies – Brazil, India, Russia, China and South Africa. Does it take a rocket scientist to figure out that the balance of power, if not already shifted, will eventually be in favour of these emerging economies? These five nations have a combined nominal GDP of US$16.039 trillion, equivalent to approximately 20% of the gross world product and an estimated US$4 trillion in combined foreign reserves. Now that's significant.

The idea of a G-7 club of industrialized countries is one that should have died long ago, but just keeps shambling along. Currently, given the omnipresent threat of global terrorism and the gravity of the world's economic and environmental concerns, it's kind of farcical and disingenuous to invite only leaders of the so-called G7 nations (US, Germany, UK, France, Italy, Canada and Japan) to partake in such a crucial and timely summit. Notwithstanding the fact that seven other leaders mostly from African countries were invited to observe on the sidelines, what has constantly discombobulated critics and commentators alike is the practice of inviting both the European Commission and European Council Presidents to contemplate solutions on behalf of the world. Why is the European Union represented in addition to having four individual EU member states and two others as observers? That is unacceptable. Besides, why is Italy, long considered "the real sick man of Europe" (Tsar Nicholas I of Russia coined the phrase to describe the Ottoman Empire) with a somnolent economy even a full-fledged member of this rich country club? Facing their own economic demons in the form of a currency and debt crisis and crippling unemployment, what advice can a sclerotic and ageing Europe provide to some of the rising stars of Asia, Africa and South America?

Given that the G-7 countries collectively account for 32% of global purchasing power parity (GDP) and represent only about 1.2 billion people, do they have the authority to speak and plan on behalf of the rest of the world? Without the active participation of the BRICS economies, the G-7 could not have hoped to achieve much at the summit, for they would not have had the mandate to tackle global crises like Ukraine unless Russia, China and other world powers were present.

As you can well imagine, the main focus of the summit was the global economy as well as other key issues regarding foreign, energy, security and development policy. Without the collective weight of China, Brazil and India that account for more than 3 billion of the world's population, a global agenda put together by mostly European countries outlining the next set of development goals and how to finance them, appeared to me at best a fleeting illusion. How on earth can such an outfit, to all intents and purposes, address critical issues such as climate change, trade, the weakness of the global recovery, combating systematic tax evasion and tackling inequality without the structural and strategic input of the BRICS economies? The Chinese and other non-Western powers share responsibility for the world's problems and it's absurd that they should be kept out of the "big" picture.

Larry Elliott, a veteran and respected business journalist with the British Guardian recently expressed these sentiments regarding the G-7: "The get-togethers started after the first oil shock in the 1970s but have long since ceased to matter. The G7 is a moribund institution and has been for the past decade. As an instrument of the internationalism it was set up to pursue, it is hopeless. It should be scrapped."

We no longer live in the 19th century, a time when the major powers met and redrew the map of the world. The new zeitgeist demands that we make institutions and mechanisms fit the new global realities and the new balance of power. There has been a fundamental change in the international economy, especially in the last decade. The Great Recession of 2007-08 led to the downgrading of Greece from developed country to emerging market status. Emerging and developing countries, especially the BRICS, have significantly increased their weight in global GDP and in global economic growth; in particular, they have been responsible for most of the growth in the world economy since the 2007–08 crisis.

Just recently the BRICS countries created a $ 100 billion BRICS Development Bank and a reserve currency pool worth over another $ 100 billion, which will no doubt counter the influence and seriously challenge the World Bank and the IMF, symbols of America's global financial hegemony. The new bank's primary focus of lending will be infrastructure projects and its modus operandi will seek to submerge the current philosophy of the World Bank and the IMF that has subsidized economic dependency and subservience.

On climate change, the G7 leaders pledged in a communique after their two-day meeting to develop long-term low-carbon strategies and abandon fossil fuels by the end of the century. But how can you discuss and develop a climate change strategy and blueprint without China at the table?

As it stands today, China is the largest consumer of coal in the world, producing 18,449 TWh of the world's total 39,340 TWh in 2009. It is one of the top emitters of all greenhouse gas emissions including building and deforestation. In fact, a new study by the London School of Economics confirms what has been increasingly clear to outside observers: "Whether or not the world will avert catastrophic climate change is now, to a large extent, in the hands of the Chinese."

According to the report's authors, "to reduce its emissions at a rapid rate, post-peak, China will need to deepen its planned reforms in cities and in the energy system, supported by a concerted approach to clean innovation, green finance and fiscal reforms."

Further, how is it practical to discuss global energy policy, energy security and oil economics without indulging the attention and participation of influential representatives from the Arab world? It would have been both wise and farsighted to invite the Arab League given the unprecedented threats and instability spreading through the Middle East. Such a move would have certainly been in the interest of superpowers like China, Europe and the USA who have several interests in this vast rich region, and are seeking to expand their influence over the oil rich countries.

Meanwhile there is "a cold peace" between Russia and the West, and currently the G-7 is pondering what they should do about Russia's aggressive behaviour in the region. But not only have the present sanctions had little impact on Russian policy, it has also not improved Ukraine's situation, which in all respects remains dire. As predicted, the G7 summit has ended with a demand to extend sanctions which are achieving none of the objectives for which they were imposed.

On the eve of the G-7 summit in Germany, the Frankfurter Allgemeine Newspaper (FAZ) opined: "One should not underestimate Beijing and Delhi's claim and desire for making this new century their own. They're realizing their own strength over the rest of the world, be it the form of downward wage pressure, competition for highly qualified jobs, or sources of energy. Both countries have quietly been expanding their international influence. We believe hand in hand, they can change the world in the not too distant future."

The G-7 has for a long time lacked the legitimacy, unanimity and leadership to tackle the world's many intractable problems, particularly cutting carbon emissions and reducing inequality. Clearly there is no future for an anachronistic and self-appointed group of supercilious nations that seek to pontificate on democratic and economic issues to the rest of the world despite the economic mess in their own homes and backyards. The G-7 is irrelevant and the idea simply perpetuates a global imbalance, and therefore should be scrapped altogether in favour of a more permanent and broader G-20 that reflects a more legitimate and realistic consensus of world opinion and circumstances.

21. The Greek Economic Drama – Lessons and Morals

Greek mythology culminates in the Trojan War, fought between Greece and Troy, and its aftermath. It's now anyone's guess how the current platonic drama unfolding between Athens and Brussels (actually Berlin) will end. It seems like not even a government ran by philosopher-kings can now save Greece from the Medusa spite of financial markets, having managed to bring the European economies to a crisis point.

Sometimes, I can't shake the feeling that I'm watching a special edition of the European debt theatre where Greece and Germany have taken centre stage. Nevertheless, it appears the battle lines have been drawn where the Greek camp, energized by the teachings of Socrates, Plato and Aristotle, are pitted against the indefatigable Germans inspired by the resolve of Kant, Engels and Nietzsche. Having mustered the discipline to think long-term, the German economy is booming with an unemployment rate of below 5 percent, while Greece is saddled with mass unemployment, alarming levels of poverty and scant hope.

In our neck of the woods (OECS and CARICOM) where we're faced with our own economic demons, a critically reflective look at the genesis and circumstances of the Greek Debt Crisis might help us better understand the psychology of capital markets and how to potentially navigate through the mindfields of politics and economic policy choices. Greece, renowned as the cradle of democracy, serves as an example, if a poor one, of the importance of economic governance, accountability and rule compliance in the dealings of a nation.

Play by the rules

For my part, if there's one thing I have learned from the Greek Debt Crisis, it's that when you don't play by the rules, and consequently lose market trust over the handling of finances, it's hard to gain it back. As previous crises in Argentina and Indonesia have demonstrated, markets sometimes ignore underlying facts and run mostly on psychology (confidence and trust). When a country has lived a life of political corruption and economic deceit, as has happened in Greece, it's only a matter of time before the financial chickens come home to roost. According to a senior spokesman from the European Commission, "While no one doubts previous Greek governments dug the economic hole the country finds itself in, the debate is over how much the rest of Europe should pay for selling Greek leaders the shovels and buckets used to dig it."

In the years leading to the introduction of the Euro in 1999, creative accounting machinated wisely by the Greek establishment was the order of the day, as attempts were made to mask the true extent of the deficit with the help of a derivatives deal that legally circumvented the EU Maastricht deficit rules. With the conniving support of Goldman Sachs, a US investment bank, cross currency swaps with fictional exchange rates and other complex financial products were devised to push part of the country's liabilities into the future, swelling the already bloated deficit. Of further disquiet is the fact that fiscal rules (Stability Pact) governing budget deficits (not more than three percent of GDP) and government debt (not exceeding 60 percent of GDP) were craftily flaunted as monetary oversight then within the currency union was weak. Greece was run almost like a third-world country with a tax collection infrastructure that was legendarily ineffective, and a civil service shot through with patronage.

A Greek departure

To be sure, the Debt Crisis shows that Europe has been anything but unified. A Grexit (Greece leaving the euro), added to the already imminent threat of a Brexit (Britain leaving the EU), would represent a significant political defeat for the euro-zone and the EU at large. Fluid market developments have once again begged the question: Was the euro-currency idea a bad one economics-wise? Economists as ideologically varied as Milton Friedman and Paul Krugman have said all along that joining a group of quite distinct European countries into a single currency would end in tears. Now economists are busy calculating:

What would abandoning the euro do to the Greek economy? How high would the costs be for the euro zone? What would be the political consequences If Athens were to turn away from Europe?

Living within your means

If anything, the ongoing crisis has drawn some uncomfortable lessons about the need for fiscal discipline. It is also a reminder of the dilemma every democracy faces in balancing tax collection with citizen expectations. Meanwhile the debate over debt servicing and management is increasingly lacking proportionality, as capital in excess of a billion euros daily take flight out of the country, hurting the banking system and the economy. As evidenced by the turmoil in financial markets, debt is a contract that must be honoured; otherwise the consequences in terms of credit ratings and long-term costs can be dire. At any rate, the message to politicians is that in the long run, you can't live beyond your means.

No free lunch

Structural reform is a serious business, particularly as it relates to taxation, pension and labour markets. When one considers the somnambulistic pace of economic reforms in Greece until now, one is left to wonder whether the Greeks have understood at all the enormity of the structural issues that confront them. The reforms proposed by the euro-zone were necessary and had to be implemented despite the amount of pain it would have inflicted on society. The reality that there is no such thing as a free lunch has already come back into fashion.

The follies of mindless austerity

One of the critical issues of European monetary and economic integration has been the reluctance and indecision of Germany in the exercise of economic leadership in the euro-zone. I would even go as far as to suggest that the present economic mess is the price the currency union is paying for five years of cowardice. The current crisis is what happens when leaders without foresight heedlessly kick the proverbial can down the road. There is no hiding the fact that plenty mistakes were made including Germany's stubborn insistence that the pain of austerity was essential to economic recovery. Europe's largest economy just didn't get the balance right. The prescribed austerity should have been tempered by a growth agenda. It is now clear that seriously bad ideas have a life of their own.

The most important step should have been to get the Greek economy out of the doldrums through collective debt guarantees and an economic stabilization programme. By focusing too much on the current state of the Greek economy, the euro-zone underestimated the fiscal risks that may have threatened future growth. Even when the economy was showing signs of recovery, instead of implementing spending cuts, the first priority should have been to ensure unnecessary burdens didn't kill off a budding economic recovery.

Early debt relief

Further, early debt relief may have helped avert the current crisis. This idea is famously supported by legendary US investor George Soros, whose speculation against the pound forced the UK to withdraw from the Exchange Rate Mechanism in 1992. Mr. Soros, who is Hungarian by birth, has called for comprehensive debt relief for Greece. "Everyone knows that it can never pay back its debt. Greece is close to a primary budget surplus after a lot of pain and suffering. And if any country were to recognize how such an approach could work, it was Germany, which ought to remember that it has benefited from debt write downs three times, with the Dawes Plan, the Young Plan and in connection with the Marshall Plan," he said in an interview recently.

Democracy isn't always a good thing

Since Alexis Tsipras's radical far-left Syriza Party came to power in January this year, the easy appeal of bad karaoke economics has been pretty disheartening to watch. Until now, the markets have not been able to tame the new Prime Minister. His government's wrong-headed policies, including the calling of a referendum this Sunday July 5th, are beyond amusement at this point; it is insanity. It is a classic example of how too much democracy is not always a good thing in the economic management of a country. According to the European Central Bank (ECB), "Prior to elections in January, the situation had been improving in the country. The government in Athens was bringing in more money than it was spending." The Organization for Economic Cooperation and Development (OECD) recently noted the country had made "impressive headway". Now with a new government, things have come to a head where Greece is demanding that Germany make war reparation payments and also pay back loans amounting to about €11 billion which the Nazis forced the Greek Central Bank to provide during World War II.

I'm not sure what advice the earlier cited philosophers of both Greece and Germany would have provided to the current power brokers, but I can make an educated guess on one thing: ethics, reason and the moral imperative would have probably guided the debate in finding a solution to the debilitating crisis. Oh Zeus, king of the Greek Gods, how could things go so wrong?

CHAPTER 2 –
GOVERNMENT, DEMOCRACY
AND LEADERSHIP

22. Leadership – Where the Buck Stops

When Eric Williams threw his hat (or his crown as some would say) into the political ring in 1956, he dazzled his compatriots with his enlightened and visionary leadership, amid all the turbulence and confusion of Trinidadian politics. As the founder of that nation's first modern political party and principal architect of independence in 1962, the brilliant scholar-politician inspired almost an entire generation of Caribbean people to dream more, become more and learn more in the pursuit of socio-political change and economic development.

Against almost insurmountable colonial odds, Williams was determined to translate his social and economic vision into reality and unlock the people's potential to become better and responsible citizens. That outstanding ability to reach people in a way that transcends the intellectual and social is the mark of a truly great leader. Eric Williams was a transformative Caribbean leader who recognized "education for the masses" as a political force. For him, politics was a continuation of education by other means. Alas, in the region today, such authentic and exceptional "servant" leaders are a rare breed – perhaps almost freaks of nature.

By all accounts, he was an indefatigable political servant committed to the welfare of his people, as well as an avid reader whose broad reading habits, by and large, defined his leadership ethos – saliently manifested in his unparalleled command of the issues, communication skills, emotional intelligence and organizational effectiveness. One of the things I admired most about him – both as an educator and politician – was the manner in which his character amplified his humility and goodwill, despite a daunted reputation for intellectual erudition and articulate oratory.

So what else defines a strong leader and what lessons can we learn from the stewardship of other luminaries? Firstly, a leader is one who inspires, an agent of change, a developer who shows the way forward and a dealer in hope. Pat Dixon, author of the book "Making the Difference: Women and Men in the Workplace", says that leadership is about "making things happen through people who are as enthusiastic and interested as you are." A good leader should be able to speak out articulately and with conviction. It's having the confidence to say "I believe" instead of "I think", maintains Dixon.

What is more, strong leaders create their own horizons and are "masters of pursuitology", i. e., they optimize the impact, nature and value of relationships, knowledge, results and excellence. It's widely accepted that almost everything a leader does is amplified in the culture of the organization. Research on leadership effectiveness has shown that institutions, especially weak ones, take on the personality of their leaders. In other words, if a leader promotes division, exercises vindictiveness and instils fear in his people or workforce, the organizational culture is likely to reflect that attitude. That very same research supports the view that the words of leaders reveal their psychological states especially in terms of their needs and defences.

At any rate, not everyone is cut to lead, and there is no magic wand for leadership success, either. Above all, it is particularly advisable to steer clear of leaders who over-promise but under-deliver, as well as those who are popular but incompetent and unproductive. There is even a special breed that pretends to be unreasonable but tactical.

Today, strong leadership, whether in business, social organizations, political parties or in government, is widely seen as a function of not only visionary thinking and competence, but also of personal character and integrity. Often people buy into the "leader" before they buy into the vision or strategy. Norman Schwarzkopf, the United States army general who led all the coalition forces in the Persian Gulf War believes: "Leadership is a potent combination of strategy and character. But if you must be without one, be without strategy." Outstanding leaders do accept and understand that the extent of their character fundamentally shapes how they engage their followers, what they observe and value, and most importantly what they decide and choose to act on. That is why a person of poor character essentially is likely to be lousy in the broader process of leadership.

Invariably, the vexing question for leaders is to determine how to get disparate groups to work together in a common interest. History is replete with examples of charismatic leaders who kept the loyalty and affection of their people and who were able to keep their organizations or countries together by showing a high degree of conscientiousness, trustworthiness and emotional intelligence.

In the same vein, Sir Winston Churchill believed influence and impact to be more important than tactics and strategy. "However beautiful the strategy, you should occasionally look at the results", he once advised.

Just as a good manager can keep an inefficient company running relatively smoothly, a good leader can transform a demoralized country or organization into a vibrant, functional and forward-looking entity. Quite instructive are the successes and transformational impacts of Jack Welsh at General Electric (GE), Steve Jobs at Apple, Ludwig Erhard in Germany and Lee Kuan Yew in Singapore. Those leaders were able to motivate, direct and organise their people and organizations to achieve a common goal and execute their vision and grand ideas by process, power and promise.

In large measure, the success of those leaders entailed the sense of direction, orientation and guidance they provided to their people and organizations – first by defining their mission and then surrounding themselves with the right people with the right mindset and skill-set to get the job done. This idea of having a leadership compass is expounded in the works of Jim Collins, a management thinker and author: "Great leaders did not start to make their companies great or successful by setting a new vision and a new strategy, but instead they got the right people on the bus, the wrong people off the bus, and the right people in the right seats – and then figured out where to drive".

Having taught leadership courses for many years, I'm fully aware of the diverse views and insights on the subject, and how leadership and management are often quoted together, incorrectly believed to be interchangeable, and misunderstood. Whereas management is a transactional position entailing work and functions performed within and according to set boundaries, leadership is a transformational quality which primarily focuses on the development and welfare of people.

I remember having a class discussion about the difference between a leader and a manager, where the German students practically rejected every idea posited by their Asian counterparts. There were times I would be amazed at the various unconventional responses given by international students on the question of leadership effectiveness. In any event, such discourses made me realize how cultural values and social structures help shape the definition, role and outlook of both leaders and managers in various parts of the world.

With so much rapid social and economic change taking place due to globalization, competition and technology, the need for strong leaders as agents of change to help strengthen and build capacity at all levels in our nation is indispensable. There is no doubt in my mind that the poor leadership in companies, schools, public hospitals and national institutions is a major cause for the declining quality of service, morale and productivity in our nation. The feeling is that in many of our institutions, there just isn't sufficient accountability and personal responsibility. Oftentimes, productivity, efficiency and morale suffer on account of that poor leadership. Those who can actually lead hesitate and instead people who shouldn't come anywhere close to leadership roles avail themselves for such.

Eric Williams, like other great Caribbean leaders, demonstrated that leadership is not about breeding or height – taller being better, as the early theorists believed. It's not simply about intelligence and charisma, either. When we're inspired by great leadership which promotes inclusive growth, social justice and institutional effectiveness, we give the best of ourselves and produce amazing work. The imperative of people empowerment should always guide the actions and motivations of a good leader.

In the final analysis, leadership is about influencing and impacting people as well as getting results. Benjamin Franklin couldn't have expressed it any more explicitly when he said: "Well done is better than well said."

23. A Vision for Growth (Part 1)

When cornered at a press conference by an inquisitive journalist on his lack of vision, Helmut Schmidt, a former German Chancellor, insolently replied, "People who have visions should go see an eye doctor." This might have been a facetious point, but it's also a serious one. For even eye doctors will admit that the only thing worse than being blind is having sight but no vision.

Predicting the future is a thankless task, especially given the rapid pace of technological development and the many uncontrollable exogenous forces circling around us. But as the saying goes, "The best way to predict the future is to create it." As I began to weave together my thoughts on visionary change and leadership, it occurred to me that a vision, while painted in the colours of the rainbow, might face a dull reality often depicted in the colours of grey, black and white.

Still, a just and sustainable society cannot be built on short-termism, adhocism and institutional inertia. Leaders need to look beyond the horizon and prepare long-term projections in pursuit of sustainable development goals. This will require them to scan the world for signals of change – what a management psychologist calls "searchlight intelligence". In striving to excel in health, tourism, the knowledge economy and creative human resources, visionary thinking lends shape to the unknown and provides a lifeline to current and future generations. Without a national vision, the ability to guide the nation's existentialism, secure national ownership and mobilize limited resources will be compromised.

Central to my vision of the future is the judgement that Saint Lucia will need to prioritize the capital budget in an era of obviously finite resources. We'll need to make higher education a priority and give the sector the resources it needs. As a matter of course, a system of vocational and technical education that combines academic studies with industrial apprenticeships and traineeships will need to be established. Furthermore and even more crucially, the Sir Arthur Lewis Community College must evolve within the next five years (by 2021) into a national university college with an international reach. What is the point of an independent nation-state in the twenty-first century without a university to call its own and an education system which attends to its specific developmental challenges? Besides, a democracy needs an educated and informed people otherwise it will be starved of vibrancy. If economics teaches us anything, it is that education improves an economy, increases its social capital and leads to prosperity.

We must commit (or recommit) to tourism both as a source of income and a catalyst for greater inter-sectoral development. Tourism's potential linkage effects render the industry a viable economic development strategy, especially as we have no real viable alternatives for economic development. Since independence, our island has struggled with problems associated with development, and these have been particularly exacerbated by the absence of an inter-sectoral growth strategy.

Given the significant patterns of consumption and resource utilization in tourism, there is enormous potential for agriculture, agribusiness, medium-scale manufacturing and the creative industries to supply the inputs needed to produce tourism and leisure services through forward, backward and horizontal linkages. There has been too much investment in recent years in hotels and retail companies and too little in manufacturing industries, which has left the structure of the economy "distorted".

With the right policies and incentives, I can envisage small and medium-sized companies (SMEs) sustaining Saint Lucia's economy in a significant way, in the absence of new foreign direct investment (FDI) flows. Economic growth alone will not solve unemployment. More creative supply-sided reforms (including expansionary fiscal policies) and active labour market policies (including job training and business development programmes) are needed to bolster the SME sector – the lifeblood of any country's economy. Further, Saint Lucia has the potential to build its SMEs on the strength of the creative arts industry. The point is if we are to truly make an economic success of the creative industries in Saint Lucia, we must aim to strengthen the sector, promote intellectual property rights and invest in the next generation of content creators to keep the flow of IP coming. The economic benefits could be huge.

The development of the agricultural sector to secure increased food production should be a cornerstone strategy if we are truly serious about sustainable development. In fact, one of the keys to sustainable development is food security. It's worth repeating that annually more than US$ 2 billion is spent by CARICOM countries on food imports, although their combined population is only six million people. If ever we needed evidence of the neglect and underdevelopment of the agricultural sector in the region, this is it. Not only have Caribbean governments failed to facilitate and exploit inter-sectoral linkage synergies, they have also done precious little to promote food security in the region.

Unlike many trading blocks of developing and emerging nations around the world, the nations of CARICOM have failed to use the region to their economic and geopolitical advantage. It is now a matter of urgency that CARICOM gets its act together if these small islands are to meet the challenges brought about by trade liberalisation and globalisation. No less a distinguished academic than Sir Ronald Sanders has weighed in on the issue, urging CARICOM to use the single market more effectively to tackle the region's bludgeoning unemployment: "Foreign investors would be more greatly attracted to a larger regional market than to the individual small markets of most CARICOM countries. It would be one effective way of creating a larger economic space for the employment of young people."

By any measure, the greatest failure of our governance system resides in the dysfunctional state of local government. For too long, our efforts as a nation have been focussed on the performance of the national economy rather than the stability and strengthening of local economies. Today within the modern nation-state, government should operate at many different levels, ranging from villages to districts, towns and cities. Hence, every single district on the island should have an elected executive mayor, assisted by a town clerk and overseen by a district council comprising of business owners, bankers and representatives of the clergy. Why hasn't Saint Lucia finally embraced the idea that "all development is local" – what development economists across the globe have known for a long time?

Essentially, the broader question is whether our mindset and work practices are compatible with economic productivity and efficiency. How do you shift a mindset of a people to align with critical national development needs? Organization and technology are only part of the solution. Transformational leadership and a somewhat revamped and upgraded national mindset will be vital in facilitating that transformation and in translating that vision into reality.

24. A Vision for Growth (Part 2)

Part of what effective leaders do is to communicate an integrative vision for change and sustainability, which eventually gets translated into reality. Going on the advice of Vance Havner, the legendary American preacher, "The vision must be followed by the venture. It is not enough to stare up the steps – we must step up the stairs."

Following in the steps of the United Nations, I believe we should create our own National Sustainable Development Goals (NSDGs) backed by an institutional capacity to implement them. These goals would embrace a new equilibrium between social welfare and economic dynamism that promotes inclusive growth, social justice and civil society. Above all, this new development thrust would necessitate a re-evaluation of the policy matrix of the country's growth strategy, as well as a wholesale revision of the factors that constitute economic development such as education, quality of life, institutional effectiveness, infrastructure, health and social cohesion.

Of course, any vision that seeks to establish a balance between social welfare and economic dynamism here in Saint Lucia, must engender a society that promotes social and economic meritocracy, supports environmental sustainability and research in agriculture, and collects and analyzes economic and social data in order to more effectively guide and inform public policy decisions.

Sustainable growth in small developing states such as ours requires reforming not only specific arrangements, such as counterproductive investment and business regulations, but also more fundamental institutions, such as the legislature and the judiciary, to make them more responsive to people's needs and to increase public and investor confidence in the dispensation of justice. It is now conventional wisdom that the functionality and effectiveness of a country's political, legal, economic and social institutions will invariably affect its rate of economic growth. Thus, it turns out a major reason for underdevelopment in small developing nations is the absence or inadequacy of independent and reliable institutions that facilitate vital economic interactions and are able to unleash the full potential of the economies and societies they serve.

The idea that sound institutions are crucial for social order and purpose is worth its weight in gold. Viewed through the prism of behavioural economics, most of our institutions and social capital are not well-developed. As I have argued before, countries with strong institutions remain stable in times of social change and socio-cultural evolution, and also do better over time.

Furthermore, there is appreciably no meaningful development without middle class activism in civil society – and certainly no sustainable democracy without a vibrant civil society. Civil society needs a strong middle class to engender social stability and to be the driver of economic change. A strong middle class supports inclusive political and economic institutions, which underpin economic growth. Further, the strength of a society can be measured directly by the strength of its middle class, which usually translates to better governance, increased corporate social responsibility and greater spending in social sectors such as public health and education. Hence, it is crucial that public policy initiatives are offered and implemented to rebuild and grow the nation's middle class.

At the same time, the need for productive public services has never been greater. The public service is the primary front office agent in our nation's attempts to improve "the ease of doing business". Any blueprint for enhancing public sector efficiency must embrace the imperative of business process re-engineering (BPR) which entails a new orientation in delivering public services based on simplification of procedures with a view to providing better quality service, increasing speed, reducing cost and transforming the workforce culture. I fully understand the public service in Saint Lucia has become something of a sacred cow. But sometimes even sacred cows need to be slaughtered. Given the present inefficiencies in the public service, we need to start questioning existing processes and systematically eliminate the duplication of functions and forms of work that do not add value to the service rendered to the public.

As far as foreign policy goes, economic diplomacy will undoubtedly play a central role in our efforts to attract foreign direct investment (FDI) into Saint Lucia. Trade policy must now become foreign policy – essentially a "Look East" policy to increase trade and investment ties with the new Asian frontier markets.

Increasingly, the foreign policy of many developed and developing nations reflect the rise of truly transnational populations, and many of these governments have made pandering to diasporas a foreign policy priority. The engagement with the Saint Lucian Diaspora offers a strategic advantage in multiple areas. Diaspora networks must be seen as true development partners that serve as a potent economic force for re-engaging disconnected citizens, driving national change and contributing to nation building. Hence, Saint Lucia needs to adopt a full-on diaspora-driven foreign policy which aims to fully utilize the skills, experiences, insights and connections of Saint Lucians overseas, in fostering economic growth, reducing poverty and increasing trade.

On the fiscal policy front, a balanced budget policy should only be a long-term goal, given the immediate problems of high unemployment and slow growth which the country faces. A balanced budget will certainly play a role in economic sustainability, but it must not become the tail that wags the dog. As economic history has demonstrated, deficits do matter, but not in the way we think.

In terms of monetary policy, the Eastern Caribbean Central Bank (ECCB) will need to show it is much more than a monetary institution that simply manages exchange-rate mechanisms and fosters financial stability. In fact, central banks around the world have become economic change-agents and pacesetters that are expected to use financial innovation and growth strategies to bolster private and public sector dynamism and advance the socio-economic interests of their respective economies. Given the economic stagnation and loss of competitiveness of the economies of the OECS, I believe the ECCB has been woefully inadequate in stimulating economic growth and bringing job security to the OECS region. Hence, new strategic leadership may be required to oversee a paradigm shift in monetary policy that can stimulate regional growth.

If Saint Lucia wants to do better as a nation, it needs to develop a balanced scorecard for growth – and leaders must rise above partisan consideration and unite people in developmental work by ensuring maximum people participation. Critically, leaders must get the questions right before proposing answers. This means they must have the willingness and emotional intelligence to listen and learn – and the stamina and perseverance to make things happen.

25. Is Saint Lucia's Birth Certificate Flawed?

Under fierce contention at a special sitting in the House of Assembly on 25th August 2015, were the recommendations of a report by the Constitutional Reform Commission – an event that the National Television Network (NTN) carried live.

At first I wasn't sure whether it was the motives of the commissioners or the recommendations of the report that was the source of the political displeasure. In any event, after listening to the edifying contributions of the Members of Parliament for Vieux-Fort South and Castries North, a part of me thought something historic was afoot to upend the country's fossilized political system. Encouragingly, most of the MPs seemed to agree that if the character of our democracy and the nature of political governance are to change, then the constitution must be changed.

Tellingly, some of the recommendations made in the report are nothing new and should have been acted upon years, if not decades ago. I have always held the view that the progress of our nation both politically and economically, has been considerably inhibited by an archaic constitution fraught with colonial undertones, which for all intents and purposes, does not reflect who we are and hasn't facilitated our political maturity and social development in any meaningful manner. Since laws must be changed to help societies adapt to emerging circumstances, I have difficulties understanding the logic of religiously holding on to a winner-takes-all first-past-the-post system that has contributed to the polarization and disillusionment of the populace.

Having observed the process of democracy in many other European countries, there is indeed no doubt in my mind that the use of a system of proportional representation makes democracies more robust; the essence of which is that all votes contribute to the result, not just a bare majority. The anomalies of a system that allocates seats not according to a party's total number of nationwide votes, but on the basis of 17 "first-past-the-post" contests, strikes me as utterly absurd and a tragic denial of people's democratic rights.

Despite all the talk about economic growth and social progress, we have been held hostage by a constitution left stranded by the shifting tides of modern democracy and globalization; and which has engendered serious deficiencies in our justice and parliamentary systems. By the commission's own admission, many of our national institutions lack the underlying structures for effective accountability and transparency, rendering our social identity and civic character questionable after 36 years of independence.

How flawed is a constitution that allows the executive branch to perform legislative functions? Doesn't a true and credible democracy require the separation of the branches of government to prevent abuse of power and to ensure the rule of law? I'm afraid unless we fix that constitutional malfunction, we cannot proudly speak of good governance in the conduct of public affairs and in the management of public resources in this country.

If after the parliamentary debate we are serious about remaking Saint Lucia, we should start by making government smaller and more accountable by abolishing the Senate (a chamber resembling the flatulent House of Lords) and establishing a unicameral system with one legislative House. For a nation our size, the amalgamation of the two legislative chambers would bring about much needed dynamism and singleness of purpose to parliament as well as end the duplication of effort which makes the upper house seem like a useless and unnecessary expense to taxpayers.

One of the issues I've always had with our present parliament is the frequency with which MPs meet to discuss the people's business. I believe any constitutional reform should mandate the House to meet twice or even three times a week to engage in policy debates on education, health, fiscal matters, etc, and for parliamentarians to have the chance to question the prime minister on a specific area of policy or on the conduct of government business -something in the mould of Britain's Prime Minister Question Time (PMQ).

If the goal of representative democracy is to bring parliament closer to the people, then more civic engagement is needed to reflect the stake that we all have in the financial performance of our government, its agenda, and its services. That's why the role of parliamentary groups and committees in the governing process is crucial in scrutinizing the expenditure, administration and policy of the relevant government departments and the performance of top public servants. Further, Parliament should be able to question civil servants directly. At all times, the electorate expects the opposition MPs to remain active in exercising their parliamentary right to scrutinize government actions.

On the "referendum" question, I believe our constitution should give more clarity on the conduct and modalities of a direct vote on issues of strategic national importance such as the Citizenship by Investment Programme (already passed by the Senate and House) and the joining of the Caribbean Court of Justice (CCJ).

Ordinary people must surely have the basic democratic right to be consulted on these issues and to have a say in any changes, welcome or otherwise, to the way they are governed. With the growth of social media, it should now be much easier for citizens to be better informed about any national issue and hence be able to participate in the democratic process – a right and obligation which too many Saint Lucians unfortunately allow to end at the ballot box.

The experience of advanced democracies shows that public awareness and involvement are the crucial forces required to establish a truly effective monitoring mechanism.

As expected, a crucial point of contention mentioned in the report is the question of whether or not the prime minister should be elected directly by the entire country. Presently we follow the Westminster model where the populace elects legislature members and in turn the leader of the party with the most members in the legislature becomes the prime minister.

Not only is the prime minister not directly elected by the people, his appointment is not even ratified by those who are elected to Parliament. On that score, I do support the idea of electing the prime minister by direct popular vote, and believe such a move would enable stronger leadership and legitimacy. Moreover, I believe a direct vote would take care of the question of term limits for prime ministers.

Essentially, the public should have the right to choose not only their parliamentary representatives, but also their leader. Parties and other political groups would nominate their candidates for the premiership, and voters would choose among them in a general election for the Lower House.

Having elected a prime minister, his or her role should be that of a chief executive rather than a minister who heads the government. Like in Britain, Australia and many other parliamentary democracies around the world, I believe prime ministers shouldn't carry any major portfolios especially one as pivotal and all-encompassing as Finance. Instead they should co-ordinate and supervise the activities and programmes of other major ministries to ensure the overall policy objectives and targets are being achieved.

Further, allowing the Finance Ministry to be managed by someone else may actually be quite helpful in terms of succession planning within government, since it is believed that the Finance portfolio affords its holder unique insights into the financial and economic operations of a government, hence allowing him or her to take on the mantle of leadership when the time comes. If you look at both Britain and Australia during the administrations of Tony Blair and Kevin Rudd respectively, the finance ministers seamlessly took over as prime minister when the need arose eventually.

In a broader context, a few other recommendations in the report struck me as worthy of consideration. Given the frequent incidents of police shootings and the slow pace of justice in Saint Lucia, perhaps the idea of a Human Rights Commission enshrined in the constitution isn't a bad one after all. Even the relationship between the executive branch and the police should be reviewed to establish more independence for the latter.

Finally, it goes without saying that a badly paid MP will be unable to perform his constituency duties effectively. I'm actually surprised that we haven't recognized the correlation between the pay of a parliamentarian and the quality of candidates who avail themselves for political office.

Perhaps, the time has come to extricate ourselves from constitutional bondage so that we can give real progress a chance – a point underscored by all of the speakers. Whether we are predisposed to and honest about implementing some of the sensible reforms proposed by the commission, will depend on how seriously and urgently we treat the concerns of our citizens; and how we view the role of a vibrant democracy. I, for one, believe our system of government, buttressed by a time-warped constitution with its many idiosyncratic provisions, is broken and needs urgent attention.

26. Do Some MPs Need a Presentation Coach?

For most IT and medical professionals, public speaking is merely an occasional engagement that requires little panache and éclat. For business executives, by and large, it is a necessary evil to be avoided. However, for legislators and elected officials, it is a fundamental requirement of their job description; a primary tool that is the key to unlocking their personal power, character and competence.

In the old Greek civilization, public speaking was relished as an academic discipline. Along with education, it served as an instrument of social mobility and intellectual influence; in large part, playing a pivotal role in the lives of politicians, philosophers and social leaders. Invariably, success in the courtroom, classroom, senate and parliament was a function of one's ability to speak eloquently and articulately. Just because one could speak didn't mean everyone would listen; individuals would have to learn the art of persuasive speaking to capture and keep the Assembly's attention.

Even in Europe and the United States, you just have to look at political history to recognize the role erudition and articulate oratory have played in electoral success. The best politicians understood that in order to communicate work and value as well as command attention, they needed to make effective use of language and possess good delivery skills.

Listening to presentations for prolonged periods of time is hard work; so politicians knew that in order to maintain focus, they needed to not only educate, but also arouse interest and inspire the audience. It was also well understood that the rhetorical approach to campaigning for political office had to be different from the actual debate presentation in parliament.

Even so, Saint Lucia's obstreperous Parliament can be both an exciting and monotonous place. Since Independence, great speakers from both parties have emerged and trod the political stage leaving indelible marks in their path. This arguably represents a period in our political history when a more discerning public took interest in parliamentary debates owing to the dynamism and educational content of such exchanges.

I still remember as a young man, the trenchant nature of those debates, serving as a source of education, enlightenment and self advancement for many. Of course, there were also angry passages during those parliamentary sessions which many of us, no doubt, will recall. Although some members of Parliament were better than others both educationally and oratorically, one still got the distinct impression that the culture of public speaking was alive and well, impacting society positively. I am one of those who believe that representative democracy is a great thing if it thrives on a contest of ideas and if people stay interested in it on the basis of its vibrancy and inclusivity.

At any rate, it is widely held that anti-politics is the prevailing mood of the times, perhaps due to a lack of inspiration. Parliamentary debates nowadays are a great bore and it's not as though the issues are not as pressing and dramatic. It's just that some of the contributions are anything but worthwhile, raising questions about the calibre of people who avail themselves for political office. The soporific speeches, the impoverished attempts at humour, inadequate research, bad pronunciation and poor diction are hardly testament to a healthy institution.

Particularly annoying is the abuse of the address form "Mr. Speaker" by members during debate presentations. At times, the nation's Lower House seems to descend to a lowly public space where members shout, jeer and hurl insults at each other. If Parliament chooses to emasculate itself in this way, it's not surprising that people take less and less notice of it.

Lurking in the minds of Saint Lucians is the notion that the role of MPs is primarily to legislate laws and to oversee the implementation of policies by the Government, including scrutiny of public financial spending. However, you can't adequately perform these functions if you don't have the ability to think and speak critically and interact with the information avalanche available at any one time. Further, debate skills are critical to winning arguments, as other politicians will have opposing views.

There is a prevailing feeling that some parliamentarians generally lack the knowledge and understanding of roles, responsibilities and issues to constructively contribute to parliamentary debates. Most people will agree that there is an urgent need for some of them to hone up their polemic and argumentative skills. How can you represent people when you can't effectively analyze policies or explain your position convincingly?

Quite apart from promoting and setting good policies for the greater good of the constituents and country, the job of a parliamentarian is to advocate and argue on behalf of a particular point of view, as well as understand and respond to counterpoints. This requires quick and critical thinking skills, and a high level of presentation skills for success.

To be fair, a few parliamentarians do give a very good account of themselves in both the Upper and Lower Chambers of the legislature.

However, in a few instances, we have parochial politicians who are elected only for the purpose of providing constituency service and are unable to contribute constructively to strategic macroeconomic planning.

Will we ever be able to nurture a political and social culture that promotes intelligent and healthy debate? The signs are not encouraging, unfortunately. Take for instance our school system. Ideally, all schools by now should have had vibrant debate clubs coached by Toastmasters volunteers. Instead of promoting inter-school SOCA competitions, we should be organizing inter-school debating competitions. Is this how we develop the minds of our young people? The promotion of debating societies would have been more productive in helping to focus more interest in debating and building an educational culture that encourages healthy discussion, non-violent communication and articulate oratory.

Not only is debating a powerful classroom tool, it is also fun and an extra-curricular activity that encourages critical and creative thinking. I believe the participation of students in debates is a good strategy that schools should adopt to empower young people with many important skills that will adequately prepare them for adult responsibilities.

Globally, many of the great debaters and orators that have graced the political landscape actually started their journey in debating societies at school. Our own brilliant wordsmith George Odlum, took part in the Drama Society and the Debating Society at the University of Bristol.

The U.S. Secretary of State John Kerry, an expert debater who has a fundamental mastery of a wide range of issues, helped found a debating society at St. Paul's School and was a star debater at Yale University.

The New York Times reports that by the time Ted Cruz, the American Republican Senator, was a senior at Princeton University in 1992, "he had developed an arsenal of rhetorical skills and theatrical gestures that made him one of the most polished performers on the college debate circuit."

Eric Williams, Tony Blair, Bill Clinton, etc, were all exposed to debating and oratory pretty early in their school education.

The emergence of Barack Obama on the political scene should have triggered awakenings about the importance of communication and debating skills to politicians.

Dean Frenkel, a vocal instructor, speech analyst, speech coach and author of "Evolution of Speech" explained: "What should our politicians learn from Mr Obama? They can start by listening to the sound-map of Mr Obama's voice and take note of his resonance, speech manner, his adroit sense of timing and musical presentation of his voice. His speech virtues begin with a combination of accurate and crisp articulation, beautifully timed speech rate and commanding presence. He has license and he willingly uses it. He is able to infuse passion into his speech and while he is understated, he does have remnants of speech gifts learned from preachers. Yet he never seems to over-do the passion. He often starts his sentences quite slowly then quickens up as he sifts through detail, then strategically slows his speech rate to emphasise strategic points...Mr Obama has a good mental library of words which helps him to responds well under pressure."

Perhaps, a mandatory long-term capacity building programme would foster and equip some parliamentarians with the presentation and research skills needed to make better contributions in Parliament. With a bit more communications training, some may feel more empowered and self-confident to participate in town council exchanges and televised debates.

27. The Peter Principle – The Cream Rises Until It Sours

A while back in 2015, I met an old friend by sheer accident whom I hadn't seen for eons. Now a retired CEO, my friend had managed companies in just about every sector in our local economy. Before long, we were sitting in a local bar having a drink, reflecting on our enduring friendship, respective careers and the general vicissitudes of life.

But it wasn't until the point when we started discussing the local private sector and the economy that he began to reminisce about the ebb and flow of his management career and what had shaped both his notion and perception of leadership effectiveness.

At one point, he complained that he had witnessed one industrial sector after another exhibit incompetence, bad service, inefficiencies and disastrous decisions. "In my professional lifetime", he lamented, "I have seen supervisors and executives promoted to positions with responsibilities that they couldn't fulfil. The result was often a depressed staff and in most instances, lagging productivity growth."

I was thrust into a management debate by his trenchant remarks, to which I replied pungently: "Apparently the cream rises until it sours!" I felt compelled to relate my own experience abroad and how I had come face to face with the spectre of managers with skills mismatches, often resulting in operational mediocrity and poor management decisions.

Of course, I'm well aware that more often than usual, the people who run those institutions and departments didn't necessarily intend to do such lousy work. They were simply victims of an immutable circumstance called promotion, which I'll explain is not always a good thing.

Now in principle, I have nothing against promotion per se, but sometimes it comes with a hidden dark side. It's called the "Peter Principle", and when it erupts it can wreak havoc on departments, government bureaucracies, personnel and productivity.

The Peter Principle, the eponymous law Dr. Laurence J. Peter (educator and psychologist) coined in his 1969 book has had far-reaching applications and implications outside of the business world. As the New York Times put it, "Dr. Peter explains why incompetence is at the root of everything we endeavour to do—why schools bestow ignorance, why governments condone anarchy, why courts dispense injustice, why prosperity causes unhappiness, and why utopian plans never generate utopias. The Peter Principle brilliantly explains how incompetence and its accompanying symptoms, syndromes, and remedies define the world and the work we do in it."

Based on systematic observations by Dr. Peter, he postulates: "Workers who do well will keep getting promoted up the ladder until they reach a point where they can no longer excel. Then they stay stuck in that role, getting by with average-to-poor performance, preventing more capable people from taking on the role. Multiply this effect across all major positions within a workplace and soon you've got a company filled with mediocrity in all its top managerial jobs."

In other words, a worker who may have excelled at his or her position is now promoted to his level of incompetence, a (reward) that eventually exceeds his field of competence.

At any rate, what obtains is a fluid situation where capable followers are promoted to be incompetent leaders or capable teachers rise to become poor administrators. Today if you look around in the various company offices and schools across the length and breadth of Saint Lucia, you might just discover the sagacity and relevance of Dr. Peter's management theory.

In the realm of international politics, when I think of the Peter Principle, ex-President George W. Bush and the inimitable Sarah Palin spring irresistibly to mind. Prior to becoming President of the United States, Mr Bush's career as a Texan oilman and governor, by published account, was reasonably successful (rewarding is perhaps a better word), having attended Harvard Business School where he earned an M.B.A degree, and subsequently made millions in the private sector through deals and business networks.

However, as America's 43rd President, his performance can best be described as "a hand with all thumbs". He received heated criticism from all and sundry over his handling of the American economy, the Iraqi War, Hurricane Katrina and countless other challenges during his presidency.

In recent years, some economists have even begun to hold his administration responsible for the Great Recession that engulfed America and the rest of the world in 2008. In the eyes of many, not only was President Bush a prodigy of incompetence and wastefulness, he was often seen and portrayed as a well-to-do stooge with a biblical and simplistic weltanschauung.

In the end, eight long years of George W. Bush left us with plenty of televised satire, both good and bad. The issue over whether he was unfairly targeted and demonized by the world's media, considering the less than stellar performance of Jimmy Carter, is still contentious.

Perhaps President Richard Nixon better understood the idiosyncrasies and challenges of the job when he declared, "It is the responsibility of the media to look at the President with a microscope, but they go too far when they use a proctoscope."

In any event, have you ever looked at your boss and wondered "Who promoted you"? Most likely he had succeeded at everything he tried, and got promoted, until he failed, and then stayed put in a job that he didn't do well. The fact is people are often promoted on false assumptions or on the wrong premise. Someone who may have done an excellent job as a mechanical engineer where technical skills are required, is now elevated to a supervisory and middle management position which calls for tactical insight, conceptual skills and executive ability. Not only might the employee lack the requisite management skills, he/she may not even have the interpersonal skills needed to lead a team.

Still, I once experienced a situation where a company had promoted a star researcher to the position of supervisor. That move had cosmic implications for the company's research output in terms of quality, hands-on creativity, the gathering of data and methodical speed. Having realized the strategic mistake, the star researcher was eventually returned to his previous post, albeit appeased by a much higher salary.

When such developments occur, a company or department ends up with a situation where it has to stomach an incompetent manager and at the same time suffer the loss of a skilled technician. The problems created by such "promotions" are compounded by the idea that an incompetent manager will make incompetent decisions – including deciding who to promote.

As is conventional in the world of human resources management, assessing an employee's potential for a promotion is often based on their performance in the current job. But why do companies, institutions and government departments employ the same old yardsticks and benchmarks when it comes to staff promotion?

No wonder, according to U.S. management research, management and leadership competence in pursuing targets, incentives and monitors, especially at the supervisory and middle management levels, have suffered serious setbacks in the last decade. Albert Einstein explained this process when he defined insanity: doing the same thing over and over again and expecting different results. Further, the research demonstrates that incompetence is on the rise everywhere. But how could incompetence be on the rise when knowledge and tools proliferate?

The observations made by Dr. Peter remain just as true today as they did in 1969. He observed that one reason so many employees are incompetent is that the skills required to get a job often have nothing to do with what is required do the job itself. "The skills required to run a great political campaign have little to do with the skills required to govern. There is nothing about being a great surgeon that prepares a doctor to run a hospital. Learning to be a great litigator in no way prepares a lawyer to run a law firm. Many organizations, from hospitals to law firms, use such standards to select new leaders—yet devote little or no attention to their management skills. They often end up with lousy leaders and lose their best individual performers."

Let's allow Dr. Peter, from the introduction to his book to have the final word: "If man is going to rescue himself from a future intolerable existence, he must first see where his unmindful escalation is leading him. He must examine his objectives and see that true progress is achieved through moving forward to a better way of life, rather than upward to total life incompetence."

28. Dropping in on Democracy's Dropouts

Is there something in the volcanic air that makes Saint Lucian politicians consume each other in campaigns of internecine fighting rather than work together in the best interest of the nation?

Over the years, what has happened is that through the constant bickering, confrontation and polarization, our democracy has been starved of its vibrancy. Perhaps for that reason, we continue to see the quixotic rise of the non-voter, or what some would call "democracy dropouts" – a term used to describe those, who over the years, have opted out of the democratic process.

Democracy is a great thing if people stay interested in it and it works. Above all, it thrives on a contest of ideas and voter participation.

At a time when the economic divide between the haves and the have-nots couldn't be sharper, and where political discussions and debates often seem to degenerate into character assassinations, we have to ask whether our system of democracy is working in terms of generating and maintaining voter participation.

Let's take a look at some statistics. As reported by the International Institute for Democracy and Electoral Assistance (IDEA), the 2011 elections recorded a 56.84% voter turn-out, the second worst since Saint Lucia attained independence in 1979. From a list of 150,996 registered voters, the total number of people who cast their votes was an abysmal 85,821. The lowest participation rate was in 2001 at 31.54%. In 2006 only 58.46% of registered voters turned out to exercise their franchise.

What this tells us is that at the last parliamentary election, almost half of the eligible population didn't bother to vote. That certainly is bad for party politics, but even worse for representative democracy. I can only make an educated guess as to the reasons: apathy, anger and frustration at the relentlessly negative tone of the campaigns and the divisive nature of party politics.

I do understand that in any democratic society, there are many different opinions and interests, often in direct opposition to one another. These are reflected in the election campaigns in which parties appeal to the electorate for support with their competing programmes, and in debates in parliament over how these policies should be translated to practical measures.

Because different groups and individuals will be affected in different ways, there are bound to be arguments about whether taxes should be raised or lowered, and how much money should be spent on what kinds of public works, whether the government should help with hospital and medical expenses, and what kind of investments the country needs for its development.

A democratic state is one in which the citizens have the right to criticize the government, to oppose or support the government, and are able to do all these things by peaceful and legal means. Where these rights are denied, the pretence of democracy is nothing more than a sham and the hollowness of the deception is at once exposed when these simple tests are applied.

Crucially, the citizenry must always be at the forefront of the debate and should determine what policies should be adopted; and unless they are intelligent in their understanding and responsible in the exercise of their judgment, the mistakes they might make could be disastrous for themselves and for their country.

The setting of the political agenda is something that too many individuals out of laziness, leave to politicians. The "big guys" at the top are allowed to frame the issues, run the dialogue and set the parameters. The population then reacts to the menu handed down to them. Precisely this may have resulted in people consistently voting against their own self-interest.

Sadly, an increasing number of voters are adopting the role of consumers; and are morphing into couch-potato voters who would like to be "offered" something by politics instead of actively informing themselves about what the politicians are proposing.

But democracy is not a delivery service or an entertainment programme. A democracy can expect a certain degree of knowledge from its citizens – a modicum of involvement. Today, more than ever, the voter bears a continuous responsibility for judgment and decision.

Civic participation is the cornerstone of a strong democracy. Under our first-past-the-post system, the actual choice of those who will govern us usually takes place at intervals of several years. The process by which the choice is determined, however, calls for attention by the voters to the issues that arise from day to day. They must try to keep informed about their nature; they must follow and on occasions take part in discussions that help to clarify opinions; they must make up their minds whether the government is doing a satisfactory job or whether some other group could do it better.

It's about time that Saint Lucians understand that democracy is not only the short process of voting. It is in fact much more than just another way of organizing and working a country's political institutions. It is a whole way of life, of which the form is only one reflection. It expresses the trust and spirit of a community that is truly self-governing in the broadest sense of the word.

Among modern prime ministers and presidents, the greatest are those who found their strength in the trust of the people, and who won that trust by their ability to embody and translate the aspirations of the democracies they serve.

The political arena can certainly use some intellectual and technocratic talent. Of course, I am not suggesting Plato's idea of a government of philosopher-kings. That's arguably something that we really don't need. The point is we need intelligent and valuable exchanges to replace the political diatribe and character assassination that have characterised Saint Lucian politics over the years.

The time has come for us to realize that politics in its true sense is a means of liberation, education and self advancement. Obviously I am not referring to the banal politics of self interest, self congratulation and rhetoric, which only aims at burying the real issues under a mask of piety and platitude, but the politics of responsibility which seeks to identify the real issues and present them to the people for decision.

In recent years, our national politics have become very boring because our leaders have failed to provide us with candid and clear-cut formulation of problems, as well as the facts necessary for intelligent choice.

Even so, in a democracy like ours where an alarmingly large number of voters are uninformed, uneducated and inherently loyal, this could be a hindrance to the execution of democratic principles and the pursuance of developmental objectives.

If voters do not take the trouble to keep themselves informed about public affairs, or allow their emotions to prevail over their better judgment, or insist on putting their own particular advantage ahead of the general interest, the affairs of the community are bound to suffer.

29. Democracy and the Poorly Educated

It was something that the polarizing and gaffe-prone frontrunner, Donald Trump said during his brief primary victory speech in Las Vegas on Tuesday February 23rd 2016, that had me musing over some of the most profound words of Thomas Jefferson that "The greatest threat to democracy is an uneducated citizenry." Salivating at the prospect of becoming the Republican nominee for President, Mr Trump declared: "We won the evangelicals. We won with young. We won with old. We won with highly educated. We won with poorly educated. I love the poorly educated."

For anyone who has watched the 2016 presidential race play out, it should come as no shock that most of the pitifully mediocre candidates on the Republican side have sought to exploit not only the anxieties of a section of the electorate, but also their ignorance and economic circumstances – by spreading calumnies and invariably presenting a sort of dystopian view of America. More than any other candidate, the political beast that is Donald Trump has fed off the ignorance of especially rural conservative voters – exploiting their cultural, economic and social fears.

As the rest of the world observe America's political spectacle with an abiding sense of smugness and foreboding, I remain cautiously optimistic about Mr. Trump's imminent departure from the race and take comfort in the words of Winston Churchill that "You can always count on Americans to do the right thing – after they've tried everything else."

In a paper on systems thinking, Jack Harich, a systems engineer and sustainologist identifies and explains five common deception strategies which politicians are likely to use to hoodwink particularly an uneducated electorate: false promises, false enemies, pushing the fear button, wrong priorities and secrecy. Sadly, in any society, all these forms of deception will work well, if illiteracy and ignorance prevail, undergirded by the ovine docility of voters. And I suppose in an election year, the deception machinery will be at its peak targeting an especially gullible section of the voting public who are looking for something that sends them into raptures rather than a political discourse that informs and educates them about the policy choices on offer.

Now, lest I be misunderstood, let me make it abundantly clear that I believe, like most reasonable people, that democracy is the best system of governance that exist and its enlightened providence should be a source of comfort and service to everyone regardless of ethnicity, class, gender or socio-economic status. There is also little doubt that the meritocratic basis of any democratic society is majority rule, further strengthened by the principle of minority and individual rights and the need to guarantee due process and equal protection under the law.

However, a system of democracy where money rules and voters are treated as famished consumers rather than active stakeholders in the process, can be a double-edged sword. By reducing democracy to just tribal voting and a rhetorical race to the bottom – or treating it as a delivery service or entertainment programme for the navel gazer and the less discerning voter, is surely a recipe for socio-economic stagnation and the collapse of civil society.

The Greek philosopher Plato saw the system of democracy as the "rule of the mob" because of the "unjust condemnation by Athenian democracy of Socrates", his mentor and friend. In fact, the original Greek Democracy was mostly based on the idea that only those that contributed to society by paying taxes had a vote. Of course this concept would most likely be rejected in today's system of democratic representation and equality under the law, although the idea may be gaining traction in some "ostensible democracies" around the world devoid of vibrancy and accountability and frustrated by poor economic performance, in large part due to electoral tribalism.

At any rate, democratic and economic progress can be stymied by an inherently loyal, un-informed and poorly educated populace only interested in short-term, incentive-driven benefits. They are the ones most likely to be bought by politicians with promises of personal benefits and utopian living standards that cannot possibly be delivered.

In an essay entitled "Democracy and Political Ignorance", Ilya Somin explains that "Democracy is supposed to be rule of the people, by the people, and for the people. But in order to rule effectively, the people need political knowledge. If they know little or nothing about government, it becomes difficult to hold political leaders accountable for their performance...Perhaps the solution is a better public school curriculum that puts more emphasis on civic education. The difficulty is that governments have very little incentive to ensure that public schools really do adopt curricula that increase knowledge."

I have said before that democracy is a great thing if people stay interested in it and it works. The success of the system is premised on the principle of "informed exchanges", i.e. citizens are expected to have a certain degree of knowledge about political matters. Above all, it thrives on a contest of ideas and voter participation. If people are not intelligent in their understanding of national development issues and responsible in the exercise of their judgement, the mistakes they might make could be disastrous for their country and for themselves. Hence, our people must embrace their civic duty and collective responsibility to rise above party politics and start putting the country first. As an Indian reformer and columnist once said, "We cannot continue to languish in 19th century politics aspiring to live in the 21st century economy."

Any attempt to solidify our system of democracy and end the degenerating vicious cycle of political pettiness will require the attention of the voter to the issues that arise from day to day and their active involvement in discussions that help clarify opinions and positions. It's a fact that voters particularly those from the lower strata of society often lack the educational background to understand the increasing complexity of many political and economic issues.

While the country has made much progress since independence, many of our people, not least the party delegates who choose leaders and representatives, have been blind to the need to educate themselves to better understand the nature of the issues that confront them. I am one of those who believe that all political party delegates should meet some minimum requirements before being allowed to participate in the process of choosing national leaders and determining the future of the country.

Let me once again invoke the wisdom of Thomas Jefferson that: "If a nation expects to be ignorant and free, in a state of civilization, it expects what never was and never will be. . . The People cannot be safe without information. When the press is free, and every man is able to read, all is safe." Does that mean in a half-literate society like ours, true democracy is only a fleeting illusion?

I've always known that a nation that stops reading will eventually stop thinking, needless to say Saint Lucians have always had an ambivalent relationship with books. How are we supposed to be safe, free and enlightened, as Jefferson noted, without doing due research, fact-checking and reading? As it turns out, the last time I checked, newspaper circulation was in decline and bookstores seemed set to go the way of the dinosaur.

30. Of Politics and the Bench

Peter Mueller, a polarizing figure who served as governor of the German state of Saarland for 12 years, is now a judge on the country's Supreme Constitutional Court. Robert French, the current Chief Justice of the High Court of Australia was once a high-profile election candidate for the Liberal Party, although he lost the election. The late T. Clark Hull, one of Connecticut's most popular politicians resigned as lieutenant governor of that U.S. state to become one of its Supreme Court justices.

These are all examples of former politicians and retired lawmakers who took up new roles in the judiciary. Of course, the Caribbean region has not been immune from this trend, which reflexively begs the question: Since democracy breathes and thrives on the distance between the branches of government, do judicial appointments of serving or former politicians pose a risk to the rule of law and democratic governance? I, for one, seriously believe this question is worth exploring, especially as judges are increasingly making political decisions.

Let me be clear from the outset that there's nothing in the respective constitutions of the countries that I've alluded to which prevents former politicians from serving in the judiciary – whether as local magistrates or regional judges. Neither am I suggesting that former politicians who become judges are automatically biased and unfair (some have in fact proved to be people of high intellectual stature and integrity). However, in an age of judicial activism and majoritarianism, concerns are being raised everywhere (especially in America and Europe) about judges becoming too powerful and acting as masters of the state (sometimes on half of their political masters) – undermining the powers of elected legislators by changing and even making laws (albeit Common Law and the process of judicial review grant such powers) instead of interpreting and applying them.

We all instinctively accept the old aphorism by the English Lord Chief Justice Gordon Hewart that "justice should not only be done, but should "manifestly and undoubtedly" be seen to be done." Thus, democratic societies must, for the sake of accountability and good governance, eschew the appointment of judges (usually lifetime) who may be ideologically inclined or appear to be beholden to a particular political outfit or pressure group (like in the U.S) – lest the respect and authority of the courts on which they serve are compromised and their rulings viewed with suspicion.

How then is justice guaranteed to be "manifestly and undoubtedly served" when erstwhile pugnacious political figures like Germany's Peter Mueller ascend to the judiciary or when U.S. Supreme Court justices – nolens volens – split "fairly reliably" along party lines dictated by their appointing presidents? Aren't such conflicted and incongruous relationships between everyday politics and the highest courts in the country a real danger to democracy?

Every schoolchild learns that democracy is built on the separation of three independent governance pillars namely; the executive, judiciary and legislature – and that none is supposed to trespass into the other's province. Now, the increasing influence of the executive branch on many aspects of democratic governance has triggered ferocious debates among the academic class and in civil society. A few years ago, there was even a debate in Germany about whether the appointment of a justice minister – who sits at the top of the justice system – is a violation of the principle of the separation of executive and judicial powers.

Recently in Saint Lucia, a case involving a French national charged with murder and sentenced to time already served on remand, have once again reignited debate about the separation of the executive branch and the judiciary, needless to say that good governance has long been comprised when one considers that both executive and legislative powers are in the same hands.

At any rate, when the above-referenced ex-governor Peter Mueller was appointed as a Supreme Court judge, the Green Party in Germany roared that the country's highest court was "no Jurassic Park for retired and worn-out politicians". The Frankfurter Allgemeine newspaper, the country's largest daily, compared Mueller's appointment to the opaque Vatican Conclaves famed for the inconclusiveness of their smoke signals which often led to confusion amongst the pilgrims gathering in St. Peter's Square.

In countries like Germany and the United States where the highest courts play a central role in mediating political and constitutional disagreements, political appointments to the judiciary have increasingly been viewed as "patronage" or deplored as "politicians in robes". Particularly in the U.S., the Supreme Court is seen as a political court, or as a CNN legal analyst put it, "a politicized judicial institution ran by legal luminaries covered in political and ideological robes". For a nation perceived to have near-impeccable democratic credentials and strong institutional underpinnings, this development is most alarming – as it represents a clear violation of the separation of powers and provokes a conflict of loyalty and interest.

According to a veteran American journalist: "It is well-understood that there are now, with Scalia's death, three very conservative Catholic justices (Samuel A. Alito Jr., John G. Roberts Jr. and Clarence Thomas), four liberal justices (Stephen G. Breyer, Ruth Bader Ginsburg, Elena Kagan and Sonia Sotomayor) and a swing justice (Anthony M. Kennedy) who is generally conservative but liberal in several important areas (such as gay rights and capital punishment of minors)." Democracies around the world are surely asking why it should matter at all whether a judge is liberal, progressive or conservative. Isn't the role of the judiciary simply to interpret laws and enforce the constitution based on the principle of strict constructivism rather than make rulings based on political beliefs, personal values and social prejudices?

I believe it makes a mockery of progressive democracy when important cases are decided by "a vote of five conservative Catholics against three liberal Jews (joined by one liberal Catholic)". Jerome Frank, a mid-20th-century legal thinker, is said to have claimed that "justice is a function of what the judge had for breakfast. Don't let their black robes, serious miens and pledges of fealty to the law fool you. Judicial decisions are not cool applications of objective legal principles. Rather, they are manifestations of personal predilections and biases." I shudder to think that any judge on a Supreme Court or High Court makes decisions based on his/her judicial philosophy and political loyalty rather than the direct interpretation of the law book.

31. It's the Debates, Stupid!

The private sector, civil society and the media have all called for it. It is, no doubt, a vital component of good governance and – as progressive and stable economies around the world will attest – the lifeblood of participatory democracies. While, in 2016, there is no shortage of issues confronting candidates here on the brink of a general election, there is only a shortage of insightful and substantive political DEBATE on subject matters ranging from the economy, healthcare and infrastructure – to foreign policy, judicial reform and national security. And if indeed political representation is about transparency, accountability and public scrutiny, why aren't such debates happening?

The fault, I can assure you dear compatriots, is not in our stars, but in ourselves – not that we are necessarily underlings; it's just that our expectations are low and malleable.

So how much have we truly evolved since independence in 1979. Economically? Reasonably well! Politically? Well umm, not so much! And the reason is not so farfetched: For aspiring candidates and politicians, we might have – to our own detriment – made the requirements for political office much too easy and set the performance bar much too low for far too long. It appears we haven't treated politics as the serious business that it really ought to be. If would-be office-holders knew they had to face serious fact-checking investigative journalists and participate regularly in formal policy debates, perhaps we would attract better-qualified candidates rather than some of the pitifully mediocre ones that we have elected over the years.

For too long, we have allowed aspiring candidates to deflect and obfuscate – hiding behind group-think structures, party colours and lately, social media. We have allowed them to delight crowds with their antics – making all sorts of vitriolic assertions and false allegations from their comfort zones and impregnable fortresses (mostly political platforms, election rallies and talk shows) instead of demanding that they face off in formal public debates both at the local and national levels to enunciate and defend their platforms.

These are serious times – and we need to open our minds to new opinions and impressions of candidates and learn more about their character and backgrounds, regardless of party affiliation. The free passes to political power without proof of professional competence and personal integrity should become a thing of the past. It's time we find a way (or make a way) to get past the silly insults, slogans, symbols and colours, and engage in constructive dialogue that will help to better evaluate the people who profess to know our needs and who wish to represent our collective voice in the nation's highest democratic institution.

Since politicians pass laws and make crucial decisions about the economy and society, I'm always surprised that relatively little attention is focused on examining closely whether they've got the requisite skills and personal attributes to handle challenging projects and fiscal matters, or to produce innovative ideas, plans and initiatives to solve community and national problems. The spectre of poor representation and economic underdevelopment should puncture any complacency about the primacy of politics and the perils of taking democracy for granted.

Clearly, the old election campaign model needs to be recharged, and rather than shine like a beacon of hope, it winks like a battery-drained flashlight. If you followed the tonal trajectory of the last few election rallies and public meetings, you would probably view the next few months of political campaigning with a sense of foreboding.

It's not too much of a stretch to say that civil society and the private sector have grown tired of the surfeit of pageantry and absence of substance that platform politics seems to incite. Thus, it's worth repeating that we have to start to reinvent our political and civic life, and reinvigorate our democracy.

Why can't we use regular political debates to force transparency, accountability and maturity in the electoral process? The nation is crying for an opportunity to hear productive exchanges which will provide the capacity to deliver intelligent analysis of economic trends and business activities. Why aren't the political leaders of all three parties going head-to-head in national debates? Given the constant campaign bloviations and political allegations going around, such a productive exercise would surely provide an opportunity to expose empty bromides and platitudes, and challenge misrepresentations and false equivalences on the spot. Further, it may even have the effect of elevating the status of third-party and independent candidates – an important electoral element in our democracy which has largely been ignored and demoralized.

Town hall meetings alone will not cut it. Televised debate – the kind that enriches and enlightens the cultural and political path of a nation – must become a regular fixture of Saint Lucian election races, if we are to truly evolve as a people. I am convinced that given the depths to which politics have sunk (not only in Saint Lucia but in the wider Caribbean) the institutionalized display of civility that organized debates represent can make a difference. The sight of more civil exchanges and handshakes, as well as competing candidates sharing the same stage – attempting to sell their respective visions to the electorate – would be a welcome development.

What is more, televised debates have the potential to open up the political landscape to the electorate, offering them an opportunity to judge the candidates and their ideas without having to trawl through manifestos. Apropos of manifestos, if political campaigning has already started, why aren't the policy proposals already out there in the public domain? How is any meaningful debate supposed to take place without first knowing the competing visions of the political contenders? We all need a direction to begin, right?

CHAPTER 3 –
NATIONAL INDEPENDENCE
AND SOVEREIGNTY

32. Our Nation at 37 – Is Sovereignty Real?

As we observe our 37th anniversary of Independence (2016), there has never been a better time to raise a few pertinent questions about the notion of national sovereignty – in an era where everything is becoming more alike, and the symbols, institutions and instruments of sovereignty are increasingly being redefined – not least by the forces of international co-operation.

There is no denying the fact that the world society and economy have entered a new age of convergence and interdependence – and the slippery idea of sovereignty has changed over time.

Against the backdrop of globalization and trans-sovereign dynamics, Saint Lucia has been affected by a range of important trends: the renewed and spreading consciousness of individual and human rights, higher development expectations, the disruptive power of the internet, the multilateral approach to decision-making and the general pursuit and inculcation of global values.

With all this convergence happening around us at breakneck speed, there is an abiding sense that nation states like ours – already handicapped by very small markets and relatively backward economies – are losing their grip on their own power as it relates to their sovereignty, territorial integrity and development interests.

The encroachment of international and multilateral regimes on the internal affairs of small and micro states – whether in the form of tax and fiscal advisories, diplomatic demands or political directives – have invoked fears of foreign subjugation and aroused distrust, skepticism, even hostility.

The Jufalli case, for instance, which has prompted furrowed eyebrows in academic and diplomatic circles around the world, shows clearly how the rights of a small country can be violated by a larger state.

The fact is, whether Dr. Juffali's appointment was ignoble or not, it is the unequivocal sovereign right of Saint Lucia to make whatever ambassadorial appointments it wishes under international law.

It's not up to a parochial London court to decide whether Dr. Juffali's appointment is "spurious" or not, having been accredited as a diplomat by the host nation. If anything, only the people of this country should demand answers and make any such determination.

Arguably, globalization has not necessarily made life any easier for small developing states. Since the idea of sovereignty is already laden with expectations, it is becoming increasingly difficult for small states to pursue their economic goals, let alone their political ones, in the rising tide of global relations and economics.

Mr Lee Kuan Yew, the late Prime Minister of Singapore, is reported to have once said: "Small island states are a political joke". Was he implying that in the modern context, the sovereignty of small states is a concept that resonates more in theory than in practice? Or was he suggesting that since the world will not change to suit the conveniences of small nations, they'll have to constantly adapt to trends set by the developed world?

Which begs another question coined by a political journalist: Is the notion of sovereignty sacrosanct, or can we describe it as fallible?

As far as I'm concerned, sovereignty is not simply an entitlement, but an obligation – and is far from being fallible. The main justification for its endowment is economic and social development – and I'm not only talking about the sovereignty of parliament, but also the real sovereignty of the people in matters of constitutional change through the use of referenda, for instance.

Without a doubt, there is a need to further entrench our sovereignty to allow our people to both think and do things differently as well as to facilitate a change in our weltanschauung.

Above all, our sovereignty should reflect a wide set of cultural norms and practices which reinforce our ideals of self-determination and self-identity.

Equally critical is the imperative of developing structures and institutions which promote participative democracy – the result and outcome of which must be a people who are responsible for their own progress and take ownership of the processes of development and growth.

At times, it appears the main threat to our national sovereignty is not necessarily some external force, but our own indisposition and incapacity to defend our democracy, patrimony and rights as citizens.

We often label ourselves "patriotic citizens" and boast about the irresistible beauty of our island. On social media and in the wider world, most, if not all citizens use the tagline "Proud to be Lucian" to express their love for country. Some genuflect before it, but few actually define it.

What does it truly mean to be a sovereign nation with the Queen of England still officially the Head of State? How does the way we are governed in small island states conflict with the need to tackle the major economic and global issues?

Sovereignty is a holistic concept which entails both personal and collective responsibility, as well as the obligation to ensure that all human and civil rights are respected. Moreover, the thinking and actions behind sovereignty should ensure that the judicial, social and economic infrastructure and institutions which underpin our development as a people are in place and function as they should.

The institutional capacity to administer justice and provide security is an existential challenge that any sovereign nation should tackle head-on. "In the absence of justice", said Saint Augustine, "what is sovereignty but organized robbery?"

However, it is Gijs de Vries, a former European Union anti-terrorism co-ordinator, who nailed the point home when he observed: "You can't get closer to the heart of national sovereignty than national security and intelligence services."

Needless to say, a breakdown in law and order in any country (think of Haiti, Grenada, Palestine or even Ukraine) is an invitation for some foreign power to either intervene or impose self-serving conditions on another country.

When we are constantly hobbled by petty and tribal politics instead of pursuing a more participative, creative and progressive approach to development, the collective energies required to strengthen our democracy and guard our sovereignty are uselessly expended.

Just the same, if we thought we could enjoy full sovereignty without some measure of food security, then we ought to think again. Today, we have to import most of our food from aboard – a serious injustice to our healthy soil and pleasant agricultural climate.

Need I remind you again that annually more than US$2 billion is spent by CARICOM countries on food imports, although their combined population is only six million people? If ever we needed evidence of the neglect and underdevelopment of the agricultural sector in the region, this is it.

As for financial sovereignty, no such thing exist for small states like ours, as the power centres of global capitalism have sought to tackle tax evasion and money laundering – problems which they themselves have bred and facilitated – by unfairly targeting Caribbean countries and restricting financial flows with little consideration for the health of these economies.

Of further disquiet is the recent labelling of Caribbean islands as "tax havens" by individual state governments of the USA – despite the fact that these islands deal with the federal government and not with its individual states.

For this and other reasons, small nations need to continuously be on the guard against the bullying and highhandedness of foreign powers that have ostensibly set "operative ideals" on how international relations ought to be conducted in the 21st century.

On that basis, I implore small nation states to remain vigilant in the fight to protect the rights and interests of their people from a few large states and global institutions that are hell-bent on ruling the world.

Response to Article
Earl Bousquet – Veteran Caribbean Editor and Journalist and recipient of the Saint Lucia Medal of Honour (Gold)

This article is very good food for thought as we observe our 37th year as an independent nation, with all the sovereignty that came with our elevated status in 1979. The writer asks the questions and offers his own answers and suggestions as to where to look.

The questions the writer raises on the reality (or lack thereof) of sovereignty ought to be answered by us all — but especially those still unable, for whatever reasons, to define sovereignty and independence. When national sovereignty is being carelessly trampled on without regard, by any state big or small, by any entity or person big or small, wherever and whenever, sages with voices of reason are always expected and called upon to offer guidance and wise counsel.

This article by Clement Wulf-Soulage is highly recommended. Indeed, it can be considered our Independence Gift to all Saint Lucians — with an invitation to use it as a basis for considering all the issues he raises, not just this weekend but for all the rest of our 37th year of independence as a small and sovereign nation.

Here's to the best for all the rest of this Independence Year!

33. Our Nation Turns 36 ... But Seriously

As we approach the 36th anniversary of our independence, I am forced to contemplate the attitude and mindset which truly make a nation independent. In an appeal to my people's intelligence rather than their emotions I ask in earnest: Is the nation at its prime at 36? Do we have a perspective and an understanding of our own problems in the context of the larger world of which we form a small part? What does independence mean and what has it brought us?

It is possible that our independence anniversary is one of the most overlooked days on the calendar owing to the fact that we haven't used that occasion to engage in vertical (problem-solving) discourse instead of the customary horizontal conversations that permeate the national airwaves around this time. This year for a change, let's have some serious discussions about the events and attitudes that have shaped the nation over the last 36 years. Critically, we should begin to view national independence as a mindset rather than an event to be celebrated out of a sense of routine obligation.

We came through the middle passage from Africa to a slave society. Under slavery and colonial subjugation, our people suffered unspeakable "mind" damage. At the onset of independence in 1979, we were supposed to have committed ourselves to the future by gaining new knowledge, insights, ideas and paradigms. At the time of the ushering in of this new era of self-government, the mood was hopeful everywhere as people were inspired by the vision of a new society free of European control.

Culturally and politically, however, the legacy of European dominance is still evident in the political infrastructure and education system of our nation. Although national independence initially produced moments of inspiration and promise, it has hitherto failed to effectively transform the island to bring about true autonomy, development and economic prosperity.

Independence was a chance to stand on our own two feet and eventually rely on our own resources. It was a time to not only "find a way" but also "make a way". It should have taught the people, what one French writer in the eighteenth century saw as the greatest danger, that they have a mind.

But the wings of independence came with a body of responsibility. If an independent nation is to responsibly develop its human, natural and structural resources, it needs to erect the following four golden pillars of sovereign strength: strong and reliable institutions, an education system which fosters innovation and creativity, a progressive culture of excellence and dedicated civic participation. Most importantly, an efficient and progressive mindset serves as the sturdy concrete footing that keeps the pillars from toppling.

Alas, attaining economic independence proved harder than gaining political independence. Safe in the knowledge that independence does not necessarily mean freedom and self sufficiency, we are at the mercy of the goodwill of the global capitalistic system and its institutional underpinnings.

High debt, an unsustainable fiscal deficit, weak economic growth, lack of institutional capacity and low foreign exchange reserves suggest anything but economic self-determination. Besides, we love everything foreign. Ironically almost everything is imported here after almost four decades of independence. Our food import bill is amongst the highest in the Caribbean and we have failed to recognize the linkage opportunities that exist between agriculture and tourism in creating meaningful employment for our people.

Half-hearted attempts at creating a strong manufacturing sector failed along the way. We say that we are a free nation but our behaviour suggests that we are still not free and depend almost slavishly on foreign aid and the largesse of developed nations. We take pride in the culture of others, but not in our own.

Since independence, there has been a steady migration of people to North America and Europe, looking for a "better" and "more stable" quality of life. We don't think independently, we often think what others make us think. Even the intervention of western economic institutions like the IMF and the World Bank has questioned the true nature of our sovereignty, not only in St. Lucia but in the wider Caribbean.

Furthermore, the colonial education system and governance structures which we inherited are constant reminders of our historical entrapment, and subsequent failure at true self-determination. It's high time that each and every citizen of our nation realises his/her responsibilities and work towards the construction of a self-sustaining nation with the least dependence on foreign culture, power and influence.

A flexible and needs-focussed education system is a necessary step towards an independent Saint Lucia. This would entail a nation where people are literate, have jobs, where through the medium of education they can rise up in the hierarchy and live a respectable life. The fact that our country has produced two Nobel Prize winners is really no measure of our educational virility. Most would argue that had Derek Walcott and Sir Arthur Lewis remained in Saint Lucia, they wouldn't have had the educational and economic opportunities that they received overseas.

Despite the gains that we have made in terms of building secondary and tertiary educational institutions on the island, there is still an incredible amount of work to be done in the areas of funding, governance, curricular standards and assessment and testing. The sad reality is that in this day and age, we still don't have our own university and research centres to allow us to become organic value providers and internationally competitive institutions. There has been a failure to "fully" serve the interests of the people through brave and innovative development programmes.

On the other hand, the truth is most people are more interested in entertainment than they are in real education. Usually the answer I get is that they don't like to read. It's not uncommon for an "educated" adult to say he/she hasn't read a serious book since leaving college or university. The result is that they remain imprisoned by old ideas, beliefs and perspectives learned all those years ago.

Meanwhile voters from the lower strata of society often lack the educational background to understand the increasing complexity of many social and political issues, and hence are not emancipated enough to make wise decisions and choices for the betterment of their communities, towns and country.

As Marcus Garvey observed decades ago, "We are going to emancipate ourselves from mental slavery because – whilst others might free the body – none but ourselves can free the mind. Mind is your only ruler, sovereign. The man who is not able to develop and use his mind is bound to be the slave of the other man who uses his mind; use your intelligence to work out the real things of life. The time you waste in levity, in non-essentials, if you use it properly you will be able to guarantee to your posterity a condition better than you inherited from your forefathers."

It seems like society as we knew it is officially over and the sharp-elbowed capitalists will continue employing their divide-and-rule tactics. While we engage daily in meaningless political chatter, our society has disintegrated into a hinterland of political tribalism. Ours is a deeply fractured nation obsessed with individualism and consumerism.

Moreover, the distance between the top and the bottom of society is growing. A process of social estrangement has set in, and no one knows where it will lead. Amartya Sen, an Indian economist and philosopher, described that process as "plural mono-culturalism" where social and political groups live side by side, but do not touch.

With the passage of time, our country seems to have lost itself in a hellish labyrinth of economic inequality, social depravity and youth recalcitrance. Just look around and you will notice plenty of social dynamite piling up in ghettos around the country. Indeed, we should stop kidding ourselves that we are still a civil society modelled on the concept of public participation, free thinking and social courtesy.

As we reflect on our journey and seek to improve our communities, it's essential to remember that building and strengthening social organizations is the key in our attempts to foster social belonging and structure social life in our country. We need to bring back the days when vibrant clubs and effective institutions conducted meaningful social projects and engaged the youth and the wider society.

Wealth inequality has not only persisted, but also grown much larger over time. The cost of living for many Saint Lucians is unbearable; the price of everything seems to be on an upward trajectory. Further compounding the problem is the fact that successive governments have stood by and allowed real estate St. Lucia to be sold to the highest foreign bidder. Land and other resources have become too expensive because foreigners with greater purchasing power have caused the price of everything from rent to food to skyrocket. Huge tracts of the best residential and agricultural land in some parts of the island have been gobbled up by wealthy foreigners, resulting in the local population being priced out of the property market. What is more, preserving public access to beaches is a constant struggle.

For all the aforementioned reasons, we need to give our independence a more profound meaning through greater democratization, collective initiative and civic oversight.

On the occasion of our 36th independence anniversary, Saint Lucians both here and abroad are called on to pay their citizenship dues in full and come forward and break all the shackles to make this country truly free. Since the welfare of any independent and progressive nation is built on education, culture and knowledge, let's continue to "emancipate ourselves from mental slavery". After 36 years of independence, I believe we still have not come of age and really can't blame it all on colonialism. We have had an equal contribution.

34. How to Leave Behind a Legacy

"We are gathered here today to remember Hunter J. Francois, and the invaluable contributions he made to education and the arts. It is only fitting that we do so, for it is important that he be remembered as a national hero." Sounds discombobulatingly familiar, doesn't it?

And while I'm at it – with no irony intended – let me use the opportunity to pay homage to George Odlum, Jeff "Pelay" Elva, Sir John Compton, Sir Stanislaus James, Geraldine Rock, Sesenne Descartes, Sir Vincent Floissac, Hilton Deterville and the many others who graced this country with their talents, visions and leadership.

Those men and women were people of great consequence and stature, and served as role models for our kids. They will continue to project an image of perseverance and greatness for generations to come.

Forgive me if I raised an issue that most of you don't seem to care about. Yet, I will persist in my quest to find answers in terms of how the lives of our national heroes should and can be celebrated, and what those fallen heroes should have done themselves to ensure that their legacies were not forgotten by a society that appears to have an incredibly short memory and a detached sense of loyalty and patriotism.

Every national hero, whether alive or deceased, has a unique and fascinating story to tell. There is no doubt that cultural heritage is enriched by the contributions of those heroes, both in deed and through written recollections of the tribulations and challenges they faced, as well as their ambitions – skilfully interweaving the personal and the historical.

Tales of political redemption, cultural nostalgia and daunting adversity can serve our society a useful contemplative purpose. A written, systematic account of an icon's personal and professional life has the inspirational gravitas to help a people become more conscientious and imaginative, and find solutions to their personal and community problems. Moreover, it adds to the knowledge capital of a society and helps leaders find their strategic composure and motivational impetus in their various roles in organizations and institutions.

Critical to the development and progress of any society is the need to record experiences and remind future generations of the unfolding of people's lives (and the large or small-scale historical processes associated with them). What better way to achieve this than through memoirs and autobiographies?

An autobiography usually covers one's entire life from birth to the present. Every great man or woman has a unique set of experiences and circumstances (triumphs, failures and hardships) that can make for a highly entertaining and worthwhile autobiography or memoir. Indeed, the more talented, famous, accomplished or successful a person is, the more interesting his/her life story becomes.

I believe autobiographies and memoirs serve an important purpose, in that, they present the authors' most outstanding achievements, tell stories about their childhood, disclose the obstacles they had to overcome, contextualize the results of their work or accomplishments, show how the society will be different, explain what it is like to be them, what satisfied them about their accomplishments and their advice on what the general or specific direction should be.

In a progressive society, social life is not only about living, but also about leaving behind something to remind of the trials and tribulations of historical life. Sadly, our heroes are dying without leaving any official account of their achievements, and thereby impoverishing our quality of life both presently and in the future.

Think of all the uplifting and amazing stories of our heroes that we would be reading today, if only sustainable interest and resolute persistence had been shown in the recording and documentation of their life journeys. Unfortunately, I get the impression that a lot of history has been allowed to go unheeded and undocumented, owing to a national disposition of indolence and indifference. We don't seem to care about the past and live only for the present. Are we truly a dead hero's society"?

Preserving social, cultural and political history (and writing it well so that it resonates with others) is a wonderful thing for posterity. Sadly, some of our great sons and daughters will not belong to posterity as instructors of future generations in the principles of steadfastness, success and perseverance. They may have read poems composed in their honour, read histories of their achievements, but never produced anything to communicate their desires, visions and aspirations. The only real question is whether or not our behaviour is leading towards creating an unliveable intellectual and civil environment for future generations.

It pains me to think that the visionary and iconic Sir John Compton, or the erudite and articulate George Odlum left this world without leaving a legacy of officially documented ideas and thoughts; a history of their lives written and told by them, even posthumously.

Where are the memoirs and autobiographies that those great men should have produced to provide critical perspectives into their lives and indulge the curiosity of young future leaders? Do we really know the true identity and understand the thought processes of these men? I would have certainly been inspired by the memoirs of the brilliant Sir Vincent Floissac or the autobiography of the business savvy Sir J.Q Charles.

St. Lucian intellectuals, statesmen and writers seemed to have failed to understand the immortal effect of written personal narratives and historical events for generational elucidation.

Ray Bradbury in Fahrenheit 451 opined that "Everyone must leave something behind when he dies . . . Something your hand touched some way so your soul has somewhere to go when you die . . . It doesn't matter what you do, so long as you change something from the way it was before you touched it, into something that's like you after you take your hands away."

We need to start locating the social, economic, political and cultural contexts in which our society has evolved and the thought processes that have sustained us. Crucially, the media and government need to document more of the life experiences of our cultural and political heroes; how they view or viewed the world and why they viewed the world in the way they did.

I dread the day when our grandchildren will ask what it was like "back in the days of Sir Allen Lewis" and we'll have nothing to tell them and/or no publication to make reference to.

CHAPTER 4 –
FOREIGN POLICY AND
INTERNATIONAL AFFAIRS

35. Trade Policy is Foreign Policy

Trade policy may no longer dominate the front pages of newspapers worldwide, but it's still a foremost factor that can make or break a nation's foreign policy vision. In most industrialized and emerging economies, the preponderance of trade issues in foreign relations remains overwhelming, as political tools are used to obtain economic benefits, and foreign policy incorporates the economic aspirations of a country. Increasingly, as issues entailing "balance of payments" and "terms of trade" invoke the concerns of citizens, trade policy has begun to move with the times.

To be sure, complications in foreign policy are likely to arise from conflict over trade policy. When countries use trade as a weapon of foreign policy, retaliatory trade warfare often ensues, and as we witnessed in the skirmish between Mexico and the U.S. in 2009, trade disputes may be serious enough to undermine free trade agreements.

Over 40 years ago, the economist Thomas Schelling observed, "Broadly defined to include investment, shipping, tourism, and the management of enterprises, trade is what most of international relations are about. For that reason trade policy is national security policy."

Today every country wants to protect its trade interests in the face of changing rules and regulations and against the backdrop of trade liberalization, suffice it to say that economic interests have always been one of the most important elements of foreign policy. But as any good student of international relations will tell you, when all the options are bad the usual rules of good foreign policy making still apply: identify the national interests that are at stake, specify the objectives that serve those interests, and design a strategy to advance those objectives (along with tactics to implement the strategy).

Nowadays, national interests mostly boil down to trade benefits and economic advantages as foreign trade can be a powerful tool in alleviating poverty and boosting development. Since issues of trade policy impinge on growth, productivity and stability, one of the goals of a modern foreign policy is to establish a country that could sell its products in the world market, thus necessitating the close co-operation between foreign and trade ministries.

At any rate, good foreign policy has a significant impact on trade growth, which is very closely linked to GDP growth. After all, prosperity is the principal means by which countries measure and exercise economic power. In today's globalizing world, the significance of economic relations in foreign policy has increased even more, and the success of specific foreign policies is now measured by their economic impact.

In 2008, for example, foreign demand supported 25% of jobs in Germany, up from around 16% in 1995, according to the OECD. When measured in terms of volume, trade is still growing faster than the world economy. Although global trade grew by only 2.8% in 2012 and by 3.2% in 2013, in the two decades up to the financial crisis, cross-border trade in goods and services grew at a sizzling 7% a year on average, much faster than global GDP. In poorer parts of Asia, the size of the middle classes has increased sevenfold since the turn of the millennium. In Latin America it has doubled. This is mostly attributable to the impact of trade.

What I think is interesting however, is the increasing convergence of foreign policy and trade policy. For instance, Germany's foreign policy is based mostly on a strategy of export promotion while China's is pure mercantilism. Seeking to maintain its export dominance, China is engaged in a two-pronged effort: fighting protectionism among its trade partners and holding down the value of its currency. An undervalued currency keeps a country's exports inexpensive in foreign markets while making imports expensive. That makes a trade surplus more likely, reducing unemployment for that country while increasing unemployment in its trading partners. Signifying the importance of currency policy in trade matters, the Swiss National Bank has said that it remains ready to intervene in foreign exchange markets to secure a competitive advantage in export markets – a scenario called "beggar-thy-neighbour policy" in econospeak.

Arguably, U.S. foreign policy has generally been about promoting commercial self-interest and free markets. As many economists will attest, global trade hasn't only helped support global development, but has also facilitated the projection of American values on the global stage.

Critically, we have observed four recent major economic trends that have changed how developing countries can use trade to facilitate their development. These trends are the economic rise of developing economies, the growing integration of global production through supply chains, the higher prices for agricultural goods and natural resources, and the increasing interdependence of the world economy.

In an era of globalization and realpolitik (politics based on practical objectives rather than on ideals), foreign policy will almost always be used as an instrument to increase trade and investment especially as more emerging economies are likely to become more dependent on global trade. Ushered in with this new era are dynamic trends toward regionalism, most favoured nation agreements, the proliferation of trade agreements and the resulting emergence of competing trade blocs that are taking us by storm.

Not surprisingly, economic diplomacy is fast replacing political diplomacy, where networks of diplomatic missions abroad are utilized to build export alliances, and trade sourcing form an integral part of the economic and commercial sections of embassies. Further, economic officers and trade negotiators constitute a large proportion of embassy staff helping to secure deals and negotiate trade laws.

Invariably, the promotion of trade issues and economic ties continue to dominate the agenda of foreign leaders on state visits. Behind the diplomatic protocol, entourages and delegations made up from trade organizations, entrepreneurs and business leaders accompany the visiting heads of state, offering an opportunity to network and develop economic, cultural and social links with industry leaders. What eventuates from these state visits (they are really and truly trade missions in disguise) is the signing of trade agreements and contracts which form part of so-called comprehensive strategic partnerships between the countries.

Thankfully, the establishment of the World Trade Organization (WTO) and other developments in international law have liberalized and greatly reduced the barriers to international trade, thus increasing its volume and importance. The integration of China and the former Soviet bloc into the world economy have been among the most dramatic economic developments of recent decades.

Unfortunately (fortunately for some) since the collapse of the Doha Round negotiations in 2008 and the contamination of the WTO process by international politics, more countries have now diverted their negotiating energies into bilateral free-trade agreements (FTAs). However, despite all the challenges and vicissitudes of global trade, I believe that the conclusion of the Doha Round would provide a strong foundation for trade in the future, and a powerful stimulus in today's slow growth environment. In the meantime, let enlightened self-interest prevail in foreign policy as international trade ought not to be a zero-sum game.

36. A Tilt Towards the East

Asia is very much on the move. It has a gigantic market of 4.4 billion people (60 percent of the world population) in need of just about everything – and by far the largest continental economy by GDP-PPP in the world, combined with a wealth of natural resources and an entrepreneurial class with a voracious appetite for trade and investment opportunities in the wider world.

Moreover, the International Monetary Fund (IMF) projects that "emerging and developing Asia will grow by 6.4 percent in 2015, making it the world's fastest-growing economic region, as it has been consistently for nearly a decade."

By 2030, it is expected that Asia will be home to over three billion middle-class consumers, who will account for over 40 percent of global middle-class consumption. No wonder they are calling it the new frontier with some of the most exciting economic prospects globally.

Even America has had to grudgingly admit that the dominant issues of the 21st century will be decided in that region. Hence, the Asia-Pacific's economic gravity should not be taken lightly – and Saint Lucia together with the other OECS territories must of necessity pursue a vigorous foreign policy that undergirds economic growth and is pivoted towards the wider Asian region in a quest to improve, strengthen and develop economic relations and forge business and trade networks.

Since foreign relations are much more than diplomacy – and the success of specific foreign policies is now measured by their economic impact, the new zeitgeist of realpolitik calls for a combination of openness, imagination, strategic vision and political coherence to maximize the economic opportunities from our international interactions. Forget the nomenclature of what conventional foreign policy is supposed to be – economic opportunity should be the soul of our foreign policy.

However, to attain the goal of foreign policy maturity and re-engagement, we need to specify objectives that serve our interests and develop a growth strategy that informs our foreign policy decisions. Above all, the Asian region should drive our foreign policy.

I have no doubt that Taiwan has a strategy to guide its dealings with our country just as China has a strategy to drive its engagement in the Caribbean. But do we have a focussed strategy which underpins our relations with Taiwan? Are we working to develop aviation and commercial ties with Taiwan and other East Asian nations? It would certainly be a welcome change to see our political parties provide some insights on their various foreign policy postures in relation to the Asian region, ahead of the general elections. This would be crucial particularly as foreign policy is now considered trade policy. Lest we forget, in the real world a misguided and feckless foreign policy can have unpleasant consequences and even lead to economic ruin. As John F. Kennedy put it, "Domestic policy can only defeat us, but foreign policy can kill us."

Caveats aside, however, the establishment of an embassy in Taiwan recently is a progressive and portentous move that represents a strategic diversification in our foreign policy relations. Diversification is not beneficial in economics and business alone; it is also needed in foreign policy as it helps to buffer the impact of complex and unpredictable changes in bilateral and regional relations.

There are windows of opportunity in Asia, but they will be opened and closed quickly if we don't act. Moreover, our local chamber of commerce should seek more international alliances in that region. Perhaps an idea would be to seek the assistance of the local Taiwanese and Japanese ambassadors in establishing an Asian-OECS chamber of commerce. Furthermore, educational and scientific exchange programmes are vital for the development of cultural ties which could later be strengthened into business and economic relations. The Taiwan Scholarship Programme that provides opportunities to young Saint Lucians to study in Taiwan for Bachelor, Master or PhD degrees is an idea worth its weight in gold. As several European nations have discovered, cultural connectivity is key to opening future trade and economic corridors.

Our long-term economic recovery at home can be bolstered by foreign direct investment (FDI) from the Asian pivot as well as the ability of local manufacturing firms to tap into the vast and growing consumer base of Asia. Given the deplorable absence in the United States and Europe of any signs of qualitative growth, the Asian region offers new opportunities for political rapprochement, economic cooperation and coordination of interests.

At the recently held United Nations General Assembly Session in 2016 to mark its 70th anniversary, our Prime Minister and his delegation met with Indian Prime Minister Narendra Modi for bilateral talks. That was indeed a welcome development and I saw much promise in the passionate handshakes and friendly gestures the parties showed towards each other. India has the potential to offer the Caribbean bilateral novelty, growth and coordination, especially as they themselves are seeking opportunities abroad.

Not surprisingly, every country wants to have a better relationship with China and the rest of Asia. The White House has indicated that economics is at the heart of American engagement in the Asia-Pacific, noting that nearly half of the world's population resides there, making its development "vital to American economic and strategic interests." The Obama administration's strategic "pivot" from the Middle East to East Asia is a policy that represents a paradigm shift in American foreign policy, whose key areas of focus are "strengthening bilateral security alliances; deepening our working relationships with emerging powers, including with China; engaging with regional multilateral institutions; and expanding trade and investment."

Just recently, the US and eleven other countries announced agreement on the Trans-Pacific Partnership (TPP), the biggest trade deal in a generation. As the Obama administration puts it: "Rules for trade and investment in the financial services sector in the TPP will ensure that American businesses and workers can serve all these varied markets, promoting economic growth and job development in the United States and throughout the Asia-Pacific region."

According to Forbes Business, the Israelis are also moving in quickly on the growth opportunities in Asia: "When we think of Israel, we usually think of the Middle East (its neighbourhood), North America (its close ally the United States) and Europe (the long history of Ashkenazi Jews). Rarely do we think about Israel and Asia, even less about Asia as Israel's new frontier... Yet, last year Israel called 2014 "the year of Asia in Israel." The Israeli government sponsored an Asian Science Camp attracting over 220 Asian students to join nearly 40 Israeli students for a week long programme of lectures by world class Israeli researchers."

The national interest of our country should boil down to trade benefits and economic advantages, as foreign trade can be a powerful tool used in alleviating unemployment and boosting development. As foreign policy scholars have long argued, a course of strategic ambiguity and agility is what's required to expand economic horizons, widen and diversify markets and take advantage of capital and advanced technology for national development and modernization.

37. The Insular Caribbean – Are We Splendidly Isolated?

In the last two decades or so, the great wave of globalization seemed to have lifted several low-income and emerging economies out of economic despondency; and may have even given them a new lease on life. The "Asian Tigers" as well as several other emerging economies, through outward-oriented strategies and modern industrial policies, were able to benefit hugely from the gains of increasing global trade, foreign direct investment and new opportunities in global capital and product markets.

In large measure, university and college curricula were updated, and research and development centres became ubiquitous in the region. Polycentric innovation was the order of the day. Although the pace of that development has somewhat slowed in many countries and regions of the world, the opportunities for economic alignment are still present if only progressive and lateral thinking were applied to facilitate better economic planning and the allocation of national and regional resources.

Admittedly, the continent of Africa was a bit slow to connect to the world economy, but now with better governance structures in place and improved research capabilities, they were able to do some catching up and in some cases a little leapfrogging. Today, the continent is being hailed as the next innovation frontier. But where does the Caribbean feature in all of this development narrative? Have we not learned any lessons from the rest of the progressive world when it comes to issues of multilateral trade and economic co-operation? Does the stock argument about size and population still hold water or is it just a convenient excuse?

Alas, the low economic level of the vast majority of our people in the Caribbean remains a basic problem. Some economists concur that every region in the world seems to be developing except the Caribbean. Is that true?

On the governmental level, it appears that economic logic has become impotent in the face of political power. Institutional leadership and initiative, including the destination stewardship of the Eastern Caribbean Central Bank has been anything but forward-looking. Considering the possibilities of modern international banking practices which can creatively be applied to create national and regional economic momentum (both conventional and unconventional), not much has been done on the part of the ECCB in the management and overseeing of OECS economies. One gets the impression that the ECCB is on autopilot. Unlike many other central banks which have, out of necessity, focussed on growth and investment in their respective countries and regions, the ECCB seems to be oblivious to the realities of the small island states and has set its sights almost pathologically on currency stability.

Essentially, the reality of the times demands a greater effort on the part of the OECS at joint marketing and investment through the pooling of resources to allow the region to enjoy economies of scope and have greater exposure to European and emerging economies. Going forward, this idea is both indispensable and inevitable. Basically, a greater presence on the world stage will necessitate a greater and more creative use of the Caribbean Diaspora; and persistent professional lobbying in the corridors of political and economic power in the US, EU and BRICS countries. As we embark on an investment offensive to save our region, more energies and resources need to be rechanneled to economic lobbying.

Once more international security has brought the Caribbean-US partnership into focus. Why can't we use that opportunity to make our case for greater social stability through foreign investment? Nothing good comes easy anymore; we need to explore creative ways to lure potential investors to our island. As is often cited in international relations, we quite often don't get what we deserve, but what we negotiate. The focus should not be on aid (although technical and financial assistance are still necessary) but on increasing trade links and presenting the region as a repository of optimism, having a stable environment with plenty of opportunities in the solar energy sector, recycling, manufacturing and the creative industries.

Another crucial point of priority is the strategic redeployment and reallocation of diplomatic resources to hitherto unexplored economic regions including Africa. For too long now, we have depended too much on North America and Europe for investment opportunities. The time has now come to explore the new Frontiers in Africa, India and China and do more partnering with their governments, universities and think tanks. Reassessing and recalibrating our relationship with international agencies and organizations will help maximize ideas on capacity building and improve international technical standards.

Like I have said before in an earlier chapter, ostensibly China has a strategy for the Caribbean and its resources, but do we have a strategy for China? Emulating the standards of developed and emerging economies as well as copying their models of productivity, education and healthcare may just provide us with the fillip and momentum needed to resuscitate our economies and pursue a more balanced and sustainable development in the long-term. As a collective entity, we must continue sourcing more technical assistance to help us balance economic development with environmental protection. Food production and exports in the OECS region should be more co-ordinated and all efforts made to reduce the region's food import bill.

In projecting the quality of life required in the Caribbean, we should ask ourselves about our collective Caribbean destiny in the next crucial ten years.

38. The UN at 70 – The Unreformed Septuagenarian

Since succeeding Kofi Annan as Secretary General of the United Nations at the start of 2007, Ban Ki-moon has had to deal with some of the world's most intractable problems ranging from civil wars and refugee crises to genocide threats and epidemics. At various junctures in the last eight years, critics have pondered whether the verecund and soft-spoken South Korean – who is just as old as the institution he governs (the UN

turned 70 on October 24, 2015) – was the right person to lead a world body facing Sisyphean and unprecedented global challenges, and also struggling to assuage the concerns of a sceptical membership about its ability to tackle issues involving institutional working methods, efficiency, legitimacy, the increasing demands on limited resources and the naked political horse trading for top jobs.

The institution itself is labyrinthian and unwieldy, ballooning over the years with a staff of 85,000 bureaucrats spread across six principal organs and fifteen specialized agencies, on an annual budget of about $40bn.

I'm sure the ubiquitous calls for reform as well as the continuous accusations of waste and corruption at the UN are not all lost in translation. Some critics have attributed these internal inefficiencies to the non-transparent manner in which resources are allocated and projects funded. In 1967, Richard Nixon, while running for President of the United States, criticized the mechanisms of the UN as "obsolete and inadequate". Above all, the trenchant criticism levelled at the venerable institution has to do with the fact that the world has changed dramatically since its establishment after World War II, yet the 193-member organization has not adapted to reflect the 21st century; and hence may no longer represent the prevailing political reality.

There is little doubt our world needs a platform (not an irrelevant debating society) where collective decisions and actions can be taken to advance the cause of global peace and to protect the vulnerable and the poor. Our present world demands action and effective leadership in so many areas; and admittedly without the UN, the planet would likely be a more dangerous and unstable place. However, the world body, owing to an outdated structure and inadequate governance, seems unable to act in a clear and decisive way when confronted with a crisis (as Syria and Sudan has shown) and lacks the resources necessary to avert humanitarian and other emergencies before they spill over and metastasize into regional and international disasters.

Mostly at issue is the need to reform the UN's governance, starting with the Security Council, the composition of which no longer reflects both global geopolitical realities and the shift in the distribution of world power. For an organization that regularly trumpets the need for good governance and democracy, some of its most pivotal structures and organs aren't entirely amenable to democracy and equal participation at the macro level.

Much to the chagrin of the general membership, any one of the five permanent members of the Security Council (The United States, China, Russia, France, and Britain) can paralyse democratic governance by simply choosing to exercise its veto right – in most cases blocking important decisions and actions already supported by a majority.

Besides, Europe and Asia are too heavily represented on the Security Council at the expense of South America and Africa. Of further disquiet is Germany's quest to become a permanent member – a move that will likely further solidify Europe's influence in global affairs. But what about the BRICS? Shouldn't the composition of a powerful UN organ like the Security Council reflect the balance of power which will eventually be in favour of these emerging economies?

It's high time that the continents of South America and Africa are given a greater voice in world affairs. According to the Global Policy

Forum (GPF): "For many years, some member-states have been advocating expansion of the Security Council, arguing that adding new members will remedy the democratic and representative deficit from which the Council suffers. Disagreement on whether new members should be permanent or have veto power has become a major obstacle to Security Council reform. Brazil, India, Japan and Germany want a permanent seat in the Council, and have threatened to reduce their financial or military troop contributions to the UN if they are not rewarded with permanent member status. African countries have also expressed the need for permanent African representation in the Council to bring an end to the hegemony of northern industrialized nations in the powerful UN organ. The Asia-Pacific region accounts for roughly 55% of the world's population and 44% of its annual income but has just 20% (three out of 15) of the seats on the Security Council."

It has now become clear to most of the UN's membership that the veto right accorded to a few powerful nations is untenable and should be scrapped. The question, however, is whether Russia and China are prepared to endorse any plans to reform the Security Council? Any time Russia votes against crucial UN resolutions and China abstains, deep disappointment and incredulity is expressed. In the past, both China and Russia have been accused of using intimidation tactics to silence their critics in the UN.

The diplomatic poker played over Syria by Presidents Obama and Putin is yet another indication of the lack of will and the frequent bouts of impotence in the UN. In 2011 and 2012 China and Russia altogether vetoed three resolutions in the UN Security Council that called upon the Syrian regime of Bashar al-Assad to desist from military actions against its own people. For selfish reasons, Russia and China have consistently frustrated the efforts of both the Security Council and the General Assembly at nipping specific problems in the bud or in taking action against regimes that violate the rights of their people or the territorial integrity of other nations. The failure to act effectively in Syria, Libya and Ukraine is probably further attributed to the skewed accountability and democracy practised at the UN.

How does an important global body with an underfunded mandate adequately perform its increasingly demanding role (including peacekeeping and fulfilling the Millennium Development Goals now dubbed Sustainable Development Goals) in delivering assistance to troubled spots around the world? Jeffrey Sachs, an American economist and director of the Earth Institute at Columbia University, agrees that the economic and political challenges are huge and will require greater resources. He beleives the MDGs have engendered impressive progress in poverty reduction, public health, school enrolment, gender equality in education, and other areas, despite the tremendous funding challenges in the future: "Spending on all UN bodies and activities – from the Secretariat and the Security Council to peacekeeping operations, emergency responses to epidemics, and humanitarian operations for natural disasters, famines, and refugees – totalled roughly $45 billion in 2013, roughly $6 per person on the planet. That is not just a bargain; it is a significant underinvestment. Given the rapidly growing need for global cooperation, the UN simply cannot get by on its current budget," he wrote.

Yet, despite some of the more glaring failures of the UN including the inability to prevent the Rwandan Genocide, the slow response to the Ebola epidemic in West Africa and the poor management of personnel which contributed to the spread of cholera in Haiti, several important triumphs have probably convinced us of the irreplaceability of certain agencies and programmes and the credit the institution deserves for some of humanity's advances. Without the UN, the nuclear deal with Iran as well as the prosecution of Charles Taylor and Slobodan Milosevic for war crimes would have been difficult, if not altogether impossible. Furthermore, the general pursuit of global peace would have been more elusive without UN proactivity (the record is not so bad as we sometimes make out). Without its own standing army and offensive military capabilities at its disposal, it was always expected that the UN would fall short in its ambition to effectively protect civilian populations, safeguard relief efforts and police the world.

Of course, there were moments when the actions of the institution defied its commitment to human rights such as when the General Assembly decided to hold a moment of silence in "honour" of North Korean dictator Kim Jong-il following his death in 2011 (perhaps a moment of levity in an otherwise orderly and decorous chamber). The reclusive dictator had violated every article of the UN Declaration of Human Rights from Article Thirteen.

Notwithstanding the frequent espousal of moral relativism and governance shortcomings, the UN has been a force for good in a world where the primacy of social responsibility has been replaced by the primacy of economic efficiency. To be sure, the global institution has helped avert potentially grave humanitarian and political disasters. Certainly, it's not yet the political elixir, but it's the best bargain we've got. Going on the declaration of a former US ambassador, "The UN was not created to take mankind to heaven, but to save humanity from hell."

39. How Much Longer, Mi Amigo?

March 20th 2016, was a day for the history books as the wheels of Air Force One, the aircraft carrying the American President, Señor Barack Obama, touched down in communist Cuba. Only a short while back, Pope Francis and French President Francois Holland had made the trip. Yesterday March 25th, the American rock band, The Rolling Stones, played a "free" show in Havana. It seems like everyone wants a chance to see socialism one last time before it dies. Even so, was the drizzle that greeted the American President at the Jose Marti International Airport on Palm Sunday a blessing in diplomatic disguise or an ominous sign of things to come?

Presidents Obama and Castro had met twice before: first at the Pan-American summit in Panama and again at the United Nations General Assembly in New York. On those two occasions, the body language of the two leaders seemed to suggest that the animosity between the two countries was waning – not that, amid the historic exchange on March 20, there was any brief moment of levity about the good old days of the Cold War or about Cuba's refusal in almost half a century to cash the U.S. Treasury checks of $4,085 per year it receives for rental of the controversial 45-square-mile Guantanamo Bay Naval Base.

Considering the rich and tortured history of U.S.-Cuba relations, the U.S. president got a surprisingly warm welcome from an island raised on revolutionary and Cold War ethos. Thus, the political noise coming from especially the Republican Party about the fact that President Obama was not personally greeted on the airport by Cuban President Raul Castro (having previously done so for other leaders), is simply "much ado about nothing". In recent times, I can't recall seeing the American President being greeted by Angela Merkel on the tarmac at Berlin's Tegel Airport or by David Cameron at Stansted Airport in London – although these two nations are close political allies of the U.S. and have both enjoyed an enduring friendship with the superpower for almost three quarters of a century.

In contrast, no one needs to be reminded that there have been several decades of diplomatic tension and economic hostility between Cuba and America – having been ideological adversaries during the Cold War. Hence, Raul Castro's failure to welcome Air Force One (One step at a time, amigo!) is perhaps a reflection of Cuba's ultra-cautious approach to the growing political and diplomatic rapprochement between the two countries. Besides, long before the presidential visit, the White House had announced that the Cuban President wouldn't be expected at the airport.

If anything, President Obama understands that the only way to influence events in Cuba is to actually engage the country. Ever since the economic embargo was imposed on Cuba in 1960 (almost two years after the Batista regime was deposed by the Cuban Revolution), precious little by way of political change has been achieved – except that the people of Cuba have been impoverished and unfairly disadvantaged.

George Schulz who served as Ronald Reagan's Secretary of State from 1982 to 1989, called the embargo "insane". In the relenting heat of the Cold War, Pope John Paul II called for an end to the embargo during his 1979 pastoral visit to Mexico. In June 2009, the Cato Institute, an influential American think tank, delivered a scathing rebuke of U.S foreign policy towards Cuba: "The embargo has been a failure by every measure. It has not changed the course or nature of the Cuban government. It has not liberated a single Cuban citizen. In fact, the embargo has made the Cuban people a bit more impoverished, without making them one bit freer. At the same time, it has deprived Americans of their freedom to travel and has cost US farmers and other producers billions of dollars of potential exports", the statement read.

If we need further proof of America's glaring hypocrisy and double standards in international relations, the embargo against Cuba is a clear example. Successive American administrations have signed trade deals and developed full diplomatic relations with China, Egypt, Russia, Saudi Arabia, et al – countries well known for violating human rights and oppressing political dissidents. In fact, 190 nations already engage politically and economically with Cuba, while the U.S. refuses to lift the economic embargo – a stance seen by many as a sort of Pyrrhic victory. In June 2009, Moisés Naím wrote in Newsweek: "The embargo is the perfect example used by anti-Americans everywhere to expose the hypocrisy of a superpower that punishes a small island while cozying to dictators elsewhere."

Despite the U.S. version of how the Cuban Crisis began, it is generally believed that the American government provoked the events that almost triggered a nuclear war. According to Cuban historical records: "In July 1960, after the removal of the Cuban sugar quota by the U.S. government, Fidel Castro announced the nationalization of all U.S. property in Cuba. The Eisenhower administration severed relations with Cuba in January 1961 and began the preparation of a mercenary brigade to invade the island. The invasion took place in April 1961 in Playa Giron, after a surprise bombing of Cuban air bases. After the defeat of the U.S.-backed invasion, the U.S. government implemented "Operation Mongoose" – a succession of aggressions which also included direct U.S. military intervention in Cuba. This altogether led to the international crisis in October 1962."

At any rate, the extending of a friendly hand to Cuba at this point amounts to nothing more than U.S. enlightened self-interest, particularly as Russia and China continue to gain influence in Latin America by carving out new markets in the superpower's so-called backyard. As for President Obama, he is surely thinking about his legacy, and would like to go down in history as the president who succeeded in ending two generations of frosty relations between the United States and Cuba.

Yet, there is not much time left for him to seal the deal, as congressional approval is required to alter or rescind the embargo. In ten months, the 45th president would have already occupied the White House, and will quite possibly show less enthusiasm than President Obama in lifting the embargo. However, history will be kind to America's first black president for the enormous positive changes he has wrought on his nation during what many will view as a transformational presidency. By attempting to re-engage Cuba, Señor Obama has recognized the wisdom in Albert Einstein's line that "doing the same thing over and over again and expecting different results is insanity."

40. Haiti, I'm Sorry Again

Where do you even start to rebuild a nation that has been traumatized by just about every conceivable crisis and human tragedy under the sun? From human slavery, foreign occupation and military coups to earthquakes, famines and epidemics, Haiti has seen it all. Convulsed by factions and political machinations, the country is notorious for violence and corruption against the backdrop of weak institutions, poor infrastructure and an ignoble reputation as the poorest country in the Western Hemisphere. Now it appears a political crisis is brewing following a decision by the electoral council to postpone a runoff presidential election, raising fears that Haiti could plunge into instability amid a leadership vacuum.

More than four years after the election of Michel Martelly in 2011, Haiti is as politically polarized as ever. Having taken just about the same amount of time to organize legislative elections, a presidential and legislative runoff vote scheduled for Jan. 24, 2016 had to be cancelled for the second time by the electoral council, amid violent protests and allegations of electoral fraud.

The chronic mismanagement and poor governance as well as the open contempt for democratic processes in Haiti have given new meaning to the term "banana republic". Meanwhile, as if the situation wasn't combustible enough, the outgoing president − no stranger to controversy − has been accused of denigrating women by releasing a song called "Give them the Banana" − taunting his critics and aiming sexually suggestive lyrics at his main target, an award-winning female journalist. All this probably explains why Haiti will remain a "banana republic" for a long time to come.

But seriously, it seems that the world has a special proclivity for ignoring or forgetting the plight and suffering of the Haitian people. Last year, the mass deportation of Haitians by the Government of the Dominican Republic, as well as the racism and xenophobia that they have had to endure in that country − initially caused an outrage but have long-since faded into the world's rear-view mirror. As for the holding of democratic elections almost five years ago in the midst of a humanitarian and economic disaster, many people believe it was an ill-advised move. Writing for an international newspaper then, a Haitian patriot residing in France expressed his abhorrence of the idea: "They could have found another way to govern the country than to stage an election over the earthquake ruins and dead bodies still warm from cholera infection or from lack of medical attention caused by the electoral chaos. My anger remains so strong against those who advocated elections to govern...what? I barely recognize my country as being such," he said.

Meanwhile, the United Nations through its Security Council has released a statement expressing deep concerns about the political paralysis in Haiti − and has underscored the urgency of seeking a quick solution to the electoral crisis. Part of the statement read: "The members of the Security Council reiterated their strong condemnation of any attempt to destabilize the electoral process, in particular by force, and urged all candidates, their supporters, political parties and other political actors to remain calm, refrain from unlawful violence or any action that can further disrupt the electoral process and political stability, resolve any electoral disputes through established legal mechanisms and to hold those responsible for such violence accountable." But even as the U.N. has provided assistance of sorts, many Haitians do not trust the U.N. peacekeepers who have been blamed for introducing the deadly cholera epidemic in 2010, which has infected over 700,000 Haitians and killed more than 8,000.

To be sure, the national election did little to alleviate conditions in the broken country, known for electing lesser evils – and given the refusal of the Haitian Opposition Alliance to meet with the OAS Mission, the way out of the impasse is unclear. The fact that 10 people are being considered for the temporary role of caretaker leader indicates the extent of the political tribalism in the country. Hence, could Haiti be days away from a full-bore leadership crisis?

In an interview with the Associated Press, Chairman of the OAS Permanent Council, Sir Ronald Sanders expressed tempered and conditional optimism that the country would lift itself out of its present predicament. "If I am to believe what people have said to us about their determination to save their country and to take it forward, then I believe there's hope that they will reach a solution," he said. Ambassador Sanders has also made it clear that "this fact-finding mission is not in Haiti to interfere, meddle or mediate in Haitian affairs."

Of course, I reacted with Pavlovian instincts to Ambassador Sander's remarks, thinking that Haiti definitely needs a great deal of support and guidance (if not interference) from especially CARICOM, which appears to be on the periphery of the discussions, seemingly satisfied to leave the influential role of mediation to the so-called Core Group – USA, Canada, Brazil, France and Spain. By the way, I couldn't help noticing that very little about the Haitian political crisis has been reported in the local press. Does that mean that we couldn't care less about how things unfold in Haiti?

There is no doubt that the task of rebuilding Haiti is enormous, as it is still reeling from the devastating earthquake which hit it in January 2010, killing more than 200,000 people. The fact that the country has only received $4 billion from the $12 billion pledged by the international community goes to show the extent to which Haiti has been ignored and treated like a failed state – earning it the unflattering title of "Republic of NGOs". Yet, the overwhelming presence of NGOs has not necessarily helped the country progress. In fact, the administration of outgoing President Martelly has consistently complained that most countries have channelled their foreign aid through NGOs (perhaps rightly so given the level of corruption in the country) rather than the Haitian Government.

At any rate, Haiti is at a crossroads and will require sustainable and inclusive leadership moving forward. Even so, have we truly misunderstood Haiti as David Rudder has lamented in song or are the Haitians themselves responsible for their own plight? One thing is certain: Haiti's problems cannot be addressed without greater international cooperation and trust. Above all, Haitians need to start taking personal and collective responsibility for their own development and progress. Although CARICOM has its own demons to deal with, it could still be leading the effort in helping Haiti contain or avert a potentially long-term crisis. Even as I sometimes doubt the capacity of CARICOM to implement and execute, I, like David Rudder – the Bob Marley of calypso – believe "one day we'll turn our heads and look inside you." I still believe with more committed political and technical assistance from CARICOM and the wider international community, Haiti will eventually turn the corner.

NB: An OAS Mission headed by Sir Ronald Sanders oversaw the signing of an agreement to bring political stability to Haiti. Under the agreement, President Michel Martelly was to demit office on February 7th, 2016. Further, the election process would go to the second round on April 24th and the new president would be installed on May 14, 2016.

41. The Demons Have Been Unleashed

A well-crystallized debate about how do handle ISIS (Islamic State of Iraq and Syria) rages on among European leaders, and less so among presidential hopefuls from both political parties in the United States.

Admittedly, it has been quite amusing listening to some of the skewed and demented suggestions coming from Republican candidates who are hell-bent on pursuing a course of Hollywood-styled military adventurism and thus spreading Middle East chaos – having convinced themselves and some of their supporters that simply invading Syria and other parts of the Middle East would eradicate the problem of terrorism and usher in more peace and democracy in the region.

By all accounts, America has spent precious resources in the Middle East floundering from one conflict to the next, with very little to show for its engagement. The helplessness of the world's only superpower shows just how little influence it has in the Middle East – and with each failure, its influence in the rest of the world erodes as well.

Notwithstanding the usual empty platitudes from Republicans, no one was under any illusion that foreign policy was going to be child's play in an age of global terrorism, increasing geopolitical conflicts and religious fanaticism. As a perspicacious diplomat once observed, the trouble with foreign policy is that it involves foreigners – and they don't always do what they are told. Now it would appear that the troublesome Middle East region has totally ignored ideas of democracy, peace and stability coming from the superpower and may well be on their way to establish their own version of hell on earth.

Although no part of the world has ever been free of depraved conflicts, the situation in the Middle East seemed to have assumed a new terrestrial dimension. Religion has truly become the opium of the people. Shias don't want to live under Sunni leadership and Sunnis are on a rampage to create their own state. The Alawite Muslims have historically been persecuted for their beliefs by the Sunnis – and the Kurds are simply not interested in sharing sovereignty with any other group. Ominously, Iraq is coming apart at the seams.

Moreover, the conflict between Israel and the Palestinians bodes ill for any eventual conflict de-escalation in the broader region. In short, the debacle in the Middle East (particularly in Iraq), serves as a poignant reminder that American ideals of democracy and society cannot be exported to the Middle East, at least not in their Western form. Perhaps the painstaking and relentless attempt to export Western democratic values (considered by many as the most dangerous American export) to the Middle East is partly to blame for the hostility and animosity towards America, and for the spread and threat of militant Islamic terrorism.

Yet there is a certain paradox about U.S. foreign policy which probably explains Obama's policy of "retrenchment" – the word Americans use to describe their retreat from the foreign policy front. Witness the results of America's engagement (or lack of it) in Iraq, Libya and Syria: In the case of Iraq, America decided to invade the country in 2003 leaving behind a trail of destruction and ruin. In Libya, its partial involvement in the country's quagmire left untold confusion and carnage. On the other hand, the decision not to get directly involved in the Syrian conflict did not alter the trajectory of monstrous events in the region. To be sure and irrespective of vantage point, foreign policy in such difficult circumstances is an unrelenting headache. Ostensibly, whether America and the West demonstrate full, partial or no commitment in this combustible region, it seems the results are likely to be equally disastrously.

Painful as it is to admit, the West, especially the United States, bears significant responsibility for creating the conditions in which ISIS has flourished. Most alarmingly, ISIS continues to function as a government, which has spun totally out of control – beheading men, crucifying Iraqi Christians and sexually enslaving teenage girls. The world's most feared terrorist group has established its presence in Iraq to such an extent that it is able to sell oil to Bashar al-Assad and U.S. allies – generating revenue to buy arms to secure a caliphate, and to finance global terrorist operations.

When America invaded Iraq on a false premise in 2003, little did it know that it was actually unleashing the demons of religious fanaticism in a notoriously unstable region. The tragic occupation of Iraq, which resulted in the deaths of almost 150,000 Iraqis and over 4,000 U.S. troops, created the conditions and provided the space for al-Qaida and subsequently ISIS to evolve to fight against the American occupation – and further destabilizing the region and spreading terror around the world. Hence the U.S. invasion of Iraq played a crucial role in the rise of ISIS and the attendant chaos, violence and sectarianism.

Meanwhile, the bombing missions in Iraq and Syria have had minimal success, as ISIS militants have continued producing oil despite the air strikes. If indeed anything has been learned from the military action in Iraq, it's that bombing Islamist extremists into submission or disappearance produces more recruits and supporters of ISIS.

Disquietingly, the practice of overthrowing governments (often regimes previously supported and financed by the U.S. itself) and installing new ones compliant with Western interests is one fraught with peril and characterized by hypocrisy. In effect, what such a practice has done is to destabilize target regions and bring great danger to America and Europe. The vicious attacks on Paris and the unfolding refugee crisis in Europe are both consequences of the absence of a comprehensive and cohesive strategy to combat this multifaceted global threat.

Further complicating the situation is the military involvement of Russia in the region – having itself played a conniving role in the unfolding humanitarian catastrophe by blocking Western-backed resolutions in the United Nations Security Council intended to expedite the fall of the Assad regime in Syria.

The Arab Spring after all (except perhaps for Tunisia) turned out to have put a spring in the step of aspiring dictators and Islamist militants. Essentially, Egypt is right back where it started. The new regime and its supporters are no more liberal and democratic than Mubarak's. Libya went from totalitarianism to anarchy, descending from Arab Spring to factional civil war. Most critically, armed conflict is spilling beyond Syria's borders into Lebanon, Turkey, Jordan, and Iraq, with absolutely no end in sight.

Being the world's only superpower, the U.S. certainly has the wherewithal and systemic reach to build alliances and tackle terrorism on a global scale. Yet can America ever be trusted to do the right thing after a failed foreign policy in Iraq, Afghanistan and Syria? When will we begin to see foreign policy realism and common sense in relation to the Middle East? Can we take solace in the words of Winston Churchill that "America can be trusted to do the right thing after it has tried everything else"? My own humble view is that there is no use stirring up an apocalyptic hornet's nest without first attempting to deconstruct the root cause of the problem and building a legitimate international alliance (including Iran, Turkey and Saudi Arabia) through the United Nations – with an action plan and strategy to exorcise the fanatical demons before this kind of barbarism turns civilization on its head.

CHAPTER 5 –
EDUCATION AND CULTURE

42. Lost in Transition

For years, Finland has been the by-word for a successful and transformative education system – recognized around the world for its innovation and pioneering approach to pedagogy and educational governance. The educational productivity and developmental performance of this small European country springs directly from the education policies which have, over the years, been introduced both in a radical and incremental manner. The British Independent daily newspaper has reported that "politicians and education experts from around the world – including the UK – have made pilgrimages to Helsinki (Finland's capital) in the hope of identifying and replicating the secret of its success."

Anchored in the belief that the idea of transformative education has in large part driven economic growth and development in industrialized and emerging economies, I was somewhat heartened to hear the idea – something very close to my heart – trumpeted at the 2016 Sir Arthur Lewis Memorial Lecture organized as part of Nobel Laureate Week, under the theme "Celebrating Excellence: Transforming Lives." Both the guest speaker, economist Dr. Hyginus Leon as well as the new Principal of the Sir Arthur Lewis Community College, Dr. Olivia Saunders, championed the idea of transformative education and the role it can play in transitioning and building sustainable societies as well as fostering economic development, in the absence of natural and mineral resources.

On account of greater international competition and the need for economic efficiency, it has become quite clear that a generic education will not suffice in producing the economic prosperity which we strive for. Instead, in the process of transforming our own system, we'll need to adopt an education and growth strategy – similar to that of the emerging economies in Asia – and adapt it to our own political, social and economic circumstances. This will mean developing an education system which should get more people innovating and collaborating in industries such as tourism, the cultural arts, manufacturing and agriculture – and also geared towards meeting the general demands of a new knowledge and services-based economy. As the Princeton economist, Alan Blinder perceptively notes: "It is clear that nations will have to transform their education system so as to produce workers for the jobs that will actually exist in their societies.... In the future, how we educate our children may prove to be more important than how much we educate them."

In our own developmental context – since tourism is our economic backbone, we'll need to develop and introduce courses such as tourism management, food and beverage management and restaurant management at the secondary school level, which could better meet the needs of the industry. I am really quite astonished that progressive ideas such as developing intercultural competencies and introducing foreign languages early in the system have been given scant attention. How can we really become competitive in tourism when we refuse to prioritize foreign language skills – something other tourist destinations around the world are already doing with much success? Besides, we are depriving our kids of an opportunity to compete globally.

Until now, why has it been so difficult to transform and transition our education system into one that is able to support our economic aspirations? Why haven't we translated the positive experiences of the industrialized world into our own socio-economic success? In a fast-paced digital world, we still seem to be stuck between one developmental phase in education and the next.

With all the discussion about globalization, most people forget that globalization is also a competition between one country's education system and another's. Unfortunately, too often we are focussed on the doors that globalization have closed, instead of looking at the opportunities ICT and other technologies offer to leapfrog our way forward. Of course, we don't need to reinvent the wheel, but instead look around the globe to see how other successful countries have used transformative education to fuel growth and prosperity. As the Asian nations have consistently demonstrated, it's possible to leap right into new technologies without having to worry about all the sunken costs of old systems.

So what can we really learn from the so-called First World? Finland has shown us that the basis for any success in transforming education is the setting of rigid standards guided by quality assurance, and by fostering a culture of educational governance, and remodelling assessment mechanisms. The German model teaches us that a vocational and apprenticeship training system that is in sync with the needs of the economy and has a primary focus on entrepreneurship, manufacturing sciences and innovation is indispensable. Australia's successful economy is driven by international education, knowledge services and skilled workers rather than resources. All these examples are based on educational models that have been tried and tested, and the results and outcomes available for assessment and application. According to an OECD source: "In all of these nations, there is a wide consensus on increasing technology, environmental sciences and entrepreneurship education – all of which seem to contribute positively to economic development and growth."

By the way, the Finns have recently introduced something quite unconventional in their education system – and the change has been hailed as one of the most radical undertaken by a nation state – scrapping traditional "teaching by subject" in favour of "teaching by topic".

Meanwhile, the country's authorities have reported that "the pre-school sector is also embracing change through an innovative project – the Playful Learning Centre – which is engaged in discussions with the computer games industry about how it could help introduce a more "playful" learning approach to younger children."

Closer to home, perhaps the most important element of educational transformation is the idea of teaching our kids to think for themselves rather than simply memorizing and absorbing someone else's ideas. As the pioneers of innovation and creativity will attest, one of the most important competencies for social and economic development is the ability to view old problems in new ways and to rethink ideas that had not been questioned before. I have mentioned in a previous article on education that our children need to engage in complex interactions that require a high level of judgment – which can help them, among other things, navigate the world to filter and sort out truth from fiction.

Even civil society must be encouraged to approach economic and social ideas critically – the idea being to nurture a culture which, according to internationally renowned journalist, Thomas L. Friedman, "thinks forward and outward instead of inward and backward". Further, let me support the Indian entrepreneur and politician, Nandan Nilekani, in his belief that "a society which has the least resistance to the uninterrupted flow of ideas, diversity, concepts and competitive signals wins, and a society that has the efficiencies to translate whatever can be done quickly – from idea to market – also wins."

Finally, as a progressive, I would like to end by asking the obvious: Why haven't we taken a closer look at the conditions and factors which have contributed to the success of the aforementioned countries? The point is: We need to adopt and adapt developmental ideas from the global village, which can help breathe economic life into our towns and villages. Perhaps we should do like the British and send our politicians and policymakers on pilgrimages to Finland, Germany and Australia to discover some of the educational ideas which could potentially translate (or transition) into economic success.

43. Education in an Information Age

It goes without saying that Google and the Internet, almost beyond measure, have revolutionized the application and use of information and communication technology. The online era in many ways has made "feature mobile phones" as obsolete as the dial-up internet. Industry is becoming more information-intensive and data-centric, and less labour and capital-intensive. Perhaps already in a couple of years, we will all be walking around with the wearable technology "Google Glass", just as the smart-phone has become a mass-market ubiquitous computer.

As time goes by, the term "literacy" will constantly be redefined and the unspoken assumptions of education policy will be challenged at every technological turn. As the American writer and futurist Alvin Toffler instructs us: "The illiterate of the 21st century will not be those who cannot read and write, but those who cannot learn, relearn and unlearn."

Most strikingly, the digital information zeitgeist has begun, to all intents and purposes, to redefine what it really means to be an "educated person".

In the book, "Success in the Information Age: A Paradigm Shift", the American Professor William G. Huitt summarized the major trends and megatrends associated with the Information Age and their implications for preparing children and youth for the future: "We are undergoing the most significant change ever experienced in human history. We have moved from the agricultural age through the industrial age and into the information age in a span of just 100 to 200 years. We have lived most of our human history in the hunter/gatherer age. In that environment the person with the best way to kill an animal or select the correct items to eat was most successful; in the agriculture age, the person with the most land and best agricultural machinery was most successful; and in the industrial age the person with the best manufacturing process or the most capital was most successful. Who will be most successful in the information age?" Alvin Toffler believes it will be the individual, group, community, society, or nation that has access to information and the ability to process it. Furthermore, he holds the view that knowledge is the central aspect of today's society.

As the knowledge and ideas economy revamp traditional models of education and thinking, our weltanschauung will increasingly be influenced and reshaped by exogenous forces, whose sole intent, it appears, is to boisterously trumpet the virtues of economic globalization, data centricity and the digital revolution.

Of further disquiet is the fact that we can't seem to remain focussed and structured when we are persistently swept by the niagara of information that fills our daily life. How can our kids process and interpret the vast quantities of news and the disinformation that swirls around them? I'm afraid, information overload (also known as infobesity or infoxication) is our new reality and the deluge of irrelevant and repetitive data promises to increase even further. The question is, does this unlimited production of data make us knowledgeable experts or is the easy access to information making us stupid? Have we indeed become intellectually lazy?

A recent study by Jason Lodge of the Griffith Institute for Educational Research at Griffith University in Australia points out that "our modern lifestyles are making us "less intelligent" than our ancestors, at least at a genetic level. This research echoes concerns Einstein had when he supposedly said, "I fear the day that technology will surpass our human interaction. The world will have a generation of idiots. The immediate availability of information has created a particular conundrum in our modern society. When it takes a mere few seconds to find information about almost any topic, the value of knowledge and expertise is being devalued as information becomes cheaper and more accessible. This is despite the fact that information, knowledge and expertise are fundamentally different entities."

The point is, there is undoubtedly more knowledge around today, but is contemporary society more intelligent and educated compared to the era of Mark Twain or John Maynard Keynes? Notwithstanding Einstein's observation that the only source of knowledge is experience, a holistic education (as a life skill) is an active, complex and perpetual process which should eventually produce an independent, self-acting, problem-solving and life-loving personality. Education therefore cannot be reduced to knowledge. Knowledge is not the aim of education but simply a means to an end. Moreover, educational attainment manifests a certain kind of judgment, reflection and critical distance to the flurry of information bombarding us and competing for our attention.

I have argued before that Saint Lucia's system of education and training is woefully inadequate in this new global order, and that curricular subjects should have a greater global scope and dimension. Further, I have urged our educators and policymakers to shape up by producing the right combination of talent in preparation for what the future proclaims as a complete transformation of motive rather than a straightforward substitution of activity. An important assertion made was that as our young people enter the workforce, the ability to deal with complex and often ambiguous information will be more important than simply knowing a lot of facts or having an accumulation of knowledge.

Countries like Finland and South Korea have demonstrated time and again that it's not necessarily technical knowledge that is the key to competitive advantage, but imaginative and lateral thinking. Hence, the educational path we are walking is not well marked, and this will make it difficult for us to traverse the information superhighway.

So what should education look like in this Information Age of enlightenment? How do you recognize an educated person today? Should we only be interested in translating technical proficiency into economic output? I believe education today should be strategically tailored to help students achieve research efficiency and impart skills to facilitate information filtration.

For the educated, educational and social informatics is like a second sun. Yet that sun doesn't seem to shine so brightly in many areas of the high-tech and knowledge economy. I'll be one of the first to bemoan the inverse relationship between technology and soft skills. The information superhighway seemed to have placed technical and conceptual skills on a pedestal, at the expense of interpersonal and intrapersonal skills. In a world where technical knowledge has to be assimilated quickly and presented simply to a wide audience, well-rounded professionals with effective communication and presentation skills are few and far between. The ironic thing about the lack of strong communication skills among IT and other knowledge workers is the fact that it's the one field where communication is so important. In order to counteract the information overload unleashed by the digital age, we'll need to employ more strategic soft skills and critical thinking to help us cut through the data clutter, present information with more clarity and make clearer decisions and choices.

So as young people move toward lives in the professional world, they have new soft skills to keep in mind. I believe some of us are so focused on one thing such as getting our degree that it can come as no surprise after leaving university when we are no good at team activities, organization, self management, social interaction and communication. There have always been—and will always be—certain soft skills, like emotional intelligence and compensation strategies, that people will need to master in the professional world. Industry leaders agree there is a growing need for these essential soft skills, and students entering the workforce who can demonstrate strong personal and social competence have a huge competitive advantage in a dynamic, data-centric and talent-intensive economy.

As someone who understands the need for a good balance between technology, social competence and traditional educational methods, I'll be glad to say good riddance to any educational culture that glorifies only technical know-how at the expense of an education touched by character and morality.

44. The School System – Challenging the Unspoken Assumptions

As a child, impetuous and rebellious, Winston Churchill suffered from a severe speech impediment and had a poor academic record in school. His life was apparently a trajectory of disparate events. However, those deficiencies and misfortunes were easily overcome by the strength of his character and the underpinnings of an enabling environment.

In a speech at Harvard University in 1943, the late British wartime Prime Minister and 1953 Literature Nobel Prize Winner indulged his audience by promulgating the vision that empires of the future would be empires of the mind. By published account, our own Sir Arthur Lewis, a development economist, also identified human capital as the main determinant of economic performance; a key to economic development.

A flourishing civil society requires an enabling environment – laws and policies that allow, favour and mainstream a socially responsible private sector and education system. Such an environment stimulates local initiative and draws inward investment, both of which can have rapid and dramatic effects on employment and human resource development. Written in stone and plastered on permanent mental billboards, a holistic education (touched by character) is relished as a fundamental prerequisite for the progress of civil society and for economic efficiency.

As most developed and emerging economies have proven, economic development depends to a large extent on the four Ts: talent, technology, tolerance and thinking (mentality). Given the fact that we have no mineral or natural resources to sustain and spur growth in Saint Lucia, the economic value that we strive to create can only be achieved by supercharging our talent machines and going against the unspoken assumptions of education policy.

With laudable regularity, our political and educational leaders take pride in emphasizing the importance of good schools and the significance of early childhood education. But is St. Lucia's system of education and training adequate in the new global environment? Are we shaping up by producing the right combination of talent in preparation for what the future proclaims as a complete transformation of motive rather than a straightforward substitution of activity?

Everywhere you turn today; the new buzzword is "talent" intensive, rather than "labour" or "capital" intensive. Large parts of industries are becoming "knowledge-based" and "service oriented", rendering old economic characterisations such as "manufacturing and industrial centres" obsolete. Even the literature on traditional economic sectors such as primary, secondary and tertiary have been revised to include "quaternary" and "quinary" sectors. Activities associated with the quaternary sector include scientific research, information technology and culture. Quinary is about the highest levels of decision making in an economy, from universities to think tanks.

By just looking at the available labour statistics in the Caribbean, it is clear that those without the benefit of a good practical education have fewer chances on the region's capricious labour markets. The corollary is that opportunities for economic advancement and social equality depend on the nature and relevance of the technical, conceptual and human skills that one has acquired through professional training.

But how and what should we be teaching our kids in modern classrooms? Traditionally, education has relied heavily on texts and lectures with precious little emphasis on lateral and critical thinking. The right approach in the 21st century should be collateral learning and contextualized training that make extensive use of case studies, business games and management exercises.

Such role plays invariably indulge the minds of our kids and help them think about old problems in new ways. It favours learning by doing rather than learning by lecture and reading. It indicates a preference for experiential and active learning rather than cognitive or reflective learning. Our children need to engage in complex interactions that require a high level of judgment, and rethink ideas that they had not questioned before. Employing such inductive methods might even help rake up a few geniuses from obscurity. My experience as a lecturer tells me that the important thing in tailoring education to an individual's brain is to let the individual do the tailoring. Didn't someone say that "the true adventure is in our heads, and if it's not there, then it can't be found anywhere else?" Like I've said before, countries such as Finland and South Korea have demonstrated time and again that it's not necessarily technical knowledge that is the key to competitive advantage, but imagination and lateral thinking.

The bottom line is that we need to readjust our national educational priorities. If we are to develop an economy that actually designs, builds and sells stuff, we'll need to produce more scientists and engineers in the future. Moving forward, our primary emphasis should be on the STEM-related fields (Science, Technology, Engineering, and Mathematics). Out of necessity, let's rise to the challenge and encourage our students to take degrees in those fields.

The process of preparing and equipping our kids for the future starts at the elementary and primary school levels. The raw materials of innovation are technical skills, insights and the commitment of teams and individuals. From an early age, our school system should be imparting innovation-related soft skills such as team building and compensation strategies, and other essential project and work-related skills like time management, intercultural competence and conflict resolution.

If Saint Lucia is to position itself educationally and economically to take advantage of the opportunities that this new world order presents, new approaches will have to be explored and more resources invested. This will include upgrading Sir Arthur Lewis Community College into a full- fledged university college. Another issue which we'll have to tackle head-on is that of foreign language instruction. In an increasingly globalized world, why aren't we exposing ours kids to foreign languages at the kindergarten level? Why should we have to wait until secondary school to commence foreign language instruction? That makes no sense to me. We are depriving our kids of an opportunity to compete globally.

Furthermore, research has shown that bilinguals tend to be more creative thinkers than those who speak one language. Exposing children to a second language from early may actually help pique their intellectual curiosity in terms of foreign cultures and development approaches, and thus broaden their professional horizons.

Education can be improved by context and adapted to our national needs. It's perhaps an opportune time to commission more studies to shed more light on the correlative and causal relationships between our education system and economic performance. In an effort to solidify our understanding and address key issues in the debate on education policy, evidence-based research would help us determine the rightful roles of national agencies and the private sector in educational development in Saint Lucia.

Total Quality Management is definitely a concept we should be looking at in order to improve standards and deliver high-quality graduates at every level of the education system. This can be achieved by setting rigid curriculum standards, fostering a culture of educational governance and remodelling our assessment mechanisms. At the same time, it's imperative that the Education Ministry embark on a quest to employ the best teachers and get the best out of them. We are reminded time and again that the quality of an education system cannot exceed the quality of its teachers.

Like successful economies already do, only the best trained teachers should staff infant and primary schools considering that this is a crucial development stage in forming and shaping our kids for the future. An unfortunate wrong start in the system can have disastrous effects on a child's development. These bold changes which I am proposing can only be pursued and brought to fruition through educational leadership and commitment.

Education is an investment in human capital that pays off in terms of higher productivity, economic engagement and even civic participation and good health. A democracy needs an educated and informed people otherwise it will be starved of vibrancy. When citizens lack the educational background to understand the increasing complexity of many social and economic issues, the result is widespread corruption, governmental complacency and eroding social capital.

45. Death of the Bookstore

The writing is on the wall. STAR publisher Rick Wayne poignantly refers to the national aversion to reading as "the curse of Derek Walcott." To the growing list of things in Saint Lucia that will be extinct in our children's world, we can now add bookstores. Does it surprise us? No. After all, to us reading seems to be an alien culture. Should we care? You bet. It's hard to imagine a nation, any nation, without bookshops. But then there is the Saint Lucian reality, however horrifying.

Visitors to Saint Lucia often encounter Nobel winner Derek Walcott relaxing or painting at the beach. What a pity they cannot buy his books and return home with an autographed volume!

One more retail clothing store, bank, fast-food outlet, or lawyer's office in an area already awash in them tends to flatten the tone of a community. But few elements enliven a public space like a good bookstore. They do more than sell books. They define the character of a street, neighbourhood, town or city. They also say much about people. They play an integral part in our ecosystem of the written word and a city's culture. Neil Gaiman, believing bookstores to be an important fabric of a community, proclaimed in his award-winning novel American Gods: "What I say is, a town isn't a town without a bookstore. It may call itself a town, but unless it's got a bookstore it knows it's not fooling a soul."

As Sunshine Bookstore and the like will attest, the times do not encourage bookselling, despite that books remain the most essential of learning tools. In the last three years or so, we have observed bookstores are disappearing overnight while those that remain carry less and less stock. The culprits behind the recent closures are many: high rents, VAT, the decline in reading, the rise of e-books and the buying and selling of used books online.

Perhaps money is a critical factor: books are expensive in a world where information on the web is largely free. As a large disheartened U.S. publisher points out: "There are many reasons for the decline of bookstores. Blame the business model of superstores; blame Amazon; blame the shrinking of leisure time; blame a digital age that offers so many bright, quick things that have crippled our ability for sustained concentration. You can even blame writers, if you want, because you think they no longer produce anything vital to the culture or worth reading. Whatever the case, it is a historical fact that the decline of the bookstore and the rise of the Internet happened simultaneously; one model of the order and presentation of knowledge was toppled and superseded by another. For bookstores, e-books are only the nail in the coffin."

Of course, to see so many local bookstores shutting their doors because they can't adjust to new economic realities is heartbreaking. But it is also bad for the business of publishing. Alas, local authors who depend on independent brick-and-mortar bookstores to promote and sell their works will not function effectively without such retail and distribution outlets.

The more discerning among us will doubtless lament the steady disappearance of a last great place for meandering. An oasis of calm in a hectic city and in suburban malls, where we go to kill time, expose ourselves to new stuff, look for a gift without something specific in mind, and maybe pick up something on impulse while we're there. A good friend of mine who is an established author frantically warned that if enough people stop taking their business to the remaining bookstores, "a beautiful cultural reality will transmogrify into a social fiction. And that, in turn, will threaten a set of values that has been with us for as long as we have had books."

For as long as I can remember, Saint Lucians have had an ambivalent relationship with books. It's not uncommon to hear adults acknowledge they haven't read a good book since they left school. Generally, today's parents hardly encourage their kids to read; the internet has become the main resource for research and recreation. Is it any wonder that many of our kids cannot think critically and are not intellectually curious? Even the adults themselves do not read for facts and have become poor listeners. Yet everyone seems to have an expert opinion on everything (a phenomenon I refer to as the ACE syndrome: Advisors, Consultants and Experts). The isle is so full of noise these days. Apparently the ubiquitous radio and TV call-in programmes have turned most of them into experts. But will a nation that won't or can't read eventually also forget how to think?

For a small chest-beating island that boasts of a Nobel Prize winner in Literature, it's kind of hard to believe local authors are not given the recognition and national attention they deserve. Why aren't the works of local writers featured more prominently at cultural events and school activities around the island? Haven't we recognized the importance of fully utilizing our intellectual and cultural capital in fostering nation-building?

Saint Lucia has great literary talent in the persons of Rick Wayne, John Robert Lee, McDonald Dixon, Kendel Hippolyte, Anderson Reynolds, Dawn French—to name only a few. We need to get these writers, poets and playwrights to our schools periodically, to present their works to our kids. Only then can they be truly inspired to read avidly, write experimentally and appreciate our local heroes and their art. I will never understand why our small nation hasn't seen the need to make greater cultural and educational use in our primary and secondary schools of our distinguished Nobel laureate Derek Walcott.

Libraries and bookstores are the keepers of community now, in addition to being centres for knowledge and recreational reading. I am therefore appealing to the state to make it a statutory requirement for every primary and secondary school in Saint Lucia to have a library, on the grounds that there are proven links between reading and attainment. One gets the impression that over the years the use of library services has been undervalued and neglected. In any event, local libraries need to actively source books from all local authors to showcase them at special events.

I am fully aware that the world is moving from analogue to digital, from products to services, and from premium to freemium-pricing models. However, no matter what one thinks of Amazon, it has been wildly effective at wiping out the competition—thanks to its demographic reach and massive used-book inventory. E-books have truly revolutionized the publishing and book-selling industries, forcing the first named to dramatically restructure their sales, marketing, and production forces, and the latter to scramble to find ways to continue to sell physical books. But no amount of digital books or online browsing can come close to finding a rare book in a second-hand bookstore, or having an author dedicate a handwritten note inside his books especially for you.

It's really no surprise that the death of the bookstore has coincided with a decline in the literary and creative arts. Saint Lucia and the wider Caribbean have the potential to build a cultural economy on the pillars of their creative industries and literary capital. Unfortunately, the neglect of the creative and literary arts industry bodes ill for our local economy since it could have given this country a unique advantage in a world evermore reliant on the knowledge economy. For all we know, this could have been the elusive answer to our unemployment problem. The point is this: if we are to truly make an economic success of the creative industries in Saint Lucia we must aim to strengthen the sector, promote intellectual property rights and invest in the next generation of content creators to keep the flow of IP coming. The economic benefits could be huge. Now the challenge for public policy is to fully embrace and invest in this dynamic sector or regret the dire consequences of ignoring it.

CHAPTER 6 –
SOCIAL AFFAIRS AND THE
ENVIRONMENT

46. A Social Policy Paradigm Shift

My deep-seated belief that the wide-ranging sphere of social policy in Saint Lucia has often been relegated to the sidelines in party-political discourse is surely not a figment of my imagination. Only a foaming polemicist would deny that social policy has everything do to with economic growth, as social development in and of itself entails the process of increasing the assets and capabilities of individuals to improve their economic wellbeing and to help them participate in the development process.

At a time of rising anxiety among the youth, and the growing awareness of the unsustainability of high unemployment and large debt repayments, this conversation could not be more important. To be sure, the burden of high youth unemployment is not unique to Saint Lucia and there have rightly been calls to find a regional approach to deal with this vexing issue. Nonetheless, youth unemployment (hovering around 50 percent) must become the focus of both social and economic policy. Economic growth for its own sake cannot be a sensible final objective of society or the only instrument to fight its ills.

We often talk about economic growth as an end in itself, as opposed to social growth as a means to an economic end. Change through social policy is a unique opportunity because it has the highest potential for economic impact in the country. Since development is about reducing vulnerabilities and increasing capacity of people and institutions, a social policy based on forward guidance must be the main instrument to improve human welfare in our small communities and to meet developmental needs in health, education, housing and economic security.

Much to our dismay, the national economy has become wildly unequal – and the way society is organized and resources allocated have probably exacerbated the inequality TRIFECTA (income, wealth, opportunity). The primacy of social responsibility has now been replaced by the primacy of economic efficiency and the virtues of the free market – with insufficient attention paid to the social dislocations caused.

Most economists agree that any economic policy discussion without its "intrinsic social-policy component" is incomplete. That is to say, not only are the two disciplines two sides of the same coin, they should also not be treated as separate domains. In effect, there can be no denial of the social multiplier effects in diverse contexts of economic stability and vice versa. When unemployment – considered an important barometer of a country's economic health – rises to unsustainable levels, it can easily foment social instability. Conversely, weak social policies that don't effectively promote equality of opportunities and people empowerment will eventually engender economic displacement and instability. Hence, good social policy is good economic policy – needless to say, poor economic decisions can have very unpleasant social consequences.

At any rate, a momentary snapshot of Saint Lucian society reveals a picture of a nation that has become disunited, indifferent and individualistic. Ours is a society of sharp elbows where money has become a deity and role models are almost non-existent. The young, and particularly students, are especially vulnerable and engage in vice owing to peer pressure, media influence, and poor guidance both at home and in society. The scourge of broken families along with a lack of employment opportunities has already taken its toll on society. Furthermore, a shameful culture of sexual violence against women and child abuse is taking root, evidenced by the recent increase in cases of rape and other sexual offences. The 2015 death of a 4-year-old allegedly at the hands of his guardians is a harrowing example of a seemingly entrenched problem that requires urgent attention. All these developments should be a spur to policy action on the social front.

Clearly a new approach is needed. While I commend the Ministry of Social Transformation for revamping the island's social policy programme to provide greater protection for the vulnerable, there is still a lot more to be done. It is obvious that social policy cannot succeed if it is focussed on the consequences, rather than the causes. First, we'll need to build strong institutions with research capability, rather than simply obedient ones. Second, an entire infrastructure of care in the form of family planning, affordable day-care, early education and after-school programmes, is needed to help families invest in the next generation. Another priority is to enhance the long-run financial viability of the social safety net for the protection of vulnerable children and the impoverished elderly.

Several studies on social development have consistently shown that higher gender-parity and female education strongly correlate with higher levels of development. On that calculus, it is to be expected that policies and programmes that boost young women's economic standing will be implemented or reinforced – which in turn will improve women's social position, reflected in better health outcomes, increased physical security, and greater political representation.

Owing to the absence of any evidenced-based research on criminality in the country, the recidivism rate among young offenders is really anyone's guess. For all we know, there's probably a viper's nest at the Bordelais prison waiting to unleash more dangerous ex-convicts on the public. Of further disquiet is the fact that released inmates have no support networks to navigate re-entry to society, and thereby face huge barriers to employment, housing, health care and education.

Essentially, the provision of social services for the homeless, disabled, mentally ill and the elderly should not be seen through the prism of costs and fiscal constraints; neither should the social sector be treated as a burden on society. Instead social services should be viewed as an essential factor for a liveable society and for economic prosperity.

Even so, lurking in the average Saint Lucian mind is the notion that government is solely responsible for creating social stability and promoting civic engagement. Yet, the private sector and civil society organizations are expected to work in partnership and contribute to sustainable development through programmes of corporate social responsibility (CSR) and social entrepreneurship. To this end, it's essential that mechanisms are built by the public service and civil society to hold the private sector accountable for development results.

Since the mid-eighties, social policy in Saint Lucia – to misquote a writer for The Economist, "has not always been in thrall to the hobgoblins of consistency". It is now time to give this area greater attention and prominence – and we can start by providing more human, financial and technical resources to the Department of Human Services. This is an issue that transcends politics and we all need to contribute constructively to the social policy conversation. Although I do understand the economic constraints that we face as a small country, I still believe greater social investments can be a game changer for our country's future.

47. Where Have All the Public Thinkers Gone?

Eric Williams' edifying lectures on world history, Greek democracy and philosophy, the history of slavery, and the history of the Caribbean drew large audiences from every social class. By his own admission, his historic crossing of the Rubicon in 1955 led inexorably to the political enlightenment of his nation. At the height of the independence movement and with a revolutionary spring in his step, he declared: "Now that I have resigned my position at Howard University in the USA, the only university in which I shall lecture in future is the University of Woodford Square and its several branches throughout the length and breadth of Trinidad and Tobago."

For many, Williams was a political visionary and a man of fine mettle who thought politics was a continuation of education by other means, and who championed the cause of political accessibility for the masses. Through his activism and advocacy, he demonstrated that political commitment and the work of the public intellectual takes many forms from writing books to engaging broader public spheres as a speaker, educator and organizer. Essentially, he taught us that we have to start to examine the power of individual historians, sociologists and economists to intervene in public affairs and provide the citizenry with ideas, insights and options.

Williams would later write in his brilliant 1969 political autobiography, Inward Hunger: The Education of a Prime Minister: "The University of Woodford square has for the past twelve years been a centre of free university education for the masses, of political analysis and of training in self-government... The lectures have been university dishes served in political sauce. They have given the people of Trinidad and Tobago a vision and a perspective... They have taught the people, what one French writer of the eighteenth century saw as the greatest danger, that they have a mind."

I suppose it's easy to be nostalgic for a period when towering intellectual figures trod the public stage. One famous publicist who captured the social change wrote, "I do recall a time, not so long ago, when formal orations seemed more eloquent, when public figures and intellectuals, some of them connected to academic institutions, dared to say more controversial things and take strong positions against the orthodox thinking of the day."

As standards in public debate have fallen, the perception across the Caribbean is that the expansion of higher education has occurred side by side with a widespread erosion of educational standards and a steady rise in cultural illiteracy. By any reasonable measure, there has been a palpable decline in the quality of intellectual life in Saint Lucia from the post-independence days of George Odlum, Hunter J. Francois, Sir Vincent Floissac and others who constituted the circle of the intellectual class. Admittedly, there are times I would reflect on the contributions of

George Odlum to the political education of the masses and think of how much I miss the intersection of literature and politics.

Yet what concerns me most is the sheer absence of public intellectuals in the social and economic development of our nation. The dearth of public intellectuals observing and commenting on the culture we live in is something I have lamented for some time. Although I do believe our nation has bright sons and daughters who can compete anywhere in the world, they just need to come out and elevate the standard of debate in our democracy. Without the active presence and contribution of public intellectuals in national development discourse, the social and economic empowerment of the masses remains a pipedream. If we are to achieve the goals of greater social inclusion and political maturity, we must encourage free, critical and independent thinking in the discussion of public affairs. As the saying goes, when everyone thinks alike, no one thinks very much and we all suffer for it.

Are there any persons alive today whose views and opinions are eagerly anticipated and sought after by all the media on a wide variety of subjects and events including education, health, urban development and economics? Where are the thinkers who can challenge the public and its complacency instead of talking down to them or rabble-rousing? Where are those people who can speak and write about their discipline and how it relates to the social, cultural and political world around it?

If you asked me to identify the nation's foremost public intellectuals who are making an impact on people's lives today, I would struggle to find any one person or institution that stands out. I mean when was the last time we heard any public intellectual call for an end to partisanship and make a clarion call for people to work together to solve the country's problems? Is the absence of public intellectuals a symptom of a larger decline in a literate audience interested in what such intellectuals have to say?

We need to bring more people and ideas into our political system and welcome any change that could reinvigorate sentiments of citizenry and patriotism. By this I mean men and women engaged in critical study, thought, and reflection about the reality of society, and who propose solutions for the normative problems of society. We owe it to ourselves and the next generation to make the nation more politically dynamic and socially viable.

Arguably, one of the problems in our system is that the media has not been sufficiently analytical and hasn't always sought through investigative journalism and explanatory reporting to make sense of complex realities in order to create public understanding. Furthermore, because the outcome of elections in our two-party system is a zero-sum game, the views of half of the electorate are usually discounted and alternative parties have no chance of making any serious impact or achieving any serious change. Unfortunately, this situation has been so since the attainment of Independence in 1979.

Of further disquiet is the fact that we live and breathe the idea that our voice must be heard irrespective of the fallacies in our arguments or the validity of our comments. In our sender-oriented society, poor listening skills, lack of conciseness, and the inability to give constructive feedback have become major impediments to our progress as a people.

Further compounding the problem is the fact that everyone seems to have an expert opinion on everything. It's not uncommon to hear people speaking out of turn or amateurs addressing social and economic issues best left to professionals. Who needs public intellectuals anyway when we can bombard radio and TV call-in programmes with ill-conceived notions and ill-informed views?

At the least, a democracy can expect a certain degree of understanding and knowledge from its citizens – a modicum of reasoning. The simplistic, political brute-force, instant-gratification answers that we provide to every problem in our daily exchanges is probably a reflection of the fossilized party system we inherited and the selfish naval-gazing mindset of our society.

If democracy thrives on good ideas, then Saint Lucia is at a crossroads. Regrettably, academia is disconnected from public debate and policy decision-making. Without independent public intellectuals and think tanks to stimulate public discussion on policy issues, I'm afraid our democracy will be starved of its vibrancy. Public intellectuals should not be bound by their profession or political affiliation. Their most important activities are action and enlightenment. They should write and speak out of obligation to society, but also out of obligation to themselves.

As is the norm in most emerging and developed countries, public intellectuals tend to have close relationships with journalists and with the policy community; a practice that has helped spread good ideas, strengthen democratic institutions and advance economic reforms. Public intellectuals may be an endangered species, but their role as thinker, dissenter and knowledge gamekeeper will always be crucial in evolving and progressive societies.

48. When Civil Society Becomes Political

Although civil society in Saint Lucia has long been perceived as weak and factionalized, the rapid decline over the years in civic engagement and personal social responsibility is perhaps both a reflection and an indication of the dwindling social capital of civil society, even as its size continues to expand. Across the Caribbean, even the discussion of the nature and role of civil society has often been obfuscated.

No way to develop a nation

It would appear that rather than having a potent and progressive society bolstered by vibrant institutions and responsive social structures, we now have a patchwork of interest groups espousing race-to-the-bottom ideas that instigate and promote division, distrust and partisan animosi-ty among our people – creating a rift through (and in some instances destroying) families, institutions, groups, clubs and communities. Un-deniably, it is a political chasm that is widening every day, limiting soci-ety's ability to both objectively address its shortcomings and establish procedures for securing whatever resources they require. Is it any won-der that nation-building has become difficult in such an environment of political tribalism and polarization?

To a large extent, the way in which civil society functions will influ-ence all the patterns of social ordering and cultural ideas that comprise it. Alas, due to the institutionalization of a dominant political culture handed down as social heritage and engrained within our national psy-che, community solidarity over the years seemed to have been eroded and all sense of civility evaporated – the cultural impact of which is profoundly unsettling.

A new strain of civic influenza

A closer look at civil society reveals a picture of a nation that has be-come angry and selfish – often demonstrating blithe indifference to the opinions and feelings of others. Ours is a society that gloats over the misfortunes of others – and hasn't yet learned to respect life, limb and property. Everywhere one turns, a new strain of civic influenza seemed to have taken hold where towns and villages are viewed as a collection of rugged individualists and navel-gazers who would rather invest their time in projects that promise direct benefits to them and their families, rather than the common good. Even on the ecological front, I am still very much dumbfounded at the level of disrespect and disregard shown to the environment by the shameless purveyors of litter. Where is our civic pride? Where is the respect for a place we call home?

A house divided against itself

On the face of it, political groups appear to live side by side but do not touch – breathing new life into the adage "a house divided against itself cannot stand". Since independence, the rapacious beast which we call party politics, has fed off the ignorance of a half-literate society with pockets of poverty and deprivation. Sadly, we now view almost every-thing through the lens of political factions. In effect, we may have al-ready moved from a civil society to a political society.

A case in point is the manner in which we promote and advocate the rights of women in this country. Why can't we vocalize women's issues through a bona fide umbrella organization rather than through the sepa-rate arms of political parties? Wouldn't such an idea better assist in the advocacy of women's rights and the promotion of gender equality?

Criminal justice

As Edmund Burke observed, "Justice is itself the great standing policy of civil society". In many ways, what continues to seriously undermine our swooning civil society is an overstretched and inadequate justice system too weak to uphold the rule of law and a demoralized police force una-ble to prevent or resolve even the simplest of crimes. Consequently criminals have become emboldened to commit more vicious crimes such as robbery, rape and murder, further contributing to the break-down of civil society. On account of ineffective laws and deterrents, street gangs have metastasized in our capital city and beyond.

I have mentioned before that we need to better understand what is really happening on our streets – otherwise we as a society stand in dan-ger of losing yet another generation as they plunge through violence and criminality to hopelessness and despair. Action on strengthening fami-lies, tackling educational failure, reforming welfare, ending drug and alcohol addiction is foundational to mending our broken society. With-out a reversal of the social breakdown and disorder that characterises life in deprived communities, we will continue to see wasted generation after wasted generation.

Social justice

Many sociologists now believe that the relationship between a robust civil society and social justice is not merely correlational but causal. In fact there is consensus that the fundamental crisis of social justice is rooted in leadership, management and persistent self-centeredness. When was the last time you heard civil society advocate for good social and community leadership – the kind that puts the interest of the community or society as a whole before those of any specific group? It is therefore the responsibility of civil society to drive action and change through its potential to influence leaders and its ability to transform the thinking of its membership. Now I am not saying that the constituents of civil society shouldn't support political parties and push for more political education. In fact, it's their right to establish ties to political parties and the State, but they must retain their independence and free-dom to criticize governments.

A vibrant middle class

As I have argued before, countries with strong civil societies remain stable in times of social change and socio-cultural evolution, and also do better over time. Moreover, a dynamic civil society needs a vibrant mid-dle class to engender economic stability and to be the driver of demo-cratic change and the backbone of democracy. A strong middle class supports inclusive political and economic institutions, which underpin economic growth. Further, the strength of a society can be measured directly by the strength of its middle class, which usually translates to better governance, increased corporate social responsibility and greater spending in social sectors such as public health and education. Hence, we shouldn't discount the role the middle class plays in the emergence and consolidation of civil society.

If we want our nation to achieve its aspirations, we as a people will have to build and strengthen a society that looks at and fights against social injustice, poverty, income inequality, poor housing, lack of ade-quate mental health provision and family support. We have to begin to build national institutions and movements that are able to negotiate, and in some cases, renegotiate the relationship between society and the State. By asking the right questions and acting as a communal unit, citizens can more effectively lobby the government and mobilize resources in an effort to help fight poverty, promote transparency and reinforce social and economic rights.

Educated, cultivated and cultured

Lest we forget, development is a mindset needed in the pursuit of personal advancement and social transformation. It is a matrix which shapes our weltanschauung and fosters democratic dynamism in our important social institutions. If we are to strengthen civil society's collective defences and character, we'll need to further improve and develop our social and education systems to produces citizens who are not only educated, but also cultured and cultivated. Joe Biden captured the essence of civil society when he said, "No fundamental social change occurs merely because government acts. It's because civil society, the conscience of a country, begins to rise up and demand – demand – demand change."

49. We Can Do Better on Human Rights

One morning in May 2011, five individuals were shot in an alleged intervention by the police to foil what they claimed was an attempted robbery at a restaurant in Vieux-Fort. After several years of political and judicial inertia, and under pressure from the United States to prosecute for alleged extrajudicial killings, the Prime Minister in a televised statement last year announced that the findings of the so-called IMPACS report revealed that "Between 2010 and 2011, twelve persons met their deaths following encounters with officers of the Royal Saint Lucia Police Force. The largest number of the civilian casualties occurred in the Castries Basin, allegedly during the execution of duly authorized search warrants." Since that moment of revelation, it seems like the country's human rights image has fallen on really hard times.

If indeed the killings were extrajudicial, to date no one has been punished, and almost no one has been held to account for any other human-rights crime committed during that period. In particular, it is far from clear whether the police acted on its own or whether they got instructions from a higher authority.

At any rate, as the prohibition of extrajudicial killings is central to human rights law, the U.S. has taken a keen interest (perhaps conveniently) in the matter, prompting the State Department to report that "the most serious human rights problems included reports of unlawful police killings" – and more specifically, "12 potentially unlawful fatal police shootings during the year."

Now I won't deny that for too long, human rights have been taken for granted in this country – perhaps as far back as the early eighties. I'll also not pretend that the United States is a moral authority on human rights. After all, Jimmy Carter once admitted: "America did not invent human rights. In a very real sense human rights invented America." Yet, any progressive society should hold human rights in the highest regard. Of course, Saint Lucia is not considered to be among the major human rights-violating countries such as Syria, Sudan and Pakistan. However, the system has shown itself often incapable of investigating human-rights violations.

Indeed there is much consensus among Saint Lucians that the country's justice system is broken – that much has become clear in recent years given the limited resources made available to foster and administer justice, amid hundreds of unresolved murders. And even as crime has become a real problem here, more problematic is the actual investigation of crime, and the swift dispensation of justice. It's not too much of a stretch to say that people's confidence in the justice system at this point is shaken. The courts are breathtakingly slow and under-funded; and even more appalling is the fact that prisoners languish in prison, remaining on remand for as long as a decade. Within any criminal justice system, protecting the rights of remand prisoners should be a priority, not an afterthought. Besides, international conventions dictate that a person is entitled to a trial within the shortest possible time.

Furthermore, there are other critical issues such as the way we treat the mentally ill and the scourge of rape and domestic violence that should be of urgent concern to us. To be sure, 2015 was not a good year for human rights as the country recorded an unprecedented number of rapes and other sexual offences including the depraved violation of a ninety-seven year old woman.

The staggering level of verbal abuse meted out to Ms Mary Francis, our Florence Nightingale of local human rights, are clear indications that quite a few of our citizens are yet to understand the distinctive idiom of human rights and how they work in practice. The constant vitriolic attacks by the "angry mob" on both radio and TV call-in programmes are perhaps an attestation to the lack of wisdom in crowds in our neck of the woods. In a country known for its divisiveness and ovine docility, it certainly takes a certain chutzpah for one courageous human rights attorney to challenge the status quo. Yet, I believe the causes she champions are just and right – and civil society needs to provide her with more support to undertake this important civic duty, as human rights transcend all political, economic and social boundaries.

Above all, it's such a great pity that more lawyers are not involved in providing legal aid and in protecting the rights and dignity of the vulnerable. Against all odds – and undaunted by all the abusive language, Ms Francis has vowed to continue championing for change – a welcome silver lining in a gathering storm cloud. On several occasions she has called for more independent investigations into human rights abuses and more recently, for the establishment of a National Human Rights Commission to safeguard the human rights of individuals. According to Ms Francis, "speedy remedy and accountability for human rights violations would help restore confidence in the justice system." Without a doubt, she is right and our young democracy needs more people of her ilk.

Even so, the failure to address our human rights issues have resulted in our island being place under greater international scrutiny and pressure. Last year, the United Nations conducted its review of Saint Lucia's human rights situation and recommended a few measures in order to strengthen the island's human rights legislative framework and establish an independent national rights monitoring mechanism. The global body has, among other things, called on Saint Lucia to do more "to further protect women and children from domestic violence, to implement gender equality polices, to adopt legislation prohibiting discrimination on the basis of sexual orientation and gender identity, and to fully prosecute all perpetrators of sexual and domestic violence."

Only recently, and much to my dismay, we were lectured by three foreign ambassadors representing the EU, Britain and France, about the failings of our justice system. Now I imagine that not only would these foreign powers have been told in other jurisdictions to take the plank out of their own eyes before worrying about the splinter in other countries, they would also have been accused of meddling in the affairs of a sovereign state. Notwithstanding the fact that the three ambassadors overstepped the mark by interfering in Saint Lucia's internal affairs and that the traditional champions of human rights – Europe and the United States – have themselves floundered, they are unfortunately right about the sad state of our country's justice system.

Apropos of "champions of human rights", where are the independent civil society organizations (NGOs, NPOs and the church) to demand swift justice and judicial accountability? So much for the primacy of independent thought and the life of the mind!

50. Public Talk Shows – Hold the Line, Please!

I don't often tune in to talk shows, but the occasions when I do it's because an interesting personality is on – and there is a chance that I may be enlightened on an important subject like, for instance the citizenship by investment programme, the scourge of domestic violence in our island or even the various economic plans of our mainstream political parties. I will also admit that even when a particular guest attracts my attention and the programme turns out to be informative and stimulating, I often end up switching channels when the show eventually gets to the call-in segment. Having held that frustration in abeyance for a while, I now suspect quite a few people will also agree that this component is the most irritating part of any public talk show, whether it be television or radio.

So why have most, if not all, talk shows in Saint Lucia consistently followed a similar concept and structure? I recently heard the host of one of the more popular TV talk shows on the island suggest that the call-in segment should be scaled down to allow more structure and focus in the presentation and discussion of national issues. Of course, I'll be the first to concur with that position, as I believe the limited time offered to featured guests to provide and explain their perspectives is insufficient – thereby defeating the very purpose and principles I suppose that undergird the idea of such public affairs talk shows – which is basically to enlighten, educate and inform. If done in a way that raises awareness and promotes fair and healthy discussion, public affairs talk shows can be a means of national education and political enlightenment as well as a source of accountability. Admittedly, there are some talk shows in Saint Lucia hosted by skilled moderators that already do just that.

Yet, I'm all for scrapping the call-in segment which often provides a platform for disputatious characters to derail a purposeful and useful dialogue – causing what sometimes started as a productive discourse to degenerate into a political proxy war. Maybe with a little luck (just maybe), discarding that part of the show can help detoxify the political atmosphere in the country. But I know you wouldn't hold your breath.

Unlike a friend of mine who believes that talk-shows are trite and therefore a waste of time, I actually think they serve an important educational and edifying purpose in a country where illiteracy is high and very few people actually bother to read. Apropos reading, perhaps it would be a good idea to expand the circulation of newspapers to all secondary schools on the island and have teachers discuss some of the issues (the non-political ones of course) with their students for about an hour or so per week. I actually witnessed such a discussion at a secondary school overseas which had me thinking of the merits and usefulness of the idea in my own country.

At any rate, a good conversation on education, health, culture, etc is often derailed when the telephone lines are opened, particularly when the featured guest is perceived or known to be associated with a particular political brand. Although I really don't want to homogenize all callers into a single mould, it's quite usual for certain individuals to call in and not ask any constructive and substantive questions – but instead verbally assault the guest(s) on the programme or make long-winded political pitches (allegedly scripted) with the calculated intention of blocking the telephone lines and depriving other callers from making a contribution. In some instances, even the host ends up being on the receiving end of various forms of verbal attack. Based on what I've witness so far and especially now in the campaign season when tensions have begun to flare, it takes a certain chutzpah to be a talk show host in this country, particularly when people are hell-bent on defending their various positions (or propagating their sometimes specious reasoning).

Now please don't get it misconstrued – there is nothing wrong with people having a strong position on any issue, even a political one at that (man is a political animal according to Aristotle) – it's just that the same people with selfish motives call in all the time and repeat the same old arguments.

As I was alluding to earlier, talk shows need to provide legislators and functionaries more time and opportunity to explain themselves, present their plans and respond to voter concerns. It is sometimes discombobulating to see talk show guests fervently attempting to shed light on an issue only to be interrupted in order to accommodate callers who often regurgitate old vapid lines – thus contributing little value to the discourse. Further, I'm sure there are so many critical questions that need to be asked – and the guests seldom get the opportunity to answer them owing to the fact that the telephone lines are opened too early – often resulting in a worthwhile discussion going off course or losing focus and cogency. Add to that the fact that some answers (especially plans and policies) may be complex and don't always fit easily into soundbites lasting only a few minutes.

Even so, given the complexity of the social and economic problems facing our small island today, it may sometimes be more useful and judicious to focus on a particular issue, say, the inefficiency of the justice system – in order to more holistically explore possible causes, consequences and implications as well as to view the issue from different vantage points. Self-evidently, that kind of productive exchange doesn't lend itself to a time-limited and unstructured format – and can best be facilitated by having perhaps, on particular occasions, two or three guests to participate in a panel discussion – allowing a more balanced educational exchange on developmental ideas, policy differences and other national interest issues. Wouldn't such a popular vehicle be a wonderful opportunity for policymakers, businessmen, functionaries and public figures to face the nation and elucidate and validate their positions?

I can already hear some of you lamenting the fact that many public officials for various reasons are sometimes reluctant to appear on such shows. Alas, it is we the people who are responsible for ensuring that they do and remain accountable. Democracy does not end at the ballot box – in fact this is only the first step in a long process of political engagement and civic participation. Hence, we have to make it our duty to pressure elected representatives to interface at all times with the taxpaying public either directly or through the media.

Make no mistake – I do believe that the voice of the people should be heard, but there are other ways and opportunities by which this could be achieved other than talk shows. For those who can't countenance the absence of audience participation in talk shows, an idea would be to have a call-in segment every second or third week. Another idea would be to have a live audience in studio that would be allowed to field relevant questions. Of course, these are not revolutionary ideas – such concepts have been part and parcel of the talk-show circuit in most countries that practice representative democracy. Besides, I'm not aware of any public affairs talk show outside our region that constitutes a call-in component.

Perhaps one of the reasons why our society has become so self-centred and quarrelsome is because we probably talk too much (and sometimes out of turn) – and don't listen attentively to others. We have all become experts on everything, even when it is clear that we aren't quite informed about many issues. One of the things I've always said is that our people must learn to listen more and cogitate before expressing their viewpoints. Above all, some of us need to read more and research the issues to enable us to better participate in constructive discourse.

51. George Odlum – Footprints in the Sand

The unflagging claim that the world was his oyster was once again validated by the UK's Bristol University in 2015, in celebration of the institution's Black History Month. The late George Odlum, perhaps the most colourful figure in Saint Lucia's political history, has received a posthumous honour from his alma mater, Bristol University, for his figurehead role in the Student's Union and his activism for the social and educational empowerment of black people.

"Two men who had a significant impact on the profile of black people in Bristol, the UK and beyond are being honoured in a special ceremony to mark Black History Month. Paul Stephenson, who led a boycott in 1963 of the Bristol Omnibus company, and George Odlum, who was the first black president of a Students' Union anywhere in the UK, are both having rooms named after them in the University of Bristol's Students' Union (Bristol SU) building", a section of the press release stated.

Samantha Budd, Chief Executive of Bristol Student Union has described Odlum as a man with a sense of purpose who "developed a vision of hope for change." In the same press release, she noted: "Stephenson and Odlum, in different ways, made a real contribution to improving the lives of black people on a global scale. Bristol SU still believes in equality and diversity and so we thought this a fitting way to mark their legacy and reaffirm our commitment to the values they championed."

This is not the first time the British university has expressed admiration and praise for the leadership of the late Saint Lucian scholar – a national hero to some and a thundering nuisance to others. A while back, the aforementioned Chief Executive had extolled the virtues of Odlum in an article written to commemorate Black History Month: "To have been a Union President, then as now, required above ordinary levels of confidence and charisma. To have achieved this, as the son of a barber, a black man from a small Caribbean island really was exceptional. Indeed even today, over 50 years later, George's feat remains remarkable as there has only been one other UBU President of Caribbean heritage, Rob Mitchell (1991-1992). Notably, George appears to have been the first black President ever of any Students' Union in Britain."

Saint Lucia lost one of its intellectual pearls in 2003 when George Odlum shuffled off this mortal coil at the age of 69. Many remember "Brother George", as he was affectionately known, as a charismatic and restless soul who frequently inspired adulation in those he encountered. By all accounts, the irrepressible Odlum was not only endowed with the gift of intellectual speculation and articulate oratory, but also an unorthodox politician with a congenitally warm personality, and very approachable and accessible to the public. I still have warm memories of the debate coaching he provided to me and my colleague at Fish Pot in Choiseul, ahead of the 1994 National Youth Council debating competition.

Odlum, like most of his political contemporaries, saw the ruthless game of politics for what it was (and still is) – a contact sport. Determined and quite resolute in his convictions, Odlum was a major player in shaping the political and social consciousness of the nation in the most turbulent period of its political history. But while he was admired for his ability to draw huge crowds at political events, many expressed undemonstrative concern over his defiant and aggressive tactics in achieving political goals.

Admittedly, some of his actions were eyebrow-raising at times – carried out with his trademark intensity, to the point of verging on incomprehensibility. We may not have always agreed with some of his methods and aspects of his ideology, but his decency and humanity were unimpeachable. It has been said that Odlum was probably discombobulated by the somnambulistic pace of educational and political development in Saint Lucia.

Widely regarded to possess one of the most penetrating minds of any politician in the Caribbean and beyond, Odlum had an adrenalized passion for Shakespeare's various chronicles of human foibles, having

studied literature at Bristol University. One of Shakespeare's most frequently quoted passages reads: "All the world's a stage, and all the men
and women merely players. They have their exits and their entrances;
and one man in his time plays many parts." Before succumbing to mor-
tality, Odlum played many intriguing parts (sometimes gallingly) almost
according to Shakespeare's playbook.

In 1972, he founded the St Lucia Action Movement (SLAM), before
joining the Saint Lucia Labour Party (SLP) and subsequently forming
his own Progressive Labour Party (PLP). Together with Sir John Compton, he flirted with the idea of a "national unity" government, which
eventually unravelled after much internal squabble and rancour. At various points in his political career, he served as Deputy Prime Minister,
Minister of Foreign Affairs and Ambassador to the United Nations. For
years, he enlightened and entertained Saint Lucians through his newspaper, the Crusader, relentlessly advocating the rights of the working
class and the poor.

In many ways, he invoked and personified the lines of Shakespearean
drama he so frequently quoted in his various written and oral produc-
tions. Admittedly, there are times I reflect on the contributions of
George Odlum and think of how much I miss the intersection of literature and politics. Who can forget the scathing admonishments so pow-
erfully laced in his incisive eulogy at Tim Hector's funeral in 2002. The
ever mournful-looking Odlum declared: "But many of you stood by
over the years and witnessed the victimization and demoralization of
Tim Hector and never lifted a finger to prevent it. Were you THERE?
Were you there when they crucified Tim Hector? Were you there? Were
you there when they nailed him to the cross? Were you there? Were you
there when they dragged him through the courts? Were you there? Were
you there when they dumped him in the prison for his views? "Were
you there? Were you there when they burnt his printing press? Were you
there? Were you there when they murdered his dear wife Arah? Were
you there? Were you there when the ballot process was contaminated to
declare him a loser? Were you there? Were you there when they denied
this prophet any honor in his own country? Were you there?"

As an orator, George Odlum understood that in order to communicate work and value as well as command attention, he needed to make
effective use of language and deliver with conviction in order to arouse
interest and inspire the masses. He also understood that the kind of

rhetoric used to campaign for political office had to be different from the one applied in debate presentations in parliament.

I suppose it's easy to be nostalgic for a period when towering intellectual figures trod the public stage in Saint Lucia. To be sure, there has been a noticeable decline in the quality of intellectual life in this country, from the post-independence days of George Odlum, Hunter J. Francois, Sir Vincent Floissac and others who constituted the circle of the intellectual class. It's just unfortunate that these national heroes who have journeyed to the great beyond didn't leave us any autobiographies describing their professional narratives and personal life trajectories.

The UK Guardian's 2003 eulogy of Odlum was further testimony of the man's outsized personality and recognition on the world stage: "George Odlum, who has died aged 69 of cancer, was a key figure in the Anglo-Caribbean "new left" movement that rattled the Reagan administration and led to the 1983 US invasion of Grenada. He also did more than anyone to arouse the people of his native St Lucia from the colonial torpor weighing on the island when Britain thrust independence on it in 1979. But his taste for squabbling with allies, coupled with the fear he inspired in local elites and in Washington, ensured that when he did gain office, he remained forever second fiddle to politicians whose more parochial vision he could rarely stomach", the Guardian wrote. His obituary in The Times described him as a man "with more flamboyance than substance".

Be that as it may, we can still argue whether Odlum would have made a good prime minister or whether there was indeed method in his occasional political madness? The idea that "All the world's a stage", particularly given his own nation's fixation on parochial matters, must have been occasionally depressing to Shakespeare's local hero. As to whether he was a man more sinned against than sinning, this I'll leave to political historians to adjudicate "sentence".

52. Are the Nation's Youth a Ticking Time Bomb?

Mince no words; a scenario in the year 2016 where more than 40 percent of a nation's young people are unemployed is indeed a national crisis. A lost generation is taking shape in Saint Lucia, and this is threatening our long-term social and cultural survival. How ever you look at it, our country seems to be losing itself in a hellish labyrinth of social depravity, youth recalcitrance economic inequality.

Everywhere from family life to national institutions, complete double standards prevail. Our contemporary culture sexualizes women, and public morality is at an all-time low. The political arena is as dusty as the old Roman Coliseums. Civic instincts and our sense of proportion have long since dissipated resulting in a shrinking process that has begun at the very heart of society. Alas, some of these wounds are self-inflicted; in important ways a reflection of a deep-rooted cavalier attitude and parochial mentality. A process of social estrangement has set in, and no one knows where it will lead.

It was several centuries ago that the Greek Philosopher Socrates wrote about the excesses and proclivities of the youth: "The children now love luxury. They have bad manners, contempt for authority; they show disrespect for elders and love chatter in place of exercise."

Several studies recently have indeed suggested today's youth may be worse than preceding generations. Whereas previous generations misbehaved as a rebellion against authorities, part of today's youth are so caught up in their own self-centeredness and consumerism that no authorities exist in their minds. The modalities of anger management, non-violent communication and good manners appear to be foreign to most. Not only are they uninterested in good conversation, they also don't listen and refuse to take an interest in anyone else. They crave for more and more in life and do not care about the damage caused to themselves and society at large or the loss of opportunity they might have to sustain.

The present scourge of gang crime is a pressing issue that must be tackled forthwith. Not only does it speak to the matter of bad parentage, but it also exposes the leadership vacuum and warped priorities on the part of the political and religious establishments. Presently, society seems to be sending so many mixed signals that young people get confused as to which model of morality to imitate. When young people cannot find an inspirational force to rally around, they will obviously turn to other dazzling things in the society that appeal to them. In the search for social belonging, gang membership – often a manifestation of their grief – becomes an attractive option.

The national outrage over crime is papered over with hysterical debates about matters of little consequence. A national security thrust espousing zero-tolerance for crime must be at the vanguard of the mission to stem the rising tide of crime. With immediate effect, the issue of gun violence must return to the top of our social and political agenda.

It is sad that our beautiful Saint Lucia has now been transformed into a new battlefield where ruthless criminals have embarked on a diabolic quest to paralyse the country. I am appalled at the chaotic nature of the approach to what is glibly referred to as gang violence. We need to better understand what is really happening on our streets, otherwise we as a society stand in danger of losing yet another generation as they plunge through violence and criminality to hopelessness and despair. Action on strengthening families, tackling educational failure, reforming welfare, ending drug and alcohol addiction is foundational to mending our broken society. Moreover, structural reforms in both the police force as well as the justice system are critically necessary in order to restore the rule of law and expedite justice.

Any action to address the rising tide of gang violence must be guided by the fact that gangs are the product of social breakdown, and are found in the most deprived and marginalised communities burdened by high family breakdown, addiction and unemployment.

The strengthening of social organizations has never been more critical especially since it can help foster social belonging and structure social life. Gone are the days when vibrant clubs and effective institutions conducted meaningful social projects and engaged the youth and the wider society. The corollary is that countries with greater organizational and institutional strength remain stable in times of social change, and do better over time.

The pervasive exposure to digital technology is rapidly transforming society as a whole. The new generation is developing unhealthy habits through the constant digital bombardment and the widespread use of smart-phones and tablets. Not only does gadget addiction destroy relationships, but they also turn us into digital slaves and robots. Social media seems to be destroying effective personal communication and good social manners, and may have already usurped the authority of parents.

Alarmingly, a strange foreboding is creeping up on us; a dawning that the familiar cultural and social routines of small-island life have been transmogrified into emblematic ugliness.

At any rate, our nation's redemption and energy lie in the talent, ideas and creativity of our young people. When people have enough room to develop themselves and are given responsibility, they are able to reach their full potential. This releases all kinds of mental energy and motivation, which ensures that people are at their best. The future of this country depends on how well we take care of our kids and youth today.

53. Beach Access – Drawing the Line in the Sand

"A simple life is good with me," exhorted Yanni, a Greek composer and music producer. "I don't need a whole lot. For me, a T-shirt, a pair of shorts, barefoot on a beach and I'm happy."

Most if not all Saint Lucians will find merit in the aforesaid sentiments, if only because the oceanfront offers them a vacation from everyday life and provides a psychological fortress against the vicissitudes of politics and urbanization. Indeed, for most of us, beach visitation has become a way of life since childhood, at anchor through our social experiences and recreational customs. Moreover, a public beach can be a sanctuary for the family and community during hot summer months, and provide harborage from the hustle and bustle of the work day. Yet, if beaches are so central to the people's identity and inner spirituality, and access to the sand is guaranteed in our constitution; why is it that many hotel developers (some with felonious intent) are laying out unwelcome mats to local beachgoers and ostensibly employing all sorts of tactics to make our people feel like trespassers?

Just a few days before Christmas in 2014, I found myself a victim of one of the most egregious examples of privatization (whether lawful or otherwise) of public space in this country. In the true spirit of the holidays, I decided to visit my ancestral hometown Soufriere, a place redolent of age and romance, to take in some of the beautiful scenery and enjoy the charcoal-grey expanse of sand and pebbles along the town's shores. Upbeat and full of festive energy, I took a water taxi and first ventured out to Anse Chastanet and then to Jalousie Bay, a sacred place right between the nation's battered breasts. As I approached Jalousie Bay, I became prostrated with grief as I realised that all beach access points had been blocked and the hotel had extended its reach and occupied a remote beach corner; the only remaining vestige of public recreational space and comfort.

Not wanting to stir a hornet's nest, we turned back and sought recreation elsewhere. All the while, with my tail between my legs, I was thinking, "stolen heritage" and "birthright violation"; all in the name of touristic development. Please understand dear reader that this isn't any abstract economic or social issue to me. This is deeply personal and I am still licking wounds from cultural humiliation and defeatism, and I'm furious. Alas, I can imagine the hundreds of Saint Lucians who are afflicted and affected by this social injustice on a daily basis. So I ask my fellow compatriots: Why do we tolerate hotel developers who erode the character of our public beaches and deny us the right to access those beaches? This is a clarion call beseeching all Saint Lucians to demonstrate importunateness and rise to protect their rights to beach access through protest, civil litigation and legislation. Today it's Jalousie Beach and Pigeon Point, tomorrow it might just be the Anse Chastanet and Malgretoute beaches in Soufriere; and there are ominous signs to indicate that they may soon be inaccessible to the public as well.

Let's take a leaf out of the book of Californian beachgoers who have resisted all efforts by multi-millionaires and property developers to block access to public beaches. Each of us has a responsibility and obligation to preserve and protect our scarce natural resources and pay homage to our heritage. There are simply no socio-economic arguments to justify the expropriation of our natural resources and the vandalism of our cultural patrimony and heritage. One vestige of human uniqueness still often cited by anthropologists is culture. Culture is central to the way we view, experience, and engage with all aspects of our lives and physical resources. The biggest determinant in our lives is culture; where we are born and what the environment looks like. But it appears like we are allowing our cultural underpinnings to sink deeper into naval-gazing irrelevance.

In Saint Lucia, beach visitation and has been a customary practice and has been part of our traditional and historical way of life. Not only is it a lifestyle for many, it's also a means of livelihood for hundreds of hardworking Saint Lucians. Hotel construction and tourism development must never interfere with the customs, practices and modus vivendi of a people. We need to balance tourism development with cultural protection.

The Surfrider Foundation, an international non-profit environmental organization dedicated to the protection and enhancement of the world's waves and beaches through conservation and activism espouses the following beach access policy: "The public should be afforded full and fair access to beaches, which are public trust resources, by minimizing the possibility of impediment; including development, subdivision or land use zoning change; or deterring obstacles, including gates, fences, hired security, misleading signage, rock walls, shrubbery or other blockades, being placed upon public rights of way to beach access."

Against a backdrop of deep distrust and cynicism in affairs of hotel development, I do have a lot of sympathy for the residents of Trouya who are raising objection to a proposal to change the land use of properties in their community from single family residential to multi-family villas and a hotel with spa and restaurant. Judging from the way things have turned out in past in Fair Helen, who is to say that agreements won't be violated and beach access blocked. Saint Lucians should be on their guard since it appears that hotel developers systematically trespass on our kindness and hospitality; give them an inch it appears and they'll take the whole backyard.

Critically, the issue of beachfront development is one that must be looked into expeditiously otherwise we will gradually lose ownership of and access to our beaches. Why are hotels constructed so close to the beach front? Shouldn't construction plans have considered public access paths and pedestrian zones? It doesn't seem like hotel developers give a damn about the cultural sensibilities and the needs of local beachgoers when they sit to devise their grand plans. Then again, how are hoteliers and developers expected to account for their actions when in the past very few "real" objections have been raised in public. Saint Lucians should have protested vehemently against the pillars erected at Pigeon Point until the issue was addressed satisfactoriy.

At any rate, I was delighted to read a trenchant piece by Earl Huntley entitled, "Saving our beaches – Not too late for the Caribbean". Writing with a ponderous gravity, Mr Huntley opined:

"If other Caribbean governments want to think that it is too late to save our beaches, then we in Saint Lucia must differ. I am of the view that there should be legislation debarring further hotel development directly next to our beaches. Copacabana shows that its is possible to have a thriving tourism industry with hotels that are not sitting almost on a beach, that are adjacent but sufficiently away from it to allow the beach to remain the accessible patrimony of the people. It is not too late to save our Caribbean beaches from the lure of the tourist dollar at any cost. I am telling this story now to show my total support for the residents of Trouya, Bois D'Orange, Gros Islet who are trying to save the small and quietly beautiful Trouya Beach from a tourism development project that will change it forever and at best condemn us to using a track to get there and at worst, debar us from it all together."

Mindful of the fact that preserving public access to beaches is a constant struggle that requires continued defense and maintenance, Mr Huntley quipped: "I support them whole heartedly and I am prepared to march, demonstrate and picket with them if necessary, not simply because as a former resident of Bois D' Orange my family and I used that beach and still do, but because there is something more valuable to us than acquiring the tourist dollar- it is to preserve our patrimony, our heritage- the gifts of nature that the Almighty bestowed upon us for our pleasure and recreation and for reminding us that he exists and is the creator. Yes we can make use of them for our economic development but not to the point of selling them to foreigners, so much so that we can no longer have access to them and our descendants know that they are there but cannot even see them."

I salute the honourable gentleman in stating his case so vociferously and incisively. I agree with everything he said and consider his contribution to be a veritable reference in the crucial debate on beach access. I still believe that we can undo the damage already done and return Saint Lucia's beautiful beaches to its people. I am growing tired of witnessing security guards shooing away Saint Lucians. Tourism cannot be allowed to be such a menace to cultural heritage.

Meanwhile, Saint Lucians must show more respect and appreciation for the environment by declaring an all-out war on littering, illegal dumping and sand mining. More public education programmes are required to help curb visitor harassment. While we are a little late in coming to grips with many critical national issues, hopefully we are not too late on the issue of beach access.

54. Fighting Climate Change in Our Own Backyard

I have very little reason to doubt global warming is the major contributory factor in the changing weather patterns that threaten the planet's bio-diversity, food security, water systems and economic growth. After all, the literature on climate change overwhelmingly supports the hypothesis that the climate system is warming and that humans are the main causal agents. As far as Small Island Developing States (SIDS) are concerned, current and future climate risks threaten both their ecological balance and prospects of sustainable development on multiple fronts, hence necessitating urgent action by the US, the European Union, China and India, the world's worst polluters. Some are hoping that a legally binding and universal accord will be hammered out when the world converges on Paris this year from November 30 to December 11 to address climate change issues (a framework agreement was in fact signed, however, adherence and implementation will be a different ballgame).

I, for one, believe that no major breakthrough should be expected on account that many countries believe any big push on their part to fight climate change will negatively impact their economies and cost jobs, especially at a time when growth prospects are low, unemployment high and inequality rising.

Nonetheless, I am pleased that Saint Lucia is at the forefront of the regional effort to focus attention on the impact of climate change through the many consultations and partnerships with various regional and international entities including the Clinton Climate Initiative. I also welcome the fact that key stakeholders in Saint Lucia have been discussing climate change mitigation and adaptation measures even as the Inter-American Development Bank (IDB) is facilitating through a US$ 10.39-million grant the enhancement of the adaptive capacity of vulnerable states across the region with support from the Climate Investment Funds (CIF) Pilot Program on Climate Resilience (PPCR).

Yet amidst all the heated debate about environmental responsibility and commitment, the contribution of SIDS to present global warming is negligible (combined SIDS annual carbon dioxide output is less than 1% of global emissions) – an ecological threat certainly not of their own making, but which will disproportionately impact their livelihoods and economies.

As with most people, my panic about climate change is equalled only by my confusion over what small islands like Saint Lucia ought to do about it. The industrialized nations that can really do much to tackle this escalating threat have been dragging their feet for more than a decade. The Kyoto Protocol, the UN's first major initiative to combat greenhouse gas emissions, has largely failed due to US recalcitrance and ill-advised exemptions to developing and emerging economies. It is reported that last year, only two dozen of the about 200 countries cut their carbon emissions, led by mostly European countries.

As I said before, I do believe the climate change initiatives and measures Saint Lucia is taking are commendable. However, there is still a lingering feeling that not enough is being done to protect and manage our own immediate natural environment by way of regulations, laws and sensitization programmes. As small island nations, our relationship with ecological sustainability is about more than the impact of climate change. Of equal importance is the relentless thrust towards environmental conservation and protection, especially as it relates to flood mitigation. Drainage systems blocked by plastic bags and other packaging waste have been identified as a major cause of flooding in many Caribbean islands. The clogging of drains and waterways through the indiscriminate disposal of plastic was the primary cause for the 2005 floods in Mumbai which killed thousands of people. Hence, unless Saint Lucians change their habits and show more respect for their natural surroundings, I see an environmental disaster heading our way.

It's so heartbreaking to see our beautiful surroundings indiscriminately littered with empty cans, plastic bags and other packaging waste. The unsightly mess after an entertainment event is a must see for anyone who wants to have a bad conscience for the right reason. The enormous amount of fast-food wrappers and miscellaneous garbage sprinkled carelessly on the shoulder of certain highways and byways is a national disgrace. It is not unusual to see a driver roll down his window and jettison garbage missiles onto the street or highway, then fearlessly drive off without any display of penitence. Alas, all this trash eventually ends up in rivers and streams – all the way to our oceans. Just where is our pride in this country? When will the revolution in our thinking begin? Our citizens need to look inward and demonstrate more personal responsibility, especially when we're talking about social responsibility, eco-tourism and sustainable development. How can we reasonably promote eco-tourism in this country given the pathetic environmental mindset of our people?

Let us begin to alert people to the dangers of the plastic in our daily lives and how it chokes our oceans and trashes our beaches. Such an educational thrust should reveal to our people how plastic particles can enter into the food chain and return to us through our dinner plates. We have to realize that litter on our streets, beaches and in the ocean isn't just ugly and nasty, it impacts everything. It can make the ocean more vulnerable to impact from climate change, coastal development and over-fishing. The research clearly shows that it impacts local economies, seafood industries and recreation, and reduces our access to beaches. Moreover, without corals many types of fish would not exist, because reefs protect fish as they mature.

At an event in the south not too long ago, it was rather unfortunate to observe not a single garbage bin had been provided for the disposal of waste, especially given the great number of children who were present at the event. What message are we sending to our young people? Should someone else have to clean up later? This is where I believe we have to nurture our people today into developing healthy habits that later form their personal and national characters. I strongly believe that the promoters and organizers of major events such as music festivals, football matches, etc., should be required by law to ensure that litter control measures are in place at the venue and in the surrounding vicinity before, during and after the event. Likewise, local authorities are responsible for keeping public places that are under their control, including public roads, clear of litter as far as is practically possible. This should include arranging cleansing programmes as often as possible, as well as providing and emptying litter bins regularly.

At any rate, the real challenge is to combat an economic model that thrives on wasteful products and packaging, and leaves the associated problem of clean-up costs. Critically, our island needs to introduce a levy system on plastic carry bags so as to encourage more people to buy durable bags for reuse when doing shopping. Let's follow the lead of other countries and introduce legislation restricting the sale of plastic bags, in a bid to reduce littering and pollution. I believe the time has come to let customers pay for their own plastic grocery bags at the nation's supermarkets. There is also the need for a national conversation on the recycling possibilities for plastic and glass bottles.

Changing the habits and attitudes of a population is a huge undertaking which will require the use of a number of educational and legislative measures to both discourage certain practices and sensitize the population of the hazards of pollution. The ongoing challenge will entail inculcating proper social habits in our children and educating consumers about their role in recycling plastics and developing new ideas for environmental conservation. This effort would also bring comprehensive programmes to the schools in which charismatic speakers would teach children about ownership and caretaking in their communities, for instance, taking an empty bag with them to the beach or park, and to ensure they take their rubbish home with them.

The establishment of a new environmental protection agency which allows people to lodge an offence using vehicle details and the time and place of the incident would be a very sensible thing. Such an agency would have the power to impose severe fines for improperly disposing of plastic waste as well as larger litter like furniture and appliances.

As I have endeavoured to explain, the debate on the impact of climate change certainly has its place in our national discourse, but conventional wisdom still maintains that charity should begin at home where awareness of our own environmental habits and proclivities must be raised. The goal is to transform environmental care into a learning experience not only for our children, but critically also for young and older adults. Littering is all about personal pride, and it is learned behaviour. Every one of us can make a difference by keeping our ecologically vulnerable island clean and litter-free.

CHAPTER 7 –
U.S. HISTORIC ELECTIONS
2016

55. The Verbal Lynching of America's First Black President

It didn't take long for the past to catch up with America and shatter the dream Dr. Martin Luther King spoke about 51 years ago. Today, the real tragedy of America's first African-American president entails the disrespectful and disparaging manner in which he has been treated by the political establishment in Washington.

Not surprisingly, the rise of the radical Tea Party and the re-emergence of Republican hard-line ideology have both coincided with the current wave of Obama-bashing around the country. Nowhere in the world or indeed in American history, has a president been constantly belittled and openly subjected to malicious insults, trash talk and derision like in America. Oprah Winfrey has advanced the view that President Obama is treated differently because he is black.

Be that as it may, America's 44th president has been portrayed as an "Islamic atheist Marxist Kenyan", and repeatedly branded a "liar", "traitor", "terrorist", "coward" and "anti-Semite" by top Republican congressmen, presidential candidates and mainstream pundits.

Everything, from his birth certificate to his intelligence and patriotism to country has been called into question. He's been ordered around by prominent sections of the mainstream media and greeted with a finger in his face by an Arizona governor in front of television reporters. Newt Gingrich, the former House Speaker, has said that Obama's policies are "a very serious threat to our way of life." From the onset of his presidency, he faced scorched-earth Republican opposition from Senate Minority Leader Mitch McConnell, who ominously announced that "Our top priority over the next two years should be to deny President Obama a second term."

Indeed, no one can find another example in American history where a U.S. president requested a date to address Congress and was refused. This was the first denial in the annals of American political history – unsurprisingly directed at the first African-American president.

If any word characterizes the current Congress, it's "obstruction".

Under a Republican Congress, truth has metastasized into lurid fantasy, and ignorance and stupidity have been held up as badges of honour. Could it really be that Republicans are incensed by a black man with a liberal agenda in the White House?

During the Baltimore riots in April 2015, Donald Trump tweeted: "Our great African-American president hasn't exactly had a positive impact on the thugs who are so happily and openly destroying Baltimore!" He also urged Obama to leave office early and play golf on one of his (Trump's) many courses. Alarmingly, there seems to be no end to the insults hurled at President Obama.

It also appears that the racial division and distrust between blacks and whites in America are more pronounced than ever. The actor Morgan Freeman has said recently that America's president may be black, but its laws are all white. To be sure, the presidency of Barack Obama appears to have once again exposed the ugly underbelly of American society.

When President Obama took office in 2008, the American economy was in a tailspin. The U.S. financial system was in a mess and the economy was hemorrhaging 800,000 jobs a month. George W. Bush's high-handed approach to foreign policy, as opposed to Obama's collaborative and common-ground approach, had contributed to the straining of relations with key international allies and in some instances, the isolation of the U.S. in some parts of the world.

Today, the U.S. economy has made a remarkable recovery against some pretty tough odds – notwithstanding Jeb Bush's implausible claim that the economy has actually gotten worse on Obama's watch. Most economists believe that the massive stimulus package introduced by the Obama administration, helped end the Great Recession. There is also much consensus around the idea that Republicans would have brought on another Great Depression if they had been allowed to implement their plan to cut federal government spending.

It has been amazing to watch how Obama's achievements in healthcare, foreign policy, energy policy, financial reform and economic management have consistently been undermined by a Republican party increasingly seen as representing the white elite – and which is hell-bent on stirring racial division and social unrest in the country.

Yet despite his ground-breaking efforts at health and social reform to assist the bottom third of American society, the vitriolic hounding has continued unabated. According to a major newspaper in America, the most radical opponents of Obama view his speeches and proposed legislation as "nothing more than a black man's attempt to exact revenge against the country's white majority."

In 2013, the conservatives within the Republican party attempted to paralyze the government and risk a federal default so they could block

Obamacare, the president's health care reforms – never mind that the reforms were endorsed by American voters, approved by a majority of both houses of Congress and upheld by the Supreme Court. In September 2009, during a State-of-the-Union address to a joint session of Congress, South Carolina Congressman Joe Wilson shouted at the top of his voice that President Obama was a "liar", as the president declared that illegal immigrants would not be covered under a health insurance reform programme proposed by the Democrats. Another Republican lawmaker last year publicly referred to the size of Michelle Obama's behind.

Critically, Obamacare was introduced to increase the quality and affordability of health insurance coverage to millions of low-income Americans, and to reduce the costs of healthcare for the government. A respected Harvard economist believes the reforms represent "The most favourable and significant regulatory overhaul of the U.S. healthcare system since Medicare and Medicaid in 1965."

Alas, the throwing of jibes at the president whether intentionally or not, has not only been confined to the American public. Upon Obama's election in November 2008, Italy's gaffe-prone and polarizing then-Prime Minister Silvio Berlusconi described him as "young, handsome and suntanned." Mr Berlusconi would later rehash the jibe on his return from the G20 summit in 2009: "Ah, Barack Obama. You won't believe it, but the two of them sunbathed together, because the wife is also tanned." Further, in a statement last year carried by the official Korean Central News Agency, a spokesman for Kim Jong-un, North Korea's reclusive leader, referred to Obama as "a monkey in a tropical forest."

Yet, a more obvious act of disrespect is hard to imagine than the occasion when Benjamin Netanyahu, Israel's recalcitrant Prime Minister bypassed the normal diplomatic protocol and accepted a Republican invitation to address Congress. Many believe this was the worst insult in living memory to a sitting American president by a foreign leader.

At the second Republican presidential debate, President Obama was viciously attacked on all fronts, and unfairly labelled "an apprentice" and "naïve". One particular presidential hopeful even bigotedly spoke of "Obama's America", as if to imply that Obama has inflamed racial tensions and divided the country. Nothing could be further from the truth.

Among the many economic pundits who were amused at the cheap rhetorical jibes thrown at President Obama at the second debate was Nobel Prize-winning economist Paul Krugman: "If the discussion of economics was alarming, the discussion of foreign policy was practically demented. Almost all the candidates seem to believe that American military strength can shock-and-awe other countries into doing what we want without any need for negotiations, and that we shouldn't even talk with foreign leaders we don't like. No dinners for Xi Jinping! And, of course, no deal with Iran, because resorting to force in Iraq went so well." Have the Republicans really pushed their once proud party (the Party of Lincoln and Reagan as they love to say) into kamikaze course?

In short, the utter disrespect levelled at President Obama, not simply from disgruntled citizens, but from people of sections of society from which respect for the Office of the President is expected, has been unprecedented. How much longer can African-Americans tolerate the insults hurled at their leaders? Bob Marley asked: "How long shall they kill our prophets while we stand aside and look?" Obama's salutary efforts, including his fight to establish a higher minimum wage, were always going to be frustrated by institutions which have been fine-tuned for many decades to work against the interests of minorities, especially blacks.

Yet despite the bigotry, intellectual buffoonery and entrenched discrimination which President Obama has faced, he has still emerged as one of the most consequential and successful presidents in American history. His leadership has been surprisingly consistent and methodical. In more ways than one, he stands for a better America, in contrast to many of his predecessors, including George W. Bush, who tried to impose their terms on the world. It is my view that economists, historians and political scientists will appreciate the scale of his successes over the long run and history will be very kind to him.

56. Have U.S. Race Relations Taken a Nosedive?

When Barack Obama assumed office in January 2009, he unequivocally announced to America and the rest of the world that he was "not the president of black America" but rather "the president of the United States of America." Predictably, African-Americans and other ethnic minorities were palpably excited that the United States had finally begun to heal its divisions over race and atone for its past disgraceful misdeeds by electing its first black president.

At any rate, the racial barrier had supposedly been broken and the historic election was celebrated and heralded by the rest of the world as the dawning of a "post-racial" era.

Now seven years later and nearing the end of his second term, Obama has traversed a tough road and the general feeling is that despite his fairly good performance in office, his presidency has not had much effect on race relations in the United States – a circumstance which a popular German newspaper has described as "the tragedy of America's first black president."

But seriously, did we really expect Obama to fix America's age-old race problem? No one expected that America's turbulent history with race would altogether stop with the momentous election of a black president. If anything, discrimination and racial profiling still remain deeply and systemically ingrained in U.S. society – a fact oftentimes revealed in official data.

In the mainstream media, racism may not always be so blatant, but it remains latent. Much to our dismay, presidential candidates continue to hold twisted notions on immigration, ethnic minorities and political history – and debates quickly devolve into a horror show of absurdities and infelicities as candidates unapologetically display disquieting prejudices and make racial appeals to mostly conservative white voters. In recent times, the nation's once proud democracy has been reduced to a noisy race to the bottom by divisive demagogues like Donald Trump and Ted Cruz.

Yet despite the ushering in of a new political era through the historic election of an African-American president, the U.S. has maintained a plethora of racialized policies over the course of its history. Deep racial schisms are evident in responses about law enforcement and the criminal justice system. Above all, the events of the past three years, including the slaying of an 18-year-old African-American man in Ferguson, Missouri and the execution of nine people in an African-American church in Charleston, South Carolina by a white Nazi adorned with the Confederate flag, have soured judgements about the current state of race relations. Of further disquiet is the fact that America still has little regard for African-American protesters who march for justice and who demand overhauls in policing through the "Black Lives Matter" movement around the country.

Some of us will recall in 2013 that the Supreme Court declared blatant racism a thing of the past and ruled that the Voting Rights Act of

1965, aimed at combating the disenfranchisement of African-Americans, was no longer valid. Needless to say, daily experience tells a different story.

But why should African-Americans still be complaining today about overt and persistent racism more than fifty years after Martin Luther King Jr. fought for equality and the end of segregation? Why does Baltimore – the city where the black teenager Michael Brown was killed, and whose population of 21,000 is two-thirds African-American – have a police force that is 95 percent white? Has the system failed African-Americans or should they themselves be held responsible for their own state of poverty and disillusionment?

A flurry of new scholarly studies have warned that as America grows richer, a large pool of African-American men are becoming ever more disconnected from mainstream society – mired in a vicious cycle of underachievement and social immobility. According to a New York Times/CBS News poll conducted recently, "nearly six in 10 Americans, including heavy majorities of both whites and blacks, think race relations are generally bad, and that nearly four in 10 think the situation is getting worse."

The irreducible truth is that the United States is still grappling with the problem of racism and with discrimination. Although the situation today is nowhere as bad as it was during the bloody 1950s and 1960s, the recent killings of young black men by white police officers and the inexorable rise in islamophobia have reignited the debate about race relations in the U.S.

Meanwhile, the rise of far-right candidates and parties in Europe and America (the Tea Party, for instance) attest to the general fear of ethnic minorities and refugees – and attitudes toward non-Christians are also perilously shifting. For many, the Paris attacks as well as the violence and chaos that erupted in Cologne on New Year's Eve (2016) may have finally brought to light what they have always been saying: that too many foreigners in the country bring too many cultural and social problems along with them. I'm afraid those events have the potential to easily trigger a radical shift in refugee and immigration policy in America, but especially in Europe.

Much to their discredit, two major 2016 Republican candidates, Jeb Bush and Ted Cruz, are advocating for the U.S. to officially discriminate based on religion, claiming implausibly that only Christians should be allowed to enter the country as refugees. Ted Cruz has even announced that he would introduce legislation to ban Muslim Syrian refugees from entering the country, following further incendiary remarks by former Governor Chris Christie that not even "3-year-old orphan" refugees should be allowed to enter the country. What is more, only recently a Muslim woman wearing a hijab was ejected from a Donald Trump campaign rally – an ill-fated action that plays further into the hands of the nationalists. Trump, the iconoclastic frontrunner, had previously called for a temporary ban on Muslims entering the U.S.

Sadly, all of this points to a desecration of American democracy and a new dangerous national mood that could trigger social unrest across ethnic, religious and other cleavages in a country that has depended and prospered on immigration. It's about time America genuinely embarks on a journey of soul-searching and contemplate what it truly means to be a "great nation". As Germany has shown, every nation has dark spots in its past, but the greatness of a country is reflected in how it deals with this past and the steps it takes to reflect and critically examine it. I believe even in modern America, it will be some time before racism truly becomes a thing of the past. Hence, in this respect, the United States is not the great nation it believes itself to be.

57. From Black Hero to Tea Party Republican

Dr. Ben Carson, the 64-year-old retired neurosurgeon who is vying for President of the United States, couldn't be more different from the suave and thoughtful Barack Obama, whom he has labelled a "liar" and "psychopath". Until now, nothing I've seen or heard suggests that the good doctor has what it takes to be commander-in- chief of a superpower.

Although people do sometimes rise to the occasion when circumstances require them to, Dr. Carson has so far been unable to convince me that he has the political intelligence and fortitude to be the world's most powerful political and economic leader – and this, despite the fact that he is presently leading the GOP field according to recent polls, although the presidential campaign still has a long way to go.

What do you make of a presidential candidate who doesn't seem to have thought through his economic and foreign policy positions and more often than usual resorts to scaremongering? Funny enough, the two candidates least qualified to lead the nation are those leading in the polls at the moment. Not only has the gaffe-prone Dr. Carson failed to provide any relevant detail of his future policies, he also seems to show very little interest particularly in broader economic matters, as his embarrassing lack of knowledge about the economy begins to manifest. Of late, his mistaken philosophy and off-script musings have begun to raise eyebrows.

If you're going to run for such high office, you'd better be sure that you're surrounded by smart people who are able to identify and analyze all the relevant issues, whether immigration, national security, taxes or foreign policy – and put together a viable plan that you as a candidate can explain to the public with little effort. I suppose the question now is, why hasn't Dr. Carson immersed himself in the economic issues the American public cares most about including employment growth, support for the middle class, the cost of education and income inequality (among other things)?

I recently read an interview conducted by Kai Rysdal of Marketplace, a business programme, which revealed the specious reasoning behind Dr. Carson's economic fantasies. When asked whether Congress and the President should raise the debt limit or default on the national debt, he equivocated: "Let me put it this way. If I were the president, I would not sign an increased budget. Absolutely would not do it. They would have to find a place to cut."

Realizing that the good doctor had misconstrued debt limit for budget, the interviewer again clarified the question with the comment: "To be clear, it's increasing the debt limit, not the budget, but I want to make sure I understand you. You'd let the United States default rather than raise the debt limit."

To which Dr. Carson replied: "No, I would provide the kind of leadership that says, 'Get on the stick guys, and stop messing around, and cut where you need to cut, because we're not raising any spending limits, period'... What I'm saying is what we have to do is restructure the way that we create debt."

Now if this sounds like Greek to you, it probably is – which of course reminds me of our own local political hopefuls who believe that we're all gutless fools to be dazzled by minimalist, gut-punching gobbledygook.

Now I'm actually quite surprised that Dr. Carson has done so well both in a country where prejudice against blacks is nauseating and in a Republican Party that espouses racist and anti-immigrant policies. Not that I believe Dr. Carson will ever clinch the Republican nomination and become President. After all, there are still many intractable hurdles to be overcome, including winning acceptance from the die-hard conservative voters of the States of the Deep South as well as rural conservative whites. But even if Dr. Carson did win the nomination (only if), the GOP doesn't seem to have a political fairy-godfather like David Axelrod (Obama's former Chief Campaign Strategist) who can package (or repackage) a black candidate to increasingly sceptical white voters.

Recently, Dr. Carson made headlines for comparing abortion to slavery, and women who have abortions to slave-owners. On the American prime-time talk show "Meet the Press", he proclaimed: "During slavery – and I know that's one of those words you're not supposed to say, but I'm saying it – during slavery, a lot of the slave owners thought that they had the right to do whatever they wanted to that slave. Anything that they chose to do. And, you know, what if the abolitionist had said, you know, 'I don't believe in slavery. I think it's wrong. But you guys do whatever you want to do'. Where would we be?"

Indeed, many pundits had trouble comprehending how Dr. Carson could be leading the other candidates in the polls after saying something so outrageous and pointless. David French of the National Review was quite astonished that Dr. Carson had expressed "an entirely mainstream, pro-life view" that "most Republican politicians dare not utter."

In his most recent book "America the Beautiful: Rediscovering What Made This Nation Great", he writes: "Many African-Americans voted for Obama simply because he was a black man and not because they resonated philosophically with his policies."

Doesn't Dr. Carson know that African-Americans have had a deep affinity for the Democratic Party since the 1960s when Lyndon Johnson signed the Civil Rights Act?

It appears that whatever small supply of goodwill the good doctor had among black voters, it has quickly dissipated after comparing the nefarious brutality of slavery with mundanely contested political issues such as abortion and healthcare. For good reason, African-Americans seem to take umbrage at any remarks that use slavery or similar historical wrongs to draw self-serving political analogies.

Yet, the controversy surrounding the thoughtless remarks Dr. Carson continues to make doesn't only expose his lack of discretion, but has also caused his personal judgment and political intelligence to be called into question. According to the BBC, he has compared gun control, political correctness, the U.S. under Barack Obama and the progressive movement in general to Nazi rule.

In an interview with NBC, he declared that Islam was not consistent with the US Constitution: "I would not advocate that we put a Muslim in charge of this nation. I absolutely would not agree with that." Apparently Dr. Carson is not aware that Article VI, paragraph 3 of the United States Constitution guarantees that "No religious Test shall ever be required as a Qualification to any Office or public Trust under the United States."

For Dr. Ben Carson, Donald Trump, or any other Republican politician to suggest that someone of any faith is unfit for political office is out of touch with the realities of American society and democracy. Hence, every citizen of the United States should be concerned that political hopefuls are engaging in and tolerating such blatant acts of religious bigotry.

Through his own words, Dr. Carson has revealed his own personal inability to serve as President of the United States. When he says, "I don't advocate anybody whose values and principles are not consistent with our constitution," he may have been recklessly brandishing his ignorance of the country's constitution and perhaps forgetting the historical racial bigotry of a nation that once turned on its own citizens, particularly the ethnic group of which he is part.

Dr. Carson has accomplished much in the field of medicine and is no doubt a role model to the African-American community and to the country at large. However, a commander-in-chief in today's crisis-ridden world is expected to have a good command of the issues and demonstrate steadfast political intelligence. Anyone can grow up to be President, but not everybody is cut out to be President. As regards past African-American presidential candidates – if, according to Republicans, Barack Obama qualifies as the devil we know, Jesse Jackson as the devil we don't know, then who the devil is Dr. Carson really?

58. Beating About the Bush

Watching the fifth Republican presidential debate on December 15, one would think the current predicament in the Middle East was child's play and the presidential contenders had just about everything figured out. The boisterous rhetoric and banal platitudes about American exceptionalism often conveyed the impression that the Republican Party already had all the answers to the scourges of Islamic fundamentalism, terrorism and illegal immigration – and that a more muscular foreign policy (like the one mistakenly pursued in the Bush Jr. years) would somehow guarantee peace and stability in the world's most volatile and conflict-ridden regions.

As expected, at the end of the night there were indeed more questions than answers. Alas, if some of the policy proposals weren't so alarming, they would be laughable. As usual, the political theatrics were on display and the incumbent president was made a scapegoat for the disasters in both Iraq and Syria. Above all, President Obama was chastised for endangering America's national security, although the country hasn't experienced a single terrorist act since he took office in 2009. Besides, it is owing to President's Obama's consensual and cautious approach (as opposed to the polarizing and belligerent style of George W. Bush) that several conflicts around the world haven't adversely disrupted the global economy and also haven't rendered the United Nations useless and irrelevant.

By any measure, this is easily the worst set of candidates the Republican party has ever fielded in an election primary and it scares me to think (God forbid) that one of them can actually become commander-in-chief of the world's only superpower. But then again, what do you expect of a political party that continually denies the reality of global warming caused by greenhouse gases from fossil fuels? What kind of nation would elevate Donald Trump to a serious frontrunner given the anti-immigrant diatribes and the malicious insults he has hurled at just about everyone – and the buffoonery he continues to demonstrate amid worsening violence in the Middle East? How can a nation of immigrants continue to tolerate candidates who divide the country along ethnic, religious and racial lines? History aside, I didn't think I would live to see America in the 21st century degenerate into such an irresponsible nation espousing religious fascism and diplomatic bigotry.

It would seem that the candidate who made the most sense on the night of the debate was the one who was most inconspicuous – and often treated as a political bantamweight. For what it's worth, I thought Rand Paul was the only candidate who understood the serious consequences of regime change and American military interventionism in the Middle East. On foreign policy and mass surveillance, he remains the best candidate by far.

It's true he didn't win the debate, but he certainly raised the most important questions of the night. When asked about his ideas to keep

America free from terrorism, he explained: "I think that if you believe in regime change, you're mistaken. In 2013, we put 600 tons of weapons – us, Saudi Arabia, and Qatar – into the war against Assad. By pushing Assad back, we did create a safe space. There are still people – the majority on the stage, they want to topple Assad. And then there will be chaos, and I think ISIS will then be in charge of Syria… When we toppled Gadhafi in Libya, I think that was a mistake. I think ISIS grew stronger, we had a failed state, and we were more at risk."

Ever the avid advocate of realpolitik, I have always thought keeping dictators in place for the sake of stability is a policy worth considering strategically. Often these dictators are the ones who keep various religious factions from descending into full-scale civil war. Soon after the regimes of Saddam Hussein in Iraq, Muammar Gaddafi in Libya and Hosni Mubarak in Egypt fell, those countries descended into chaos and confusion – destabilizing the entire region.

Thankfully, Rand Paul's was a rational voice in an otherwise polemical wilderness of delusion and sophistry. "Regime change hasn't won. Toppling secular dictators in the Middle East has only led to chaos and the rise of radical Islam. I think if we want to defeat terrorism; I think if we truly are sincere about defeating terrorism, we need to quit arming the allies of ISIS. If we want to defeat terrorism, the boots on the ground – the boots on the ground need to be Arab boots on the ground," the Kentucky senator asserted.

Meanwhile, the presidency of George W. Bush seemed to have attained a new status of nobility, and his policies are being acclaimed by some candidates as the new gold standard. This is the same George W. Bush who left office with a 28% job approval rating. It's difficult to find any president who did more economic damage and left the country in worse diplomatic shape than George W. Bush.

Yet, Senator Lindsay Graham – already trailing badly in the polls – believes that the George W. Bush era was the best thing that happened to American foreign policy. "I blame President Obama for ISIL. I'm tired of beating on Bush. I miss George W. Bush," he fumed. "I wish he were president now. We wouldn't be in this mess. I'm tired of dictators walking all over us. I'm tired of siding with the Iranians and the Russians."

Of course, such implausible claims elicit derision. If dictators are walking all over America now, it's because America's policy of conveniently supporting and deposing dictators has somehow backfired. Apropos Iran, I was under the distinct impression that given the alternatives (military strikes and partly effective sanctions) the nuclear deal between Iran and the P5+1 nations, which got global support, was the best option available at this time in blocking Iran from acquiring nuclear weapons.

Furthermore, the idea that America should not talk to countries it deems "enemies" or "recalcitrant" is deeply flawed. I think it is profoundly irresponsible to label Russia an "enemy", despite Putin's inflated ego and revisionist approach to history. This just goes to show the dangerous lack of diplomatic sophistication and political ignorance in the Republican camp.

How on earth can you refuse to talk to China and Russia – both of them members of the United Nations Security Council? Could you believe the loose rhetoric coming from Ohio Governor John Kasich, a Republican presidential candidate, that it was time the U.S. "punched the Russians in the nose"?

As for Dr. Ben Carson, his implausible call during the debate for a moment of silence for the San Bernardino victims was nothing short of opportunism and eccentricity. Having chronicled most of his meaningless utterances and false equivalences, I believe once again Dr. Carson has demonstrated that he, like Donald Trump, is unfit to lead America on both the foreign and economic policy fronts. By the way, Dr Carson made some strange reference to "death by a thousand pricks". What does he mean? I haven't a clue – but neither does he I suspect.

By now it should be clear that a Republican presidency would be disastrous for America and the rest of the world. There are just too many critical economic and global issues to entrust the presidency to this current bunch of misleading, evasive and delusional candidates. When candidates begin to pull out their worst sloganeering and scaremongering tactics – and extol the reverence of the Bush years – then you know it's time to appreciate the saying that "A bird in the hand is worth two in the bush."

59. How to Blow a Dog Whistle

Frenetic and race-based electioneering is America's fate for the next few months until the presidential election in November 2016. The stakes couldn't be higher for America and the rest of the world in a consequential presidential election that will test the nation's meritocratic foundations and reveal its true commitment to the ideals of a free and open society, civil liberties, and even human decency.

On account of his bloviating and populist ranting, it's become crystal clear that Donald Trump is a danger to all of the above-mentioned democratic and human virtues – spouting absurdly discriminatory rhetoric under the guise of wanting to "Make America Great Again" (he has even filed a trademark application to protect that slogan). Now there is little doubt that his presence in the presidential race has had a wretched effect on race relations in America – taking recourse in a bogus slogan that has proved to be really just a dog-whistle strategy for saying "Let's Make America White Again".

Although the practice of dog whistling has been rampant in American electoral politics for the last several decades (remember Richard Nixon's appeal to 'law and order' at the height of the struggle for civil rights), the term itself is said to have originated in Australia to describe the coded rhetoric used by former Prime Minister John Howard (for instance, "un-Australian" and "mainstream") to appeal to white Australian voters.

For the enlightenment of those not familiar with the term "dog whistle", the New Urban Dictionary defines it as "a type of communication strategy that sends a message that the general population will take a certain meaning from, but a certain group that is 'in the know' will take away the secret, intended message."

Tony Quinn, a Republican political analyst in California, has concluded that Trump knows perfectly well how to dog whistle the race card, suggesting further that his racially-loaded rhetoric does not at all target white Europeans. In a recent interview, he asserted: "The Republican electorate is overwhelmingly white and elderly. In 2009, Republicans were mystified that an African American with a funny name took over the country. Then their worst fears were realized when his appointees and his policies seemed to many to favour non-whites over white people; and in these seven years deep white resentment has built up."

Apropos of Mr. Trump's outlandish claims that America is weak and needs to be rescued from its downward spiral, the reality and statistics on the performance and strength of America's economy do not support that contention. The United States is indubitably the planet's only superpower and has sat on top of the world for almost a century. Furthermore, it remains the world's largest economy, has the largest military by far, and its companies and entrepreneurs are notable pioneers and leaders of the ICT Revolution.

Since President Obama has often been accused by Republicans of contributing to America's ostensible "weakness", it's both instructive and edifying to note that under his watch the U.S. economy recovered from the Great Recession of 2008 brought on by the misguided macroeconomic policies of former President George W. Bush and the uncontrolled excesses of the hypertrophied and dysfunctional financial sector. One can even argue that if America today is less successful than in previous decades, it's probably because its own runaway success has made it complacent and sclerotic.

Yet Donald Trump, whose dog whistles have been heard loud and clear by the most incorrigible racists from the Old South, has never been interested in facts and evidence – his sole intention being to undermine America's democracy by exploiting the insecurities of the undiscerning, and preying on the angst of an electoral cohort, mostly white Christians, in order to win the presidency.

Mr Trump together with his Republican colleagues continue to use coded expressions such as "food stamps", "we'll bring back the glory days of America" and "America doesn't have smart leaders anymore" as surreptitious appeals to the worst prejudices of certain segments of the GOP base.

Further compounding the situation, I believe, is the seemingly innocuous use of the term "non-whites" by the mainstream media which probably helps perpetuate prejudices against minorities and delude us by distorting our perception of the true electoral make-up of contemporary American society.

In any event, the rhetorical deception coming from the Republicans reminds me of Mitt Romney's "vision of American society" – defining it as "makers and takers". His many equivocations as a Republican candidate during the 2012 presidential election are well documented, when he often delivered one message to the overall electorate while at the same time delivering quite a different message to private fundraisers. How can we forget Mr. Romney's infamous "48, 49 percent" remark about President Obama's voters who he claimed "pay no income tax"?

The purveyor of unmitigated gloom that is Donald Trump has conveniently ignored the fact that the social, economic and electoral demographics in America have changed dramatically and that America's strength is derived from its multiculturalism, external forces of change and meritocracy. Thus, I have difficulties comprehending the Republican Party's pathological obsession with CONSERVATISM in a country built by immigrants and which has prospered on the entrepreneurship, dynamism, resources and skills of Arabs, Europeans, Jews, Hispanics, Blacks and Asians.

The fact that America is the only developed country without a "CULTURE MINISTER" is testimony to the fact that its socio-cultural makeup is too diverse to warrant "the advocacy, promotion and systemization of a single American culture." Perhaps this is the reason why Americans by and large make greater reference to shared values and constitutional rights rather than collective culture.

Of course, by no means am I suggesting that the practice of dog whistling is only racially motivated and is only prevalent in countries with predominantly Caucasian populations. In fact, I could identify plenty of examples of it in society and politics right here in Saint Lucia. However, dear reader, I'll let sleeping dogs lie and allow you to figure this out yourself, especially in an election season when you're most guaranteed to be hit by some rhetorical dog dung.

INTERVIEW

60. Cuba and the Caribbean (with Ambassador Jorge Soberon)

In Dialogue with Ambassador Jorge Soberon

Cuba is on the move. Business opportunities are opening up in many of its semi-untouched markets – and international business leaders are seeing dollar signs as the Obama administration moves to restore economic and diplomatic ties with the island. From airlines, hotel chains and telecommunications firms – to business consultants, exporters and retailers, private capitalists are all jostling for a piece of the pie.

Since the Cuban government loosened restrictions on private enterprise – reflecting changing times – hundreds of thousands of small enterprises have been started by Cuban nationals. For its part, Cuba's Communist Party, which held its Seventh Congress this month, appears to be moving cautiously towards increased trade and private enterprise. In an interview with His Excellency Jorge Soberon, Cuba's Ambassador to Saint Lucia and the O.E.C.S, I asked about the economic and political future of Cuba and the impact of the normalization of U.S/Cuba relations on CARICOM economies.

CWS: Mr. Ambassador, thank you for agreeing to sit with me and talk about the economic and political intrigues of Cuba at this historic juncture, and the implications for Caribbean economies. What's the exact nature of the economic evolution taking place in Cuba presently?

AMB: I would first like to extend fraternal greetings to the dear people of Saint Lucia and to thank them for the expressions of support and sympathy for Cuba which I have witnessed since I took up duties on this beautiful island. Cuba is working to build a prosperous and sustainable socialism. To achieve this goal, we are updating our economic and social model and a 2030 development plan has been launched, having taken into account the popular opinion. Essentially, the development of the economy is our fundamental goal. We have decided that no one will be left behind in Cuba as a result of this process, and that we will not apply any "shock therapy". Thus we will not privatize social services, or apply any measures that will harm the unity of the people or which will generate instability or uncertainty. We will advance on the basis of consensus and national organization, and not in an improvised or desperate manner. The resources that determine the development of the nation will remain in the hands of state enterprises. Until now, we have managed to restructure our foreign debt. We will never depend on either a market or a product. At the same time, we have put in place a new "Law on Foreign Investment" which protects the environment and allows for the efficient use of our natural resources. We recognize the market's role in the functioning of our economy, particularly in terms of planning and private enterprise. However, we also wish to protect our history, our identity and our culture. In this process we have considered the idea of our national hero José Martí that "to govern is to foresee".

CWS: Cuba is a market of 11 million people. As its economy grows and the purchasing capacity of its population increases, its attractiveness as a place for investment will rise correspondingly. What are the implications for Saint Lucia and the wider Caribbean of U.S. President Obama's visit to Cuba and the opening-up of the Cuban market?

AMB: Cuba will work towards the sustainable development of its economic and trade relations with its neighbours. The new "Law on Foreign Investment", the Economic Zone of Mariel (west of Havana) as well as the development of the Cuban economy, offer important opportunities for Saint Lucia and the Caribbean. We are interested in the increased presence of Saint Lucia and the wider Caribbean in our relatively huge market of 11 million people that sees more than 3.5 million tourists per year. Our relations have their own dynamics and the gradual elimination of U.S. economic, trade and financing restrictions, which have cost us more than 121 billion dollars since the U.S. severed ties in 1961, will definitely facilitate closer economic ties with Saint Lucia and the Caribbean and will promote peace in the region.

CWS: According to the Peterson Institute of International Economics, U.S. exports to Cuba totalled $360 million last year. If the trade embargo were to be eliminated, that number could increase to as high as $4.3 billion. If the trade embargo is fully rescinded, could Cuba be the new emerging economy in the Caribbean, and should CARICOM be worried?

AMB: The lifting of the U.S embargo can contribute significantly to the sustainable development of Cuba in the economic, social and cultural spheres, and would therefore help raise the living standards of our people. As our Government has stated, even if the U.S. embargo is lifted, the expansion and diversification of economic and trade relations with CARICOM will remain a priority. Of course, we won't forget those who have accompanied us in all these difficult years. Cuba is an emerging opportunity for the Caribbean, not a threat. Saint Lucia and the Caribbean have demonstrated their ability to compete successfully with regional economic actors greater than Cuba. We will always defend the legitimate economic and environmental interests of the Caribbean nations, including Haiti. Our approach is not to advance at the expense of any other country or group of countries, but to work with all for the good of all. We need to continue to strengthen our co-operation in order to address our vulnerabilities and to broaden our economic and trade relations.

CWS: Sir Ronald Sanders, a respected Caribbean diplomat, has said and I quote: "The game has changed. The rest of the Caribbean should have seen this coming and prepared themselves to cope with it. There were certainly enough warnings…Caribbean countries will have to improve their own competitiveness and create better and smarter conditions for business. They should waste no time in doing so. The challenges will come in two crucial areas: Tourism and investment from the US." Is he right?

AMB: I have always read with great interest the approach and perspectives of Sir Ronald Sanders. Just allow me to say this: Cuba believes that the Caribbean as a whole needs to move forward together to achieve its rightful place in the world. Let's work together to turn these challenges into opportunities.

CWS: An event last year at Havana's Panorama Hotel provided a unique view into the future of Cuba. Some 50 would-be business owners attended Cuba's first-ever Startup Weekend, listening to presentations, holding workshops and refining business models. Is it reasonable to say that venture capitalists seeking an opportunity that could rival the type of explosive growth seen in Vietnam need look no further than to Cuba?

AMB: We recognize that foreign investment should play an important role in the development of our country and therefore we offer significant incentives and legal certainty to investors, needless to say that the updating of our economic policies offers plenty of advantages to potential investors: stability, qualified personnel, a favourable location, natural resources, a new port and economic zone at Mariel, ten international airports, the investment protection agreements signed with different countries, the existence of an Investment Promotion Agency and a Chamber of Commerce. Information about foreign investment can be found at *camaracuba.cu.*

CWS: Cuba is known to have one of the best healthcare systems in the world. Of course, Cuba's contribution to healthcare in Saint Lucia is well-documented. How do you see this relationship developing with the eventual commissioning of two new hospitals in Saint Lucia?

AMB: As a starting point, let me mention that Cuba has been cooperating with Saint Lucia on health for fifteen years now. During that period, our medical staff in Saint Lucia have treated more than 164,000 patients and performed more than 17,000 surgeries, including eye surgeries. More than 240 Saint Lucians have completed programmes in the health sciences through our scholarship programme. Cuba is willing to expand the presence of its medical services and products in Saint Lucia. One example is the possible use of the Cuban product Heberprot-P, an effective therapy for diabetic foot ulcers that reduces the risk of limb amputation by 70%, and this has been used in 180,000 patients in 26 countries. Cuba is willing to further strengthen relations with Saint Lucia in the health sector, both through technical co-operation and through economic partnership that brings mutual benefits.

CWS: How can Saint Lucia and Cuba better co-operate in the area of education?

AMB: Let's look at the effective and low-cost Cuban adult literacy programme known as "Yes I Can", which is recognized by UNESCO and has been used successfully in about thirty countries. "Yes I Can" has resulted in more than nine million people becoming literate, from the Caribbean to New Zealand. Also, we see great opportunity in a potential language learning initiative, whereby Cubans learn English and Saint Lucians learn Spanish. Further, Cuba supports the promotion of teacher exchange programmes and other cultural exchanges between our countries.

CWS: Finally Mr. Ambassador, with the eventual opening up of Cuba, do you see the Cuban economy eventually transforming into a (hybrid) state-led market economy like China or a social market economy based on the Scandinavian model?

AMB: We want a sovereign, socialist, democratic, prosperous and sustainable nation. Our economic model must take into account our history, our culture, our internal conditions and the international situation, and crucially learn from the experience of countries like China and Vietnam. Our socialism has been sufficiently democratic to successfully combat unemployment, to guarantee the livelihoods of people unable to work and to ensure access for all to health care, education, culture and sports. That notwithstanding, Cuba will become more democratic and will ensure that the citizens increasingly participate in the fundamental decisions in the society and economy.

CWS: Thank you, Your Excellency.

EPILOGUE

Let me end with a few last points. My instincts tell me that there is a silent minority in this country who are tired of inhaling the toxic plume of partisan politics and yearn for healthier and more measured debate on all things political, economic, social and environmental.

The collective task of identifying Saint Lucia's economic interests and then designing strategies to pursue and foster growth is unlikely to happen within the present framework of the country's fossilized party system. The engineers, economists, educators, sociologists, health professionals, urban planners and scientists among us need to storm the barricades as it were, and force entry into politics' closed situation rooms.

There are serious questions we should be asking such as how we can best invest in our young people for growth and development, as well as how we can make our health and education systems the wealth of the nation. Our people deserve no less than a fully-functioning democracy with visionary leadership and solid institutions.

I know that we have bright men and women in this country who have the ambition and intellectual capacity to build our nation – and together, I'm hopeful we can find and develop solutions to make our education system serve the needs our economy, and provide economic insights that can help foster fiscal and macro-prudential stability, as well as nurture the growth potential of the economy.

I have argued that since development is about reducing vulnerabilities and increasing the capacity of people and institutions, change through social policy is a unique opportunity because it has the highest potential for economic impact in a small country like ours. We need to see more vitality and vibrancy in our country's economic and social metabolism – more targeted policies and programmes that engender the change we wish to see in our families, clubs, schools and institutions.

There are plenty of challenges abroad and at home; injustices and imbalances that need to be corrected and reformed. Without a doubt, we'll need to develop a growth and progressive mindset that will drive the change that we wish to see. In the final analysis, progressivism is about action, change and results. It's about affecting your country in the most profound way.

At this point as we approach the end of an inspirational journey, let me repeat one of my favourite quotes by the Indian entrepreneur and politician, Nandan Nilekani: "A society which has the least resistance to the uninterrupted flow of ideas, diversity, concepts and competitive signals wins, and a society that has the efficiencies to translate whatever can be done quickly – from idea to market – also wins."

Let this book be a lodestar of our aspirations and hopes for a better Saint Lucia. It is time to re-ignite the flame of hope and progress which brighten the path of our nation, in our aspiration to join the ranks of the modern, industrialised economies. I have the reason, will and ability to shape my country's future. My mind is set, my mood is right, the journey has already started!

Clement Wulf-Soulage

NOTES AND QUOTES

Chapter 1 – Economic and Business Affairs

1: How Keynes changed the world

British economist John Maynard Keynes was regarded as the founder of macroeconomics. He published his magnum opus, "The General Theory of Employment, Interest and Money" in 1939.

John Maynard Keynes was the greatest economist of the 20th century.

Paul Samuelson is quoted to have said, "Funeral by funeral, theory advances" – and so have the works of Keynes.

John Maynard Keynes – "I believe myself to be writing a book on economic theory which will largely revolutionize – not, I suppose, at once but in the course of the next ten years – the way the world thinks about its economic problems."

The main plank of Keynes' economic theory is that government intervention through active fiscal policy can stabilize an economy – and that spending by households, businesses and the government is the most important economic driving force.

Government should "keep its hands off the economy, cutting back on regulations, and instead allow the free market – supply and demand – to determine prices and wages."

Keynes argued that demand creates its own supply – in direct opposition to Jean Baptiste Say's Law which posits that supply creates its own demand.

Joseph Stiglitz (Article) "After The Financial Crisis We Were All Keynesians", but all too briefly.

The real policy debate isn't about Keynesianism versus the free market, it is about magnitudes and techniques: How much stimulus is necessary? And how should it be divided between government spending and tax cuts?

How much stimulus is necessary? And how should it be divided between government spending and tax cuts?

2: Can a nation grow without developing?

A German economist famously called the notion of GDP "laboured and overwrought", as it measures income but not equality, growth but not development, and it ignores values like social cohesion and the environment.

Economic growth in many instances, whether market-led or government-facilitated, is still widely confused with economic development, even by economists themselves.

Economic growth entails only an increase in quantitative output; it may or may not involve development.

Economic development is the "increase in the standard of living in a nation's population with sustained growth from a simple, low-income economy to a modern, high-income economy."

Development is "both a human condition and a progressive mindset that facilitates people upliftment, cultural advancement, and the harmonious and social integration of society."

The six factors that constitute economic development are education, incentives, quality of life, infrastructure, health and social cohesion.

Growth and development do not have to conflict; they can reinforce each other.

Amartya Sen points out, "economic growth is one aspect of the process of economic development."

The tiny remote Himalayan kingdom of Bhutan invented its own Gross National Happiness (GNH) index in 1972.

If an undeveloped country or corporation was flooded with money it would be richer but no more developed. On the other hand, if a well developed country or corporation was suddenly deprived of wealth, it would not be less developed.

Does growth come before development or do they occur simultaneously?

Research has shown that high economic growth may not necessarily result in increased economic development of the overall population, and targeting human development indicators will not automatically translate into higher level of economic growth.

Some economists believe that a lack of resources can limit growth but not development.

3: The middle class – who they are and why they matter

The middle class is a fluid group of people who are not poor but not truly rich.

Middle-class economics means "helping working families feel more secure in a world of constant change. That means helping folks afford childcare, college, health care, a home, retirement – lowering the taxes of working families and putting thousands of dollars back into their pockets each year."

In many developed countries like the UK and Germany, political parties are often elected to office on a "middle class" campaign pitch.

In France, the middle classes helped drive the French Revolution that overthrew the monarchy and established a republic.

It is middle class workers who grow the economy and promote the development of human capital and a well educated population, not the rich.

Brazilian economist Eduardo Giannetti da Fonseca, describes members of the middle class as "People who are not resigned to a life of poverty, who are prepared to make sacrifices to create a better life for themselves, but who have not started with life's material problems solved, because they have material assets to make their lives easy."

The Washington Post poignantly states that "the middle class took America to the moon. Then something went horribly wrong." The British Guardian indulged our attention recently when it wrote, "Who are the new middle classes around the world? You'd be surprised how poor some are."

Let's hope that politicians don't see the middle class as something to create with the gains of economic growth, as opposed to an actual source of economic growth.

4: SMEs – the answer to unemployment

SMEs are the lifeblood of a country's economy; they are essential to generating good jobs. Long recognized as crucial to economic development, entrepreneurs and SMEs are increasingly seen as crucial for sustainable recovery and for a strong middle class – a source of economic growth.

How can we promote an enterprise culture or forge an entrepreneurial spirit in Saint Lucia which can help catapult greater wealth and job creation?

5: When the most productive sector is the weakest link

With all the great promise that tourism holds for our resource-starved nation, it is still the weakest link in our economic system.

Given the significant patterns of consumption and resource utilization in tourism, there is enormous potential for agriculture, agribusiness, small-scale manufacturing and the creative industries to supply the inputs needed to produce tourism and leisure services through forward, backward and horizontal linkages – resulting in greater resource efficiency and encouraging large-scale production.

Why haven't we worked harder to overcome the obstacles blocking inter-sectoral linkages, since many economists believe this approach to be our sole means of long-term survival?

Stuart McCook, in a trenchant review of the book, Last Resorts: The Cost of Tourism in the Caribbean authored by Polly Pattullo, posits the view that what Caribbean tourism presently engenders among other industries is not "linkages" but indeed "leakages".

6: All development is local

By any measure, the greatest failure of our governance system resides in the dysfunctional state of local government – an institution considered by many as the most fundamental form of grass-roots democracy and the lodestar of community welfare.

In 1945, the West India Royal Commission wrote, "the improvement of the social conditions in these territories depends in (a) large measure on co-operation between the central administration and the people through properly constituted and well-conducted local authorities."

The late Professor Rex Nettleford noted in 1998 that "local government is an investment in human capability for self-governance over the long haul in building a nation and a society."

Shouldn't a vibrant democracy be giving more power back to the people at the local level where the economic and social impact are likely to be most pronounced?

The closer a representative government is to the people, the better it works. In the final analysis, we can all appreciate that all development, like all politics, is local.

7: Development is a mindset

Development is a mindset; a frame of mind needed in the pursuit of personal advancement and social transformation.

The broader question is whether our mindset and work practices are compatible with economic productivity and efficiency.

Thomas L. Friedman in his book "The World Is Flat": "Every morning in Africa, a gazelle wakes up. It knows it must run faster than the fastest lion or it will be killed. Every morning a lion wakes up. It knows it must outrun the slowest gazelle or it will starve to death. It doesn't matter whether you are a lion or a gazelle. When the sun comes up, you better start running."

Poor work ethics hinder economic progress as they cripple productivity, and hence competitiveness becomes a difficult game to play.

The public service is the primary front office agent in small nation-states like ours.

Any blueprint for enhancing public sector efficiency must embrace the imperative of Business Process Re-engineering (BPR).

8: Are retirees distorting the labour market?

If a group enters the labour market and stays in it beyond their normal retirement date, others will be unable to gain employment. This best explains the lump of labour.

According to Paul Krugman, a Nobel-prize winning economist: "The "lump-of-labour thinking – and the policy paralysis it encourages – feeds protectionism. If the public no longer believes that the economy can create new jobs, it will demand that we protect old jobs from new competitors..."

Rick Newman, a senior economics writer explains: "The economy can only support so many jobs, and as older workers stay on the payroll longer, it impedes the creation of new jobs, many of which would go to younger workers. Older people remaining on the job later in life are stealing jobs from young people."

9: Are commercial banks out of balance?

Retail banking is not what it used to be. The relationship between banks and customers no longer feels personal.

Why do customers in this modern age of banking have to waste so much time just to conduct a simple transaction?

Technology was supposed to reduce the cost of banking for both banks and customers, but it appears the value impact of technology at local banks is yet to be felt. A more competitive banking sector will translate into economic gains and provide access to the organised financial sector for more people. Customer service should be seen as an attitude rather than a department.

On its website, the Laborie Co-operative Credit Union declares, "We are not a bank, we are better. To others you are a risk, to us you are family

10: Diaspora capital – wheresoever you may roam!

Kingsley Aikins of the Diaspora Forum: "There is growing awareness now that there is such a concept as 'diaspora capital' to go alongside financial, human and social capital. Countries are coming to the realization that this is a resource to be researched, cultivated, solicited and stewarded. Many see this as a way of addressing tough domestic economic challenges and as a key piece of their economic recovery. They also see it as more than just economic remittances as there are also social remittances in the form of ideas, values, beliefs and practices."

Canada openly boasts of adopting a full-on diaspora-driven foreign policy shaped out of a combination of its interest and values, and its attentiveness to the sensitivities of the country's diverse and sundry ethnic and immigrant communities.

Diaspora networks can serve as a potent economic force for re-engaging disconnected citizens and driving national change.

Diaspora capital is the new foreign exchange.

11: Categorical imperative or new deal

Christine Largarde writes: "Today, we understand better than before how a restrictive fiscal policy weighs on growth."

Paul Krugman has made reference to "the lesson that the Obama administration unfortunately failed to learn until very late in the game – that the economic strategy that works best politically isn't the strategy that finds approval with focus groups; it's the strategy that delivers results."

Recent research demonstrates that bond market confidence might even rise on the prospect of faster growth.

12: PPP – timely solution to pressing fiscal gaps

One can well appreciate that when investors have their own money in the game, they have a major incentive to avoid budget overruns and missed deadlines because this cuts into profits.

The World Bank admits: "Given the present fiscal constraints and the need to stabilize debt-to-GDP ratio, governments are increasingly turning to the private sector as an alternative source of funding to meet infrastructural needs in order to spur badly needed economic growth."

Public-private collaboration has been a key driver in countries' strategies for diversification, competitiveness and development, and for successful integration into the global economy.

13: Is C.I.P a solution waiting for a problem?

Citizenship should have nothing to do with economics.

Should the Caribbean region become havens for investment citizenship?

While a few Caribbean governments have decided that the heft of the applicant's wallet is the answer to their economic woes, several economists view economic citizenship as the bastard children of economic policy.

What precisely does citizenship mean today for a society and what values are associated with nationality?

Sharing citizenship with people you have nothing in common with sounds like a sardonic business model.

There are three big snags with the idea of economic citizenship. Firstly, issues of transparency and accountability are still cast in a cloud of suspicion. Secondly the question of whether these islands will and can attract the right people is disquieting. And finally, how do we reconcile the putative economic gains with the resulting social costs?

The International firm Henley and Partners advise clients on the best place to spend their money and estimates that every year, several thousand people spend a collective $2bn (£1.2bn; 1.5bn euros) to add a second, or even third, passport to their collection.

14: CSME – still an empty shell after 25 years

Sir Ronald Sanders, a regional diplomat: "Foreign investors would be more greatly attracted to a larger regional market than to the individual small markets of most CARICOM countries. It would be one effective way of creating a larger economic space for the employment of young people."

David Rudder: "Tiny theatres of conflict and confusion better known as the isles of the West Indies."

Membership of a single market is commonly assumed to be a key factor in encouraging foreign investors to choose to invest in a region.

We in the Caribbean are still stuck in the eighties' mindset of preferential treatment in trade matters.

The future challenges of economic development give rise to three foundational principles on which economic development investments should be based: exports, productivity and sustainability.

China seems to have a strategy for the Caribbean. But do we have a strategy for China?

15: ECCB leadership – thinking outside the bank

While central banks have a monopoly on the issuance of fiat money, the people who actually lead such banks cannot be said to be sole custodians of economic and financial knowledge.

Alan Greenspan has been called: "An economist's economist".

When asked about his perspective on Sir Dwight's lengthy tenure, former SVG Prime Minister Sir James Mitchell pointed out: "I was one of the persons who put him there, but...same way we have to look for succession in politics, we have to look for succession in our institutions. And it is very, very sad what has happened there with Building & Loan."

16: The economics of corruption

Corruption is defined as the misuse of public power for private benefit.

Research has revealed the negative impact of corruption on levels of investment, which is "the most important causal link to the impact of corruption on the growth of GDP."

Corruption exacerbates the inequality trifecta (income, wealth and opportunity).

Graf Lambsdorff: The "invisible foot" (which shows that the unreliability of corrupt counterparts induces honesty and good governance) is a novel strategy to fight corruption.

Corruption is highly context-specific as it depends on the institutional setup, stage of development, but also norms and culture.

17: The IMF's new groove

The IMF acronym has been re-labelled: "Its Mostly Fiscal".

The former French President Francois Mitterand admitted that the debt repayments demanded by the IMF since the 1980s have been a major mechanism for the transfer of wealth from the South to the North.

The Nobel Prize-winning economist Joseph E. Stiglitz notes in his book, "Making Globalization Work": "Advanced industrial countries, through international organizations like the International Monetary Fund (IMF), the World Trade Organization (WTO), and the World Bank, were not only not doing all that they could to help these [developing] countries but were sometimes making their life more difficult. IMF programs had clearly worsened the East Asian crisis, and the "shock therapy" they had pushed in the former Soviet Union and its satellites played an important role in the failure of the transition."

When Mr. Strauss-Kahn took over the reins, the outstanding credit at the fund was US$ 10 billion as opposed to US$ 91 billion fours years earlier. Upon leaving office, the figure was at US$ 84 billion. Owing to prudent economic management, the total capital of the fund had quadrupled to US$ 250 billion.

A statement released by the IMF in 2014 recommended: "Ambitious, credible medium term fiscal consolidation to put public debt on a sustainable path and create the fiscal space for counter cyclical policies."

18: The anatomy and insanity of debt

The Grammy Award-winning American singer James Taylor: "People should watch out for three things. Avoid a major addiction, don't get so deeply into debt that it controls your life, and don't start a family before you're ready to settle down."

How will small vulnerable states like ours face the growing challenges of high debt and low growth?

How can emerging and middle income states reconcile local democracy with international debt obligations?

But if debt is an ingenious substitute for the chain and the whip of the slave-driver, as Ambrose Bierce puts it, why is the world so addicted to borrowing?

A sovereign rating assessment is based in equal measure on a government's willingness to pay as its ability to do so.

Thomas Jefferson: "Never spend your money before you have it."

19: Between debt and the deep blue Caribbean Sea

In a report entitled, "The Silent Debt Crisis", the U.S. rating agency Moody's provides some further perspective: "Unlike elsewhere, the build-up of debt in the Caribbean region was not sudden or caused by the global financial crisis. It happened gradually and almost unnoticeably over many years."

The rating agency Moody's explains that: "The industries in which Caribbean economies specialize are highly cyclical in nature, exposed to external shocks, and dependent on the performance of the external economic environment. Therefore, Caribbean countries remain vulnerable to external shocks and balance of payments difficulties, and their economic performance will continue to exhibit cyclical features."

Moody's estimates: "The debt-to-GDP ratio is over 60 per cent for 12 of the 20 Caribbean countries for which it has data. Six have debt-to-GDP ratios of over 80 per cent, and four have over 100 per cent."

20: More BRICS in the G-7 wall

The phrase, "The sick man of Europe" was coined by Tsar Nicholas I of Russia.

A new study by the London School of Economics confirms: "Whether or not the world will avert catastrophic climate change is now, to a large extent, in the hands of the Chinese."

Is there a "cold peace" between Russia and the West?

The Frankfurter Allgemeine Newspaper (FAZ) opined: "One should not underestimate Beijing and Delhi's claim and desire for making this new century their own."

21: The Greek economic drama – lessons and morals

The battle lines have been drawn where the Greek camp, energized by the teachings of Socrates, Plato and Aristotle, are pitted against the indefatigable Germans inspired by the resolve of Kant, Engels and Nietzsche.

Senior spokesman from the European Commission: "While no one doubts previous Greek governments dug the economic hole the country finds itself in, the debate is over how much the rest of Europe should pay for selling Greek leaders the shovels and buckets used to dig it."

What would abandoning the euro do to the Greek economy? How high would the costs be for the euro zone? What would be the political consequences If Athens were to turn away from Europe?

George Soros: "Everyone knows that it can never pay back its debt. Greece is close to a primary budget surplus after a lot of pain and suffering. And if any country were to recognize how such an approach could work, it was Germany, which ought to remember that it has benefited from debt write downs three times, with the Dawes Plan, the Young Plan and in connection with the Marshall Plan."

Too much democracy is not always a good thing in the economic management of a country.

Oh Zeus, king of the Greek Gods, how could things go so wrong?

Chapter 2 – Government, Democracy and Leadership

22: Leadership – where the buck stops

Politics is a continuation of education by other means.

Leadership is about "making things happen through people who are as enthusiastic and interested as you are."

Norman Schwarzkopf, the United States army general who led all the coalition forces in the Persian Gulf War believes: "Leadership is a potent combination of strategy and character. But if you must be without one, be without strategy."

Sir Winston Churchill believed influence and impact to be more important than tactics and strategy. According to him: "However beautiful the strategy, you should occasionally look at the results."

Jim Collins, a management thinker and author: "Great leaders did not start to make their companies great or successful by setting a new vision and a new strategy, but instead they got the right people on the bus, the wrong people off the bus, and the right people in the right seats – and then figured out where to drive."

Benjamin Franklin couldn't have expressed it any more explicitly when he said: "Well done is better than well said."

23: A vision for growth – part one

German Chancellor: "People who have visions should go see an eye doctor."

Peter Drucker, the management guru: "The best way to predict the future is to create it."

This will require them to scan the world for signals of change – what a management psychologist calls "searchlight intelligence".

24: A vision for growth – part two

Vance Havner, the legendary American preacher: "The vision must be followed by the venture. It is not enough to stare up the steps – we must step up the stairs."

The factors that constitute economic development are education, quality of life, institutional effectiveness, infrastructure, health and social cohesion.

The Eastern Caribbean Central Bank (ECCB) will need to show it is much more than a monetary institution that simply manages exchange-rate mechanisms and fosters financial stability.

25: Is Saint Lucia's birth certificate flawed?

I have difficulties understanding the logic of religiously holding on to a winner-takes-all first-past-the-post system that has contributed to the polarization and disillusionment of the populace.

By the commission's own admission, many of our national institutions lack the underlying structures for effective accountability and transparency, rendering our social identity and civic character questionable after 36 years of independence.

How flawed is a constitution that allows the executive branch to perform legislative functions?

Doesn't a true and credible democracy require the separation of the branches of government to prevent abuse of power and to ensure the rule of law?

26: Do some MPs need a presentation coach?

In the old Greek civilization, public speaking was relished as an academic discipline.

Dean Frenkel, a vocal instructor, speech analyst, speech coach and author of "Evolution of Speech" explained: "What should our politicians learn from Mr Obama? They can start by listening to the sound-map of Mr Obama's voice and take note of his resonance, speech manner, his adroit sense of timing and musical presentation of his voice. His speech virtues begin with a combination of accurate and crisp articulation, beautifully timed speech rate and commanding presence. He has license and he willingly uses it. He is able to infuse passion into his speech and while he is understated, he does have remnants of speech gifts learned from preachers. Yet he never seems to over-do the passion. He often starts his sentences quite slowly then quickens up as he sifts through detail, then strategically slows his speech rate to emphasise strategic points...Mr Obama has a good mental library of words which helps him to responds well under pressure."

27: The Peter Principle – the cream rises until it sours

The Peter Principle, the eponymous law Dr. Laurence J. Peter (educator and psychologist) coined in his 1969 book has had far-reaching applications and implications outside of the business world.

As the New York Times put it, "Dr. Peter explains why incompetence is at the root of everything we endeavour to do—why schools bestow ignorance, why governments condone anarchy, why courts dispense injustice, why prosperity causes unhappiness, and why utopian plans never generate utopias. The Peter Principle brilliantly explains how incompetence and its accompanying symptoms, syndromes, and remedies define the world and the work we do in it."

Dr. Peter postulates: "Workers who do well will keep getting promoted up the ladder until they reach a point where they can no longer excel. Then they stay stuck in that role, getting by with average-to-poor performance, preventing more capable people from taking on the role. Multiply this effect across all major positions within a workplace and soon you've got a company filled with mediocrity in all its top managerial jobs."

Richard Nixon better understood the idiosyncrasies and challenges of the job when he declared, "It is the responsibility of the media to look at the President with a microscope, but they go too far when they use a proctoscope."

Albert Einstein: "Doing the same thing over and over again and expecting different results."

28: Dropping in on democracy's dropouts

Politics in its true sense is a means of liberation, education and self advancement.

As reported by the International Institute for Democracy and Electoral Assistance (IDEA), the 2011 elections recorded a 56.84% voter turn-out, the second-worst since St. Lucia attained independence in 1979. From a list of 150,996 registered voters, the total number of people who cast their votes was an abysmal 85,821. The lowest participation rate was in 2001 at 31.54%. In 2006 only 58.46% of registered voters turned out to exercise their franchise.

Civic knowledge is the cornerstone of a strong democracy.

29: Democracy and the poorly educated

Thomas Jefferson: "The greatest threat to democracy is an uneducated citizenry."

Donald Trump: "We won the evangelicals. We won with young. We won with old. We won with highly educated. We won with poorly educated. I love the poorly educated."

Jack Harich, a systems engineer and sustainologist identifies and explains five common deception strategies which politicians are likely to use to hoodwink particularly an uneducated electorate: false promises, false enemies, pushing the fear button, wrong priorities and secrecy.

Greek philosopher Plato saw the system of democracy as the "rule of the mob" because of the "unjust condemnation by Athenian democracy of Socrates."

In an essay entitled "Democracy and Political Ignorance", Ilya Somin explains: "Democracy is supposed to be rule of the people, by the people, and for the people. But in order to rule effectively, the people need political knowledge. If they know little or nothing about government, it becomes difficult to hold political leaders accountable for their performance...Perhaps the solution is a better public school curriculum that puts more emphasis on civic education. The difficulty is that governments have very little incentive to ensure that public schools really do adopt curricula that increase knowledge."

Democracy is a great thing if people stay interested in it and it works.

An Indian reformer and columnist once said: "We cannot continue to languish in 19th century politics aspiring to live in the 21st century economy."

Thomas Jefferson; "If a nation expects to be ignorant and free, in a state of civilization, it expects what never was and never will be. . . The People cannot be safe without information. When the press is free, and every man is able to read, all is safe."

30: Politics and the bench

English Lord Chief Justice Gordon Hewart: "Justice should not only be done, but should "manifestly and undoubtedly" be seen to be done."

Green Party in Germany: "The country's highest court is "no Jurassic Park for retired and worn-out politicians."

CNN legal analyst: "A politicized judicial institution ran by legal luminaries covered in political and ideological robes."

According to a veteran American journalist: "It is well-understood that there are now, with Scalia's death, three very conservative Catholic justices (Samuel A. Alito Jr., John G. Roberts Jr. and Clarence Thomas), four liberal justices (Stephen G. Breyer, Ruth Bader Ginsburg, Elena Kagan and Sonia Sotomayor) and a swing justice (Anthony M. Kennedy) who is generally conservative but liberal in several important areas (such as gay rights and capital punishment of minors)."

Jerome Frank, a mid-20th-century legal thinker, is said to have claimed: "Justice is a function of what the judge had for breakfast. Don't let their black robes, serious miens and pledges of fealty to the law fool you. Judicial decisions are not cool applications of objective legal principles. Rather, they are manifestations of personal predilections and biases."

31: It's the debates, stupid!

The old election campaign model needs to be recharged, and rather than shine like a beacon of hope, it winks like a battery-drained flashlight.

If would-be office-holders knew they had to face serious fact-checking investigative journalists and participate regularly in formal policy debates, perhaps we would attract better-qualified candidates rather than some of the pitifully mediocre ones that we have elected over the years.

The free passes to political power without proof of professional competence and personal integrity should become a thing of the past.

Chapter 3 – National Independence and Sovereignty

32: Our nation at 37. Is sovereignty real?

Lee Kuan Yew, the late Prime Minister of Singapore, is reported to have once said: "Small island states are a political joke."

Is the notion of sovereignty sacrosanct, or can we describe it as fallible?

What does it truly mean to be a sovereign nation with the Queen of England still officially the Head of State?

How does the way we are governed in small island states conflict with the need to tackle the major economic and global issues?

Saint Augustine: "In the absence of justice, what is sovereignty but organized robbery?"

Gijs de Vries, a former European Union anti-terrorism co-ordinator observed: "You can't get closer to the heart of national sovereignty than national security and intelligence services."

33: Our nation at 36 ...but seriously!

Is the nation at its prime at 36? Do we have a perspective and an understanding of our own problems in the context of the larger world of which we form a small part? What does independence mean and what has it brought us?

Independence should have taught the people, according to a French writer in the eighteenth century that they have a mind.

Marcus Garvey observed decades ago: "We are going to emancipate ourselves from mental slavery because, whilst others might free the body, none but ourselves can free the mind. Mind is your only ruler, sovereign. The man who is not able to develop and use his mind is bound to be the slave of the other man who uses his mind; use your intelligence to work out the real things of life. The time you waste in levity, in non-essentials, if you use it properly you will be able to guarantee to your posterity a condition better than you inherited from your forefathers."

Amartya Sen, an Indian economist and philosopher, described the process of "plural monoculturalism" as a situation where social and political groups live side by side but do not touch.

I dread the day when our grandchildren will ask what it was like "back in the days of Sir Allen Lewis" and we'll have nothing to tell them or no publication to make reference to.

34: How to leave behind a legacy
How do we make connections between the profoundly local and individual on the one hand, and the global and world historical on the other hand?

St. Lucian intellectuals, statesmen and writers seemed to have failed to recognize the importance and immortal effect of written personal narratives and historical events for generational elucidation.

Ray Bradbury in Fahrenheit 451 opined: "Everyone must leave something behind when he dies . . . Something your hand touched some way so your soul has somewhere to go when you die . . . It doesn't matter what you do, so long as you change something from the way it was before you touched it into something that's like you after you take your hands away."

Chapter 4 – Foreign Policy and International Affairs

35: Trade policy is foreign policy
Complications in foreign policy are likely to arise from conflict over trade policy.

When all the options are bad, the usual rules of good policy making still apply: identify the national interests that are at stake, specify the objectives that serve those interests, and design a strategy to advance those objectives (along with tactics to implement the strategy), with a system of monitoring and review to ensure that corrective action is taken if the expected results are not forthcoming.

Foreign policy has a significant impact on trade growth, which is very closely linked to GDP growth.

Economic diplomacy is fast replacing political diplomacy, where networks of diplomatic missions abroad are utilized to build export alliances and trade sourcing form an integral part of the economic and commercial sections of embassies.

Economist Thomas Schelling observed: "Broadly defined to include investment, shipping, tourism, and the management of enterprises, trade is what most of international relations are about. For that reason trade policy is national security policy."

36: A tilt towards the East

John F. Kennedy: "Domestic policy can only defeat us, but foreign policy can kill us."

As the Obama administration put it: "Rules for trade and investment in the financial services sector in the TPP will ensure that American businesses and workers can serve all these varied markets, promoting economic growth and job development in the United States and throughout the Asia-Pacific region."

By 2030, it is expected that Asia will be home to over three billion middle-class consumers, who will account for over 40 percent of global middle-class consumption.

Since foreign relations are much more than diplomacy – and the success of specific foreign policies is now measured by their economic impact.

Forbes Business, the Israelis are also moving in quickly on the growth opportunities in Asia: "When we think of Israel, we usually think of the Middle East (its neighbourhood), North America (its close ally the United States) and Europe (the long history of Ashkenazi Jews). Rarely do we think about Israel and Asia, even less about Asia as Israel's new frontier... Yet, last year Israel called 2014 "the year of Asia in Israel."

37: The insular Caribbean

The low economic level of the vast majority of our people in the Caribbean remains a basic problem. Some economists concur that every region in the world seems to be developing except the Caribbean. Is that true?

The reality of the times demands a greater effort on the part of the OECS at joint marketing and investment through the pooling of resources to allow the region to enjoy economies of scope and have greater exposure to European and emerging economies.

The continent of Africa was a bit slow to connect to the world economy, but now with better governance structures in place and improved research capabilities, they were able to do some catching up and in some cases a little leapfrogging.

Food production and exports in the OECS region should be more coordinated and all efforts made to reduce the region's food import bill.

38: The unreformed septuagenarian

There is little doubt our world needs a platform (not an irrelevant debating society) where collective decisions and actions can be taken to advance the cause of global peace and to protect the vulnerable and the poor.

Richard Nixon in 1967, while running for President of the United States, criticized the mechanisms of the UN as "obsolete and inadequate".

A former US ambassador: "The UN was not created to take mankind to heaven, but to save humanity from hell."

39: How much longer, mi amigo?

George Schulz who served as Ronald Reagan's Secretary of State from 1982 to 1989, called the embargo "insane".

In June 2009, the Cato Institute, an influential American think tank, delivered a scathing rebuke of U.S foreign policy towards Cuba: "The embargo has been a failure by every measure. It has not changed the course or nature of the Cuban government. It has not liberated a single Cuban citizen. In fact, the embargo has made the Cuban people a bit more impoverished, without making them one bit freer. At the same time, it has deprived Americans of their freedom to travel and has cost US farmers and other producers billions of dollars of potential exports"

In June 2009, Moisés Naím wrote in Newsweek: "The embargo is the perfect example used by anti-Americans everywhere to expose the hypocrisy of a superpower that punishes a small island while cozying to dictators elsewhere."

40: Haiti, I'm sorry again!

A Haitian patriot residing in France expressed his abhorrence of the idea: "They could have found another way to govern the country than to stage an election over the earthquake ruins and dead bodies still warm from cholera infection or from lack of medical attention caused by the electoral chaos. My anger remains so strong against those who advocated elections to govern...what? I barely recognize my country as being such."

United Nations through its Security Council has released a statement expressing deep concerns about the political paralysis in Haiti – and has underscored the urgency of seeking a quick solution to the electoral crisis. Part of the statement read: "The members of the Security Council reiterated their strong condemnation of any attempt to destabilize the electoral process, in particular by force, and urged all candidates, their supporters, political parties and other political actors to remain calm, refrain from unlawful violence or any action that can further disrupt the electoral process and political stability, resolve any electoral disputes through established legal mechanisms and to hold those responsible for such violence accountable."

Haiti has been dubbed a "Republic of NGOs".

David Rudder: "Haiti, one day we'll turn our heads and look inside you."

41: The demons have been unleashed

Religion has truly become the opium of the people. Shias don't want to live under Sunni leadership and Sunnis are on a rampage to create their own state. The Alawite Muslims have historically been persecuted for their beliefs by the Sunnis – and the Kurds are simply not interested in sharing sovereignty with any other group. Ominously, Iraq is coming apart at the seams.

America has spent precious resources in the Middle East floundering from one conflict to the next, with very little to show for its engagement.

A diplomat once observed: "The trouble with foreign policy is that it involves foreigners – and they don't always do what they are told."

Winston Churchill: "America can be trusted to do the right thing after it has tried everything else."

Chapter 5 – Education and Culture

42: Lost in transition

The British Independent daily newspaper has reported: "Politicians and education experts from around the world – including the UK – have made pilgrimages to Helsinki (Finland's capital) in the hope of identifying and replicating the secret of its success."

Princeton economist, Alan Blinder perceptively notes: "It is clear that nations will have to transform their education system so as to produce workers for the jobs that will actually exist in their societies…. In the future, how we educate our children may prove to be more important than how much we educate them."

OECD source: "In all of these nations, there is a wide consensus on increasing technology, environmental sciences and entrepreneurship education – all of which seem to contribute positively to economic development and growth."

The Finns have recently introduced something quite unconventional in their education system – and the change has been hailed as one of the most radical undertaken by a nation state – scrapping traditional "teaching by subject" in favour of "teaching by topic".

Indian entrepreneur and politician, Nandan Nilekani: "A society which has the least resistance to the uninterrupted flow of ideas, diversity, concepts and competitive signals wins, and a society that has the efficiencies to translate whatever can be done quickly – from idea to market – also wins."

43: Education in an information age

The American writer and futurist Alvin Toffler instructs us: "The illiterate of the 21st century will not be those who cannot read and write, but those who cannot learn, relearn and unlearn."

Knowledge is not the aim of education but simply a means to an end.

44: Our school system – challenging the unspoken assumptions

The four Ts: talent, technology, tolerance and thinking (mentality).

The right approach in the 21st century should be collateral learning and contextualized training that make extensive use of case studies, business games and management exercises.

Education is an investment in human capital that pays off in terms of higher productivity, economic engagement and even civic participation and good health.

A democracy needs an educated and informed people otherwise it will be starved of vibrancy.

45: Death of the bookstore

Star Publisher Rick Wayne poignantly calls the lack of bookstores in Saint Lucia, "the curse of Derek Walcott".

Neil Gaiman, believing bookstores to be an important fabric of a community, proclaimed in his award-winning novel, American Gods: "What I say is, a town isn't a town without a bookstore. It may call itself a town, but unless it's got a bookstore it knows it's not fooling a soul."

As a large US publisher disheartenedly points out: "There are many reasons for the decline of bookstores. Blame the business model of superstores, blame Amazon, blame the shrinking of leisure time, blame a digital age that offers so many bright, quick things, which have crippled our ability for sustained concentration. You can even blame writers, if you want, because you think they no longer produce anything vital to the culture or worth reading. Whatever the case, it is an historical fact that the decline of the bookstore and the rise of the Internet happened simultaneously; one model of the order and presentation of knowledge was toppled and superseded by another. For bookstores, e-books are only the nail in the coffin."

But will a nation that stops reading eventually stop thinking?

Chapter 6 – Social Affairs and the Environment

46: A social policy paradigm shift

Most economists agree that any economic policy discussion without its "intrinsic social-policy component" is incomplete.

Social policy cannot succeed if it is focussed on the consequences, rather than the causes.

Several studies on social development have consistently shown that higher gender-parity and female education strongly correlate with higher levels of development.

47: Where have all the public thinkers gone?

Eric Williams: "Now that I have resigned my position at Howard University in the USA, the only university in which I shall lecture in future is the University of Woodford Square and its several branches throughout the length and breadth of Trinidad and Tobago."

Eric Williams, Inward Hunger: The Education of a Prime Minister: "The University of Woodford square has for the past twelve years been a centre of free university education for the masses, of political analysis and of training in self-government... The lectures have been university dishes served in political sauce. They have given the people of Trinidad and Tobago a vision and a perspective... They have taught the people, what one French writer of the eighteenth century saw as the greatest danger, that they have a mind."

One famous publicist who captured the social change wrote: "I do recall a time, not so long ago, when formal orations seemed more eloquent, when public figures and intellectuals, some of them connected to academic institutions, dared to say more controversial things and take strong positions against the orthodox thinking of the day."

In our sender-oriented society, poor listening skills, lack of conciseness, and the inability to give constructive feedback have become major impediments to our progress as a people.

Public intellectuals may be an endangered species, but their role as thinker, dissenter and knowledge gamekeeper will always be crucial in evolving and progressive societies.

48: When civil society becomes political

Edmund Burke observed: "Justice is itself the great standing policy of civil society."

The strength of a society can be measured directly by the strength of its middle class.

Joe Biden captured the essence of civil society when he said: "No fundamental social change occurs merely because government acts. It's because civil society, the conscience of a country, begins to rise up and demand – demand – demand change."

49: We can do better on human rights

Jimmy Carter once admitted: "America did not invent human rights. In a very real sense human rights invented America."

Ms Mary Francis, human rights advocate: "Speedy remedy and accountability for human rights violations would help restore confidence in the justice system."

50: Public talk shows – hold the line, please!

Aristotle: "Man is a political animal."

Democracy does not end at the ballot box.

51: George Odlum – footprints in the sand

Saint Lucia lost one of its intellectual pearls in 2003 when George Odlum shuffled off this mortal coil at the age of 69.

Odlum had an adrenalized passion for Shakespeare's various chronicles of human foibles.

William Shakespeare: "All the world's a stage, and all the men and women merely players. They have their exits and their entrances; and one man in his time plays many parts."

The Times described Odlum as a man "with more flamboyance than substance."

The idea that "All the world's a stage", particularly given his own nation's fixation on parochial matters, must have been occasionally depressing to Shakespeare's local hero.

Whether Odlum was a man more sinned against than sinning, this I'll leave to the political historians here and abroad to determine.

52: Are our youth a ticking time bomb?

Greek Philosopher Socrates wrote about the excesses and proclivities of the youth: "The children now love luxury. They have bad manners, contempt for authority; they show disrespect for elders and love chatter in place of exercise."

The future of this country depends on how well we take care of our kids and youth today.

53: Beach access – drawing the line in the sand

Yanni, Greek composer and music producer: "A simple life is good with me. I don't need a whole lot. For me, a T-shirt, a pair of shorts, barefoot on a beach and I'm happy."

Give them an inch it appears and they'll take the whole backyard.

54: Fighting climate change in our own backyard
The real challenge is to combat an economic model that thrives on wasteful products and packaging, and leaves the associated problem of clean-up costs.

Chapter 7 – U.S. Historic Elections 2016

55: The verbal lynching of America's first black president
America's 44th president has been portrayed as an "Islamic atheist Marxist Kenyan", and repeatedly branded a "liar", "traitor", "terrorist", "coward" and "anti-Semite" by top Republican congressmen, presidential candidates and mainstream pundits.

Newt Gingrich, the former House Speaker, has said that Obama's policies are "a very serious threat to our way of life."

Minority Leader Mitch McConnell, announced that "our top priority over the next two years should be to deny President Obama a second term."

Nobel Prize-winning economist Paul Krugman: "If the discussion of economics was alarming, the discussion of foreign policy was practically demented. Almost all the candidates seem to believe that American military strength can shock-and-awe other countries into doing what we want without any need for negotiations, and that we shouldn't even talk with foreign leaders we don't like. No dinners for Xi Jinping! And, of course, no deal with Iran, because resorting to force in Iraq went so well."

56: Have U.S. relations taken a nosedive?
Barack Obama inauguration speech, January 2009, "I'll not be the president of black America" but rather "the president of the United States of America."

A German newspaper has described race relations in America under Barack Obama as "the tragedy of America's first black president."

Has the system failed African-Americans or should they themselves be held responsible for their own state of poverty and disillusionment?

According to a New York Times/CBS News poll conducted recently, "nearly six in 10 Americans, including heavy majorities of both whites and blacks, think race relations are generally bad, and that nearly four in 10 think the situation is getting worse."

57: From black hero to Tea Party Republican

Dr. Ben Carson, in his most recent book, "America the Beautiful: Rediscovering What Made This Nation Great", writes: "Many African-Americans voted for Obama simply because he was a black man and not because they resonated philosophically with his policies."

Dr. Ben Carson: "I would not advocate that we put a Muslim in charge of this nation. I absolutely would not agree with that."

58: Beating about the bush

United States Constitution: "No religious Test shall ever be required as a Qualification to any Office or public Trust under the United States."

Lindsay Graham: "I blame President Obama for ISIL. I'm tired of beating on Bush. I miss George W. Bush!"

59: How to blow a dog whistle

Dog whistle is a type of strategy of communication that sends a message that the general population will take a certain meaning from, but a certain group that is "in the know" will take away the secret, intended message."

The fact that America is the only developed country without a "CULTURE MINISTER" is testimony to the fact that its socio-cultural makeup is too diverse to warrant "the advocacy, promotion and systemization of a single American culture".

"Lets Make America Great Again" is a bogus slogan that has proved to be really just a dog-whistle strategy for saying "Let's Make America White Again".

"Hope is not the conviction that something will turn out well, but the certainty that something makes sense, regardless of how it turns out."

– Former Czech president and writer Vaclav Havel

ALSO BY CLEMENT WULF-SOULAGE

- Management English Intelligence (2010)

- Market Economy – English for International Economics (2011)

www.ingramcontent.com/pod-product-compliance
Lightning Source LLC
Chambersburg PA
CBHW071335280526
45787CB00001B/109